PRINCIPLES OF INSURANCE LAW

REVISED THIRD EDITION

2006 SUPPLEMENT

EMERIC FISCHER

Professor of Law, Emeritus
Marshall-Wythe School of Law
College of William & Mary

PETER NASH SWISHER

Professor of Law
T.C. Williams School of Law
University of Richmond

JEFFREY W. STEMPEL

Doris S. & Theodore B. Lee Professor of Law
William S. Boyd School of Law
University of Nevada Las Vegas

D1319467

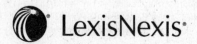

Editorial Offices
744 Broad Street, Newark, NJ 07102 (973) 820-2000
201 Mission St., San Francisco, CA 94105-1831 (415) 908-3200
701 East Water Street, Charlottesville, VA 22902-7587 (434) 972-7600
www.lexis.com

(Pub.333)

Acknowledgments

Thanks as always to our colleagues at the Boyd School of Law-UNLV and the T.C. Williams College of Law-Richmond and to Deans Dick Morgan and Rod Smolla. Special thanks also to our friends and fellow insurance affectionados in the academy and in private practice, including Ken Abraham, Julia Adams, Tom Baker, Hazel Glenn Beh, Keith Bruett, Michael Cashman, Corey Esch-weiler, Jim Fischer, Roger Henderson, Bob Jerry, Randy Maniloff, Leo Martinez, Marc Mayerson, Ellen Pryor, Susan Randall, Jim Reece, Adam Scales, Jeff Thomas, and Eric Van Vugt. Thanks also to editor Jennifer Beszley and LexisNexis publishing.

About the Supplement

Supplements, usually done annually or biannually, are a feature of casebooks in required or core law school courses. They are less common in elective courses, particularly where the subject matter has a certain venerable stability. However, in writing the Third Edition, we came to believe that the modern era of insurance litigation warrants a change in thinking about supplementation of insurance casebooks. Since the advent of the mega-coverage battles growing out of the asbestos mass tort phenomenon in the late 20th Century, insurance issues have been more frequently litigated, more hotly contested, and involved far larger stakes than in the past. As a corollary, state law on cutting edge insurance issues has tended to exhibit greater differences than in the past, with insurance law developments proceeding at a faster pace. Legislation has also become a battleground and new or modified insurance products are introduced with greater frequency.

In light of these developments, we determined to provide supplementation between new editions of *Principles of Insurance Law*. The Supplement attempts to give instructor and students an updated picture of the casebook's leading topics, with particular emphasis on important new decisions or current events affecting insurance or illustrating its operation and attendant litigation. In addition, some of the cases in the Supplement are designed to expand upon the coverage of the main text by including cases and materials on topics that, for reasons of space limitations, were only lightly touched upon in the Third Edition.

Note Regarding Edited Cases

The cases excerpted in this Supplement, like those in the main volume casebook, are edited. Omitted materials are identified through asterisks, ellipses or brackets. However, these signals are not used when the only editing is to delete citations to caselaw or other authority or to make only trivial and non-substantive changes such as condensing paragraphs or eliminating headings in the original text. In addition, case excerpts and case citations in the Supplement, like those of the main volume, ordinarily do not reflect subsequent history of the case.

Supplement Highlights

The 2006 Supplement to *Principles of Insurance Law* provides updates since publication of the Third Edition in 2004, including citation to and excerpting of new cases of significance. In addition, the Supplement addresses in more detail some topics that received only brief discussion in the main volume due to space limitations. Among the topics receiving particular focus in the Supplement are:

- Fortuity and the Expected or Intended Exclusion

- The U.S. Supreme Court's Most Recent ERISA cases

- The Role of Agents and Brokers and Their Exposure to Liability Claims

- Amendments to Policy Language

- Lost Policies

- Transfer of Rights to Insurance Policy Benefits

- Hurricane Katrina Coverage Cases

- Title Insurance

- The Business Risk Exclusions to General Liability Coverage

- Recent Pollution Exclusion Decisions

- Punitive Damages After *State Farm v. Campbell*

- Advertising Injury Coverage Under the CGL

- Additional Types of Liability Insurance (e.g., Directors and Officers coverage)

- Suretyship

- Financial or Finite Reinsurance

- Excess and Umbrella Coverage

TABLE OF CONTENTS

Page

Chapter 1

INSURANCE HISTORY AND FUNDAMENTAL CONCEPTS

§ 1.04   FORTUITY, ADVERSE SELECTION AND MORAL HAZARD

[A]   Fortuity Generally

Page 58: [Add immediately prior to § 1.04[A][1]:]

As discussed in the previous section, the concept of fortuity and accident are important to insurance theory. Insurance is available to protect against the losses that may occur by chance—so-called "fortuitous" losses—and should not be available to provide payment for things that are certain to happen or are within the effective control of the policyholder. Life insurance fits the model because there is risk and uncertainty about the length of life even though death itself is inexorable. Warren Buffett, who is not only the world's second richest person but also an owner of insurance and reinsurance companies, captured the concept of risk well when commenting on the dangers of insuring property subject to hurricane loss. "If you like to watch football, you probably enjoy the game a little more if you have a bet on it. I like to watch the Weather Channel." *See* Liam Pleven, Ian McDonald & Karen Richardson, *As Hurricane Season Begins, Disaster Insurance Runs Short*, WALL ST. J., July 10, 2006 at A1, col. 5. Or, as Buffett put it on another occasion, predicting future loss experiences is always something of a guess and insurers "get paid to guess." Although Buffett is refreshingly candid and willing to suffer the consequences of risk, he did not get rich by being exploited and would not want to insure events that were subject to the control of the policyholder rather than fate.

The notion that losses must take place inadvertently because of oversight, chance or bad luck rather than intent dominates judicial concepts of what constitutes a covered loss for purposes of property insurance (Chapter 10) or an "occurrence" for purpose of liability insurance (*see* Chapter 11). Courts get this concept wrong with surprising frequency and may apply 20-20 hindsight to label a loss non-fortuitous or intentional even when the requisite intent to bring about harm or loss is lacking. For example, some courts have found even negligent misrepresentations not to be accidents or occurrences because the person making the representation intended to induce reliance. *See, e.g., Green v. State Farm Fire & Cas. Co.*, 127 P.3d 1279 (Utah App. 2005). The problem with this line of thought is that it confuses volitional conduct (which takes place constantly in life and

1

business) with intent to injure, which is thankfully relatively rare. *See, e.g., Aetna Casualty & Surety Co. v. Metropolitan Baptist Church*, 967 F. Supp. 217 (S.D. Tex. 1996) (negligent representation an "occurrence."); *Sheets v. Brethren Mut. Ins. Co.*, 342 Md. 634, 679 A.2d 540 (Md.1996) (misrepresentation without intent to injury can still be covered accident or occurrence). The same analysis applies to questions of whether liability insurance provides coverage for foolishly reckless acts. *See, e.g., Metropolitan Prop. & Cas. Ins. Co. v. Pittington*, 841 N.E.2d 413 (Ill. App. 2005) (shooting incident may be sufficiently accidental and fortuitous for potential coverage even where policyholder was criminally convicted for reckless conduct in connection with deadly shooting; court reasons that policyholder may have behaved abominably but injury may not have been intentional or practically certain to take place); *Cumberland Mut. Fire Ins. Co. v. Murphy*, 183 N.J. 344, 873 A.2d 534 (N.J. 2005) (injuries caused by teenagers shooting BB gun at cars sufficiently accidental because insureds did not expect or intend injury but were negligent in use of gun); *Allstate Ins. Co. v. McCarn*, 683 N.W.2d 656 (Mich. 2004) (same).

The requisite degree of fortuity or "accidentalness" may exist for some persons insured under a policy even if others are engaging in intentional destruction. *See, e.g., Illinois Farmers Ins. Co. v. Kure*, 846 N.E.2d 644 (Ill. App. 2006) (allegations of negligent supervision by parents sufficient to come within potential coverage even where child intentionally caused injury). *But see American Family Mut. Ins. Co. v. Corrigan*, 2005 Iowa. Supp. LEXIS 64 (Iowa May 6, 2005) (criminal act exclusion in homeowner policy precludes coverage where innocent parents were negligent in supervising their child, who was subsequently convicted of endangering another child).

Staged or fraudulent claims, of course, clearly are not accidental and do not satisfy the fortuity concept. Unfortunately, they abound in spite of serious insurer and government efforts against them. *See, e.g., Insurance Scam Plotted by Mich. Prison Inmates Takes Fatal Twist*, Ins. J. (April 28, 2006) (describing scam in which prisoners created phony business and then insured one another as business partners; original plan to mutually stage fake deaths went awry when one prisoner killed co-conspirator in effort to take sole possession of fraudulently obtained payments).

A particularly memorable, tragicomic case involving the issue of when a loss (in this case a self-inflicted loss) was sufficiently unintended to be adequately fortuitous for insurance purposes. In *Federal Ins. Co. v. ACE Property & Cas. Co.*, 429 F.3d 120 (5th Cir. 2005) (applying Texas law). Electronic Date Systems (EDS), perhaps best known as the computer company started by former presidential candidate Ross Perot, was approached by a man identifying himself only as "Colonel West," purporting to be a representative of NATO (the North Atlantic Treaty Organization) and expressing interest in perhaps contracting with EDS as general contractor for a covert operation requiring purchase of electronic goods. Eager for the business, EDS induced two prospective subcontractors to provide "Colonel West" with exemplary equipment worth millions of dollars as part of EDS's effort to land the job.

"Colonel West" turned out to be a con man and the equipment was never seen again. The subcontractors sued EDS for the cost of the lost equipment. EDS sought insurance coverage for its potential liability to the subcontractors. The court denied coverage, ruling that there was nothing accidental about these events (in spite of the story's film noire/O. Henry-style ending) because EDS and the subcontractors always intended that the equipment be given to the mysterious colonel in hopes that this would induce future business worth much more than the electronic products given as "samples." Those hopes were dashed when the colonel turned out to be an imposter but the court treated the mater as an intentional loss rather than an accidental loss or "occurrence" within the meaning of the EDS liability policy.

And some people say insurance is boring. More important for our purposes, the case illustrates sometimes murky boundaries of fortuity and insurability. On one hand, as the court noted, EDS and the prospective subcontractors intended to give the equipment to the mysterious Colonel West. But was the loss of the equipment intended? Even if EDS et al. were not assured of future business from the Faux Colonel, can it not be said that the subcontractors lost their equipment because of an EDS negligent mispresentation about the bona fides of Colonel West? Even if the subs were willing to use the equipment as a loss leader, could they not have changed their minds and sought its return from a legitimate business? But that avenue was foreclosed due to the alleged negligence of EDS in implicitly vouching for Colonel West even though he proved to be just a Matchstick Man in a uniform. Now you see why courts divide on insurance issues.

The correct outcome of the EDS case, in our view, turns on the factual context. If the subcontractors completely parted with their expensive equipment with no expectations of its return in the absence of landing a contract with the Cardboard Cut-Out Colonel, then the court's decision is right. EDS and the putative subs would then only have been engaging in the type of ordinary loss leader business practices that are not insurable events. For example, a fast food restaurant may for a time sell its hamburgers at "1960s prices" hoping that the losses on each hamburger sale will be more than made up by increased consumer traffic that includes purchase of other items on which the company earns good profits. If the restaurant guesses wrong, it loses money, but this is not "accidental" within the meaning of insurance. On the other hand, if a vendor lends equipment for a customer "tryout" and expects to get the equipment back in the absence of purchase, there has been a fortuitous loss if the customer skips town with the vendor's property (and without paying). Ordinarily, the vendor would sue the customer but that was foreclosed in the EDS case, but the event could still be fortuitous under the right set of facts.

Also, of course, fortuity and liability should be distinguished. Even if the loss is accidental because a vendor and EDS both expected to have the equipment returned if there was no purchase, EDS may or may not have said or done things to make it legally responsible for the vendor's loss. On one hand, EDS could have said "We have a really good shot at landing this military contract," which arguably implies that it is vouching for Colonel West, or it could have said "We're not sure about this outfit, but we're willing to gamble, are you?" The latter presentation would seem not to create any misrepresentation or similar liability. But as we will learn in Chapters 9 and 11, liability insurance exists to defend claims against the policyholder even when the claim lacks merit. Why? Because part of the purpose of liability insurance is to provide "litigation insurance" and remove from the policyholder the albatross of defending and resolving claims (some valid, some meritless). Absent collusion, the existence of a claim by a third party is almost always fortuitous. Even the most careful of policyholders cannot prevent others from suing.

[1] The Intentional Act Exclusion

Page 68: [Add the following at the end of § 1.04[A][1]:]

After all this description of the expected or intended injury exclusion, perhaps its time to look at a couple cases applying it.

AUTOMOBILE INSURANCE COMPANY v. COOK

2006 N.Y. LEXIS 1400 (N.Y. June 8, 2006)

CIPARICK, J.:

The issue in this declaratory judgment action is whether the insurer has a duty to defend its policyholder under his homeowner's insurance policy in an underlying wrongful death action, resulting from a shooting committed in self defense. We conclude that the insurer here is obligated to defend under the policy.

On February 20, 2002, Alfred Cook shot and killed Richard Barber inside his home. At the depositions, the witnesses testified that the two men had known each other for many years, but became involved in a dispute relating to their business relationship. Barber, weighing about 360 pounds, was approximately three times Cook's size and had previously attacked the smaller man, causing injury to his leg. On the morning of February 20, Barber and another man were outside of Cook's home, hurling objects at the house. They left without further incident, but Barber returned later that day with two other companions. When Cook, who was standing outside his door, saw them approaching, he asked a person visiting him to leave because he expected trouble. He returned inside, locked the door and, anticipating a confrontation, retrieved a .25 caliber hand gun from his bedroom.

There was further testimony that the group burst into Cook's home. The four individuals gathered in the kitchen where Barber began demanding money from Cook while pounding his fists on the kitchen table. Cook, alarmed, drew his gun and demanded that they leave his house. Barber apparently laughed at the small size of the pistol, at which point Cook withdrew to his bedroom for a larger weapon. He picked up a loaded, 12 gauge shotgun and stood in his living room at the far end of his pool table. Cook again ordered them to leave the house. Although Barber started to head toward the door with his companions, he stopped at the opposite end of the pool table, turned to face Cook and told his companions to take anything of value, and that he would meet them outside because he had some business to attend to. When Barber menacingly started advancing toward Cook, Cook warned him that he would shoot if he came any closer. Cook aimed his gun toward the lowest part of Barber's body that was not obscured by the pool table — his navel. When Barber was about one step away from the barrel of the gun, Cook fired a shot into Barber's abdomen. Barber died later that day at a hospital.

Cook was indicted for intentional and depraved indifference murder. At trial he raised a justification defense. A jury acquitted him of both murder counts and of the lesser included offenses of manslaughter in the first and second degrees. * * * The administrator of Barber's estate, Victoria Pruyn, commenced a wrongful death action against Cook. The first cause of action alleges that "injury to the decedent and the decedent's death were caused by the negligence of the defendant, Alfred S. Cook." Specifically, the complaint alleges that Cook's behavior "consisted of negligently playing with a loaded shotgun; negligently pointing that shotgun at the abdomen of the decedent; negligently discharging that shot gun into the decedent's abdomen; and engaging in unruly behavior at the Defendant's residence on February 20, 2002." In a separate cause of action, the complaint alleges that Cook intentionally shot Barber causing Barber's death. At his examination before trial, Cook testified, "I knew the [shot from the] shotgun would injure Mr. Barber because I had to stop him, but I did not anticipate it killing him."

Cook sought homeowner's personal liability coverage from his insurer, the Travelers's Insurance Company, appearing in this action as the Automobile Insurance Company of Hartford. Hartford disclaimed coverage explaining that the incident was not an "occurrence" within the meaning of the policy and furthermore that the injury inflicted upon Barber fell within a policy exclusion, as it was "expected or intended" by Cook. The insurer commenced this declaratory judgment action against both Cook and Pruyn for a declaration that it was not obligated to defend or indemnify Cook in the wrongful death action. After depositions, Hartford moved for summary judgment and Cook cross-moved, seeking a declaration that the insurer was required to defend and indemnify him in the underlying tort action.

Supreme Court denied Hartford's motion and granted Cook's cross motion to the extent of declaring that the insurer had a duty to provide a defense for Cook in the wrongful death action. The court found that Hartford failed to prove that the incident was not an occurrence covered by the policy or that Cook's actions were subject to the exclusion for injuries expected or intended by the insured. The court held that the insurer had a duty to defend because the negligence allegations in the complaint could potentially be proven at trial.

The Appellate Division reversed, concluding that since Cook intentionally shot Barber, his actions could not be considered an accident or "occurrence" and, thus, were not covered by the policy. The court also noted that the acts came within the policy exclusion for bodily injury "expected or intended" by the insured. One Justice dissented and voted to affirm, holding that if the negligence claim were established, Cook's actions would be covered by the policy. This Court granted leave to appeal and we now reverse.

Our inquiry is two-fold: whether an "occurrence" is involved that gives rise to policy coverage and, if so, whether it falls within the "expected or intended" injury policy exclusion. As relevant here, the insurance policy defines an "occurrence" as "an accident . . . which results, during the policy period, in . . . bodily injury." The policy also contains an exclusion for bodily injury "which is expected or intended by any insured." The policy represents that it will provide a defense and pay—up to the policy limits—the amounts for which the insured is legally liable, "if a claim is made or a suit is brought against any insured for damages because of bodily injury . . . caused by an occurrence to which this coverage applies, even if the claim or suit is false."

It is well settled that an insurance company's duty to defend is broader than its duty to indemnify. Indeed, the duty to defend is "exceedingly broad" and an insurer will be called upon to provide a defense whenever the allegations of the complaint "suggest . . . a reasonable possibility of coverage" * * * "If, liberally construed, the claim is within the embrace of the policy, the insurer must come forward to defend its insured no matter how groundless, false or baseless the suit may be". * * * The duty remains "even though facts outside the four corners of [the] pleadings indicate that the claim may be meritless or not covered" For this reason, when a policy represents that it will provide the insured with a defense, we have said that it actually constitutes "litigation insurance" in addition to liability coverage. Thus, an insurer may be required to defend under the contract even though it may not be required to pay once the litigation has run its course. * * * When an insurer seeks to disclaim coverage on the further basis of an exclusion, as it does here, the insurer will be required to "provide a defense unless it can 'demonstrate that the allegations of the complaint cast that pleading solely and entirely within the policy exclusions, and, further, that the allegations, *in toto*, are subject to no other interpretation.' " In addition, exclusions are subject to strict construction and must be read narrowly.

An examination of the wrongful death complaint leads to the conclusion that Cook's claim is covered by the policy. Among other things, the complaint alleges that Cook negligently caused Barber's death. If such allegations can be proven, they would fall within the scope of the policy as a covered occurrence. The policy defines an "occurrence" as an accident, and we have previously defined the term "accident" albeit in a life insurance policy "to pertain not only to an unintentional or unexpected event which, if it occurs, will foreseeably bring on death, but equally to an intentional or expected event which unintentionally or unexpectedly has that result." Thus, if Cook accidentally or negligently caused Barber's death, such event may be considered an "occurrence" within the meaning of the policy and coverage would apply. The fact-finder in the underlying action may indeed ultimately reject the notion that Cook negligently caused Barber's death given the evidence of intentional behavior, but that uncertain outcome is immaterial to the issue raised here—the insurer's duty to defend in an action where it is alleged that the injury was caused by the negligent conduct of the insured.

Turning to the exclusion—as an allegation of negligence implies an unintentional or unexpected event, Hartford necessarily has failed to demonstrate that the allegations of the complaint are subject to no other interpretation than that Cook "expected or intended" the harm to Barber * * * In light of this disposition, it is unnecessary to address the remaining arguments—specifically, whether acts of self defense are intentional acts precluding coverage under a homeowner's policy. Suffice it to say that a reasonable insured under these circumstances would have expected coverage under the policy. As to a duty to indemnify, that determination will abide the trial. Accordingly, the order of the Appellate Division should be reversed, with costs, and the order of Supreme Court should be reinstated.

MINNESOTA FIRE AND CASUALTY COMPANY, v. GREENFIELD

579 Pa. 333; 855 A.2d 854 (Pa. 2004)

MADAME JUSTICE NEWMAN

We must decide today whether an insurance company owes a duty to defend or indemnify a homeowner for the wrongful death of his houseguest occasioned by his selling heroin to her. For the reasons that follow, we affirm the holding of the Superior Court, albeit on different grounds, that no such obligation exists.

At 8 p.m. on February 9, 1998, eighteen year-old Angela Smith (Smith) arrived at the home of Michael J. Greenfield (Greenfield) at 600 North Third Street, in Wormleysburg, hoping to obtain some heroin from him. Another young woman, Brook Broadwater (Broadwater), was with Smith. When they arrived, Greenfield had been drinking Mad Dog beer and was under the influence of marijuana and heroin. * * * Greenfield was no stranger to the use of heroin, having lost consciousness three times from it in the past. He was using heroin on a daily basis. He had used heroin with Smith before, and she, too, had become unconscious twice from it. Greenfield had sold heroin to Smith on other occasions and was arrested in 1995 for possession of marijuana. Greenfield acknowledged that he sold drugs out of his house "occasionally;" for the most part, he sold "mostly just weed" and "didn't really sell heroin to too many people."

In exchange for some marijuana and a small sum of money, Greenfield provided Smith with a bag of heroin, which was labeled "Suicide." At approximately 8:20 p.m., Smith voluntarily injected herself with the heroin. From that time until 10 p.m., Smith lay in a chair and communicated only when directly addressed. Greenfield put out some blankets for her, and she went to sleep on the floor. Greenfield left with Broadwater, returning to the house approximately 10:45 p.m. Smith remained in the residence, and when Greenfield awoke around 6:30 a.m., he found Smith still on the floor. When he left for work, he told Smith to lock the door if she left, and Smith groggily responded.

When Greenfield came home from work later that day, he found Smith dead on the floor where he had left her that morning. Greenfield knew that she was dead because "she was pale and not breathing." Autopsy results showed that Smith died from a heroin overdose. Greenfield called a friend, Robert Rollins (Rollins), who came to his residence. Wearing gloves because he "didn't want to touch" Smith's dead body, Greenfield, with his friend, took the body and put it in a vehicle owned by Greenfield. They drove around the area, and then dumped the body in York County near the Yellow Breeches Creek. Greenfield then contacted the police and concocted a story to the effect that he had simply found a body near the creek. Rollins initially told the same story, but recanted and told the truth. The men were arrested later that same day.

Greenfield was charged criminally for the outcome of the death of Smith; he pled guilty and was sentenced on counts of involuntary manslaughter, abuse of a corpse, and unlawful delivery of heroin. * * * Greenfield obtained a homeowner's policy (the Policy) from Minnesota Fire and Casualty Company (Insurance Company) when he purchased his residence. This was the Policy in place when Smith died . . . . The Policy defines "**occurrence**" as "**an accident**, including exposure to conditions, **which results,** during the policy period, **in: a. bodily injury**; or b. property damage. "Bodily injury" is "bodily harm, sickness or disease, including required care, loss of services and death that result." However, **the Policy excludes coverage for bodily injury "which is expected or intended by the insured."** Bodily injury "arising out of business pursuits of an insured" is also excluded. "Business" is defined as a "trade, profession or occupation."

On June 10, 1999, Sharon L. Smith and Arlin C. Smith, the parents of Smith, filed wrongful death and survival actions against Greenfield in the Court of Common Pleas of Cumberland County (trial court), individually and on behalf of all the other beneficiaries of the Estate of Angela C. Smith, as administrators of that Estate. They alleged, *inter alia*, that: (1) Greenfield had sold heroin to Smith; (2) he knew of, or should have foreseen, the harmful and dangerous consequences of selling heroin to Smith; (3) he made no attempts to check on her condition during the evening of February 8, 1998, and the following morning; and (4) he made no attempt to revive her, instead, leaving her and going to work. * * * The Insurance Company filed a Declaratory Judgment Action in the trial court, claiming, *inter alia* that:

The allegations of the Smith Complaint do not trigger an obligation on the part of Minnesota Fire and Casualty to either defend
or indemnify [Greenfield] for the allegations of liability set forth
herein. The damages sought in the Smith Complaint are alleged
to have been caused by the sale of heroin by Greenfield to [Smith]
resulting in [Smith's] death. These allegations do not constitute "an
occurrence," i.e., an accidental event; rather the allegations are premised solely upon the intentional and criminal act of the insured of
selling heroin, a controlled substance.

The Insurance Company further alleged that it had no legal obligation to
defend or indemnify Greenfield on the ground that public policy bars the
insurance coverage asserted.

On March 14, 2001, the trial court ruled on the parties' Cross-Motions
for Summary Judgment, which sought summary judgment regarding a duty
of the Insurance Company to defend and indemnify Greenfield in the
wrongful death and survival action. * * * The court found that the record
"does not, as a matter of law, show that the Smiths' claim is excluded under
Minnesota's policy." The trial court, however, did not grant the Smiths'
Motion for Summary Judgment on the issue of indemnification, finding that
the Insurance Company was required to defend Greenfield until the claim
could be confined to a recovery that was not within the scope of the Policy.
* * * The Superior Court reversed and determined that two factors precluded coverage: (1) its expanded doctrine of "inferred intent," which had
been applied previously in Pennsylvania only to cases involving child abuse.
The court noted "compelling public policy reasons" to deny coverage, for,
"in effect, the courts are being asked to help provide insurance for heroin
dealers . . . . The legislature . . . has already determined the inherent
danger of heroin . . . . It should not be the public policy . . . to insure the
sale of such a . . . dangerous and illegal narcotic . . . ."

Relying on Aetna Casualty and Surety Company v. Roe (Pa. Super. 1994),
which adopted in Pennsylvania the idea of inferred intent in child abuse
cases, the Superior Court in the instant matter stated that "inferred intent
results when there is an intentional act on the part of the insured and it
is inherent in that act that harm will occur. In child abuse cases, the actor's
abuse will frequently cause long-term harm to the child." Reasoning that
it was frequently certain that harm would occur to the buyer of heroin, the
Superior Court extended the doctrine of inferred intent, vacated the trial
court Order, and remanded with instructions to enter an Order holding that
the Insurance Company had no duty either to defend or to indemnify
Greenfield. Judge Olszewski dissented, rejecting the extension by the majority of the concept of inferred intent, noting that the doctrine was intended
only for "exceptional cases involving sexual child abuse . . . ."

For the reasons that follow, we determine that although the Superior
Court erred in expanding the inferred intent doctrine, it reached the correct
result in determining that public policy precludes the Insurance Company
from any duty to defend or indemnify Greenfield. As we explained, the

question before us is whether the Insurance Company must defend or indemnify Greenfield for the wrongful death of Smith resulting from heroin that he sold to her.

The interpretation of an insurance contract regarding the existence or non-existence of coverage is "generally performed by the court." "Where a provision of a policy is ambiguous, the policy provision is to be construed in favor of the insured and against the insurer . . . . Where, however, the language of the contract is clear and unambiguous, a court is required to give effect to that language." In light of the fact that the appropriate construction of the Policy poses a question of law, our standard of review is plenary.

> The Superior Court asserted two reasons for reversing the trial court: (1) Greenfield intentionally supplied Smith with the heroin that caused her death and, although he may not have intended her death, the known risks of heroin use make an adverse reaction an "expected occurrence;" and (2) "it should not be the public policy of this Commonwealth to insure the sale of such a notoriously dangerous and illegal narcotic, limited only by an express clause denying such coverage." We will address only the issues that the parties raised, although there appears to be an argument based on contract interpretation that the Insurance Company did not advance.

The Superior Court and the Insurance Company focused their analyses on that part of the Policy that excludes coverage for injuries that are "expected or intended by the insured." The question concerning whether Greenfield "expected or intended" Smith to die when he provided her with heroin is certainly difficult to answer, as reflected by the fact that the trial court and the Superior Court came to opposite conclusions. The trial court found that the averred facts support that the death of Smith was caused by the **negligence** of Greenfield; and the Superior Court inferred that "an intent to cause injury existed as a matter of law due to . . . Greenfield's providing Angela Smith with what . . . all too predictably, proved to be a fatal dose of heroin."

When this Court first considered the effect of a similar exclusionary clause in a homeowner's policy, we stated that "the vast majority of courts which have considered such a provision [an exclusionary clause] have reached the conclusion that before the insurer may validly disclaim liability, it must be shown that the insured intended by his act to produce the damage which did in fact occur." We emphasized in that case the difference between intending an **act** and intending a **result**. [W]e [have] held that the exclusionary clause did not preclude coverage for damages caused by a house fire during the course of a burglary. Further, we found that although the perpetrators intended to burglarize the house, they did not anticipate or plan the resulting house fire occasioned by their use of matches to light their way in the dark.

The trial court found that "the facts averred support Smiths' allegation that the death of Angela Smith was caused by Greenfield's negligence." It is in the context of this jurisprudential background that the Superior Court extended and applied the doctrine of **inferred** intent, presumably for the reason that it was unable to establish **actual** intent, given the absence of allegations that Greenfield expected or intended Smith to lose consciousness or die. * * * The Superior Court stated that "the notion of inferred intent is accepted in Pennsylvania," however, the concept has not been extended beyond child sexual abuse cases. "In adjudicating general liability insurance cases, as opposed to those **exceptional** cases involving child sexual abuse, Pennsylvania courts presently follow." [Precedent has stated] the very narrow applicability of inferred intent and stated that "in cases that do not involve child sexual abuse, Pennsylvania has adopted a general liability standard for determining the existence of this specific intent that looks to the insured's actual subjective intent."

Jurisprudence in Pennsylvania does not support the extension of inferred intent to cases other than exceptional ones involving child sexual abuse. Although this Court is not bound by the precedent established in a subsequent diversity case based on the law of Pennsylvania, we note that the Third Circuit has refused to extend the doctrine of inferred intent to preclude coverage for harm suffered by a female college student after a sexual assault by the homeowner's son.

* * *

In our state, the exclusionary clause applies only when the insured intends to cause harm. Insurance coverage is not excluded because the insured's actions are intentional unless he also intended the resultant damage. The exclusion is inapplicable even if the insured should reasonably have foreseen the injury which his actions caused.

* * *

Although [Pennsylvania precedent] mandates a 'subjective intent' analysis for determining coverage under an exclusionary clause in most Pennsylvania insurance cases, a different analysis is applied in 'those exceptional cases involving sexual child abuse.' In 'those exceptional cases,' many jurisdictions have adopted what is called the 'inferred intent' rule: This rule 'allows a court to infer an actor's intent from the nature and character of his or her acts' and to 'establish conclusively the existence of intent to harm as a matter of law.' This presumption is conclusive 'notwithstanding the insured's assertion of an absence of subjective intent to harm. Intent may be inferred only 'if the degree of certainty that the conduct will cause injury is sufficiently great to justify inferring intent to injure as a matter of law . . . . The more likely harm is to result from certain intentional conduct, the more likely intent to harm may be inferred as a matter of law.'

The incursion by the Superior Court into the territory of inferred intent was unnecessary with respect to reaching a determination of non-coverage. If it had followed its own analysis in [a prior case] it would have arrived at the same place without the detour. In that case, an insured went on a shooting spree, killing several occupants of a house. The court held that there was no coverage pursuant to the perpetrator's homeowner's policy for the reason that the conduct of shooting was intentional and, in applying the [correct] standard, the conduct was excluded under the policy "as it is exactly the type of injury against which insurance companies are not and should not be expected to insure." The court found no evidence that the shooting was "accidental or negligent" and also determined it irrelevant that the insured did not know the identity of one of the victims or that the victim was present in the house. Further, the court held that notwithstanding its finding that coverage was excluded under the terms of the policy, "we would also find coverage excluded as violative of the public policy of Pennsylvania." "The courts of Pennsylvania have refused to require an insurer to defend an insured for his own intentional torts and/or criminal acts." Based on this and the facts in the case *sub judice*, there is no coverage under the Policy given that Greenfield and Smith were voluntary participants in a criminal transaction involving heroin, a Schedule I controlled substance, that directly caused Smith's death.

We cannot know with certainty what Greenfield's state of mind was, a fact neither necessary to nor dispositive of our decision. We do ratify existing principles of our jurisprudence and, by doing so, we reject the Superior Court's extension of inferred intent, which established, as a matter of law, that Greenfield intended the harm that befell Smith. Having said that, however, the Superior Court's determination that the Insurance Company is not required to defend or indemnify under the Policy is correct. In addition to applying an expanded inferred intent doctrine, the court based its determination on the "compelling public policy reasons for denying a claim such as this where, in effect, the courts are being asked to help provide insurance for heroin dealers." * * * In [a prior case], we rejected an argument that allowing recovery pursuant to an insurance policy where property damage arose out of the commission of a crime by the insured would contravene public policy. We did so for two reasons: (1) the insurance contract itself did not contain a "violation of law" clause; and (2) our analysis that "under the facts of this case, we are not confronted with any overriding public policy which would preclude recovery." Our decision in that case determined that an insurance company was required to indemnify against losses caused by a carelessly lit match that was dropped when teenagers were burglarizing a home. We supported our holding on two bases: (1) the widely accepted principle that "before the insurer may validly disclaim liability, it must be shown that the insured intended by his act to produce the damage which did in fact occur[;]" and (2) the absence of any "overriding public policy" to preclude recovery.

Using our analysis in the case at bar, and providing further refinement of [prior precedent], we find that recovery is precluded for damages that arise out of an insured's criminal acts regarding a Schedule I substance, as a matter of overriding public policy. Therefore, in situations when an insured commits a criminal act, with respect to a Schedule I controlled substance, and unintended or unexpected injuries or losses occur as a result, whether by accident or negligence, public policy will not allow coverage under the contract of insurance. However, in cases that do not involve a criminal act by an insured with respect to a Schedule I controlled substance, our decision in Eisenman, reiterating the test traditionally required for an insurer to disclaim liability; i.e. the insurer must prove that the insured intended by his act to produce the damage which did actually occur, retains its validity.

* * *

"Only in the clearest cases, therefore, may a court make an alleged public policy the basis of judicial decision." Regardless of whether the insurance contract listed the possession, use and sale of heroin as an exclusion, the fact is that the legislature has criminalized the conduct that resulted in the damages in the instant matter. This exemplifies the clearest of cases.

Moreover, the Insurance Company argued that public policy prohibits indemnification under the Policy, citing, among other statutes, the Controlled Substances Act, which criminalizes the possession, use, or transfer of heroin as a felony violation infringing upon public health, safety, morals, and welfare. This comports with our requirement that

> [A] Plaintiff must do more than show a possible violation of a statute that implicates only her own personal interest. The Plaintiff in some way must allege that some **public policy** of *this* Commonwealth is implicated, undermined, or violated because of the employer's termination of the employee. **Public policy** of the Commonwealth must be just that, the **policy** of the Commonwealth.

Our Commonwealth, from the legislature to the Secretary of Health, has made its policy on the illegality of heroin abundantly clear: "heroin has a high potential for abuse, has no accepted medical use within the United States, and . . . is unsafe for use even under medical supervision." Given this clear enunciation of public policy regarding Schedule I controlled substances, we find that the Insurance Company is not required to defend or indemnify against damages arising out of its insured's criminal acts where the voluntary participation of the victim in an illegal heroin-transaction caused her death. * * *

CONCURRING OPINION (MR. JUSTICE CASTILLE)

I concur in the result of the lead opinion, but not in its reasoning. I do not seriously doubt that considerations of public policy would warrant denying coverage here, where liability would be premised upon the putative insured's deliberate criminal conduct in selling heroin. In my view, however, this case is resolvable, and the result is the same, by resort to bedrock principles of contract construction. Specifically, I would find that the deliberate conduct here, which would form the basis for homeowners' insurance liability, did not constitute an "accidental occurrence" which would trigger coverage under the plain language of the policy. * * * As the lead opinion notes, the homeowners' policy at issue here promises personal liability coverage for, *inter alia*, bodily injuries which are caused by a covered "occurrence." The policy then unambiguously defines an occurrence as "an accident" which results in bodily injury or property damage. The unfortunate teenage victim in this case, Angela Smith, did not trip down the stairs in Michael Greenfield's home, or fall upon a knife, or die in a fire. Rather, Smith and Greenfield engaged in a common, commercial transaction of a criminal nature, which just happened to occur in the home: Greenfield delivered heroin to Smith in exchange for a quantity of marijuana and, possibly, a small amount of cash. Smith then voluntarily injected herself with the heroin, thereby causing her own death from heroin intoxication. Greenfield did not inject Smith with the drug; instead, the basis for his liability was premised upon the simple fact of his delivering the narcotic to Smith, and her later dying from it while still in Greenfield's home.

Whatever else Greenfield's delivery to Smith may have been, it was not an accident. Smith wanted heroin; Greenfield accommodated and delivered it to her. Smith's decision to inject herself with the heroin, as she had done in the past, likewise was not an "accident" for that act, too, was deliberate and voluntary. Following upon the heels of the intentional and illegal activities of both Greenfield and Smith, the fortuity of the fatal overdose, while tragic, can hardly fall into the category of a covered "accident." As appellants themselves note:

> "Accident" has been defined in the context of insurance contracts as "an event or happening without human agency or, if happening through such agency, an event which, under circumstances, is unusual and not expected by the person to whom it happens." Black's Law Dictionary (6th ed. 1990). "Accident" has also been defined as an "unintended and unforeseen injurious occurrence." Black's Law Dictionary (7th ed. 1999). The Superior Court has defined an accident as an "untoward or unexpected happening."

The overdose here plainly resulted from human agency. Moreover, the prospect of heroin intoxication, including death from heroin intoxication, was no less plainly foreseeable. Although the overwhelming majority of heroin users do not die from a single injection of the narcotic, it nevertheless is an inherently dangerous drug and the risk of such a lethal result certainly is foreseeable. * * * There having been no "accident," there was no covered occurrence. I therefore agree with the plurality's determination to affirm the Superior Court's holding that Minnesota Fire does not have a duty to defend or indemnify Greenfield, albeit I concur only in the result because I arrive at that conclusion as a matter of contract construction, rather than resorting to an external ground for decision, such as public policy.

CONCURRING OPINION (MR. JUSTICE SAYLOR)

I join the lead opinion's disposition and the core of its analysis, namely, that on the facts of this particular case, public policy may be invoked to deny a defense and indemnification under a homeowner's insurance policy for liability resulting from the criminal delivery and ingestion of a powerful narcotic substance such as heroin. This conclusion does not, in my view, improperly or unfairly rewrite the policy to correct the absence of an appropriate exclusion, particularly since it cannot be reasonably maintained that the parties to the insurance contract anticipated that the homeowner's involvement in the drug overdose death of another would give rise to a covered risk. See generally RESTATEMENT (SECOND) OF CONTRACTS § 178(2)(a) (providing that, in weighing the enforcement of a contractual provision in connection with public policy grounds, the parties' justifiable expectations must be considered). Like the lead, I strongly prefer this rationale to support the result in this case over the attribution of "inferred intent" to Greenfield. Indeed, in effect, the inferred intent approach seems to me merely to represent an unnecessarily indirect and somewhat strained route to the implementation of a judicial, public policy exclusion.

Centrally, prevailing Pennsylvania law establishes that "an insured intends an injury if he desired to cause the consequences of his act or if he acted knowing that such consequences were substantially certain to result." Appellee's concession that "the prospect of a fatal overdose may be statistically remote as a function of the number of regular heroin users on a national basis," thus answers the contractual coverage question under the law as it presently stands. * * *

DISSENTING OPINION (MR. CHIEF JUSTICE CAPPY)

Because I cannot agree with the majority's decision to rewrite the insurance policy at issue, I must respectfully dissent. * * * We are not here confronted with the question of whether an insurer may enforce an exclusion which excludes from coverage damages arising out of the sale of heroin or any other illegal drug. Rather, at issue is whether this court may insert, via the invocation of public policy, such an exclusion into an insurance policy. The majority finds that this court may rewrite the contract on the basis that an insured should be precluded from receiving coverage where damages result from the insured's criminal act.

In my opinion, this court should not rewrite the contract for the insurance company. The [insurer] drafted the insurance policy. It is beyond cavil that it was capable of writing an exclusion which would exempt from coverage damages arising out of the sale of illegal narcotics, and yet it did not do so. Arguably, this was a failing on the part of the insurance company. Yet, is it the role of this court to act as super-scrivener, correcting the apparent errors in business judgment committed by insurers? With all due respect to the majority, I submit that this is not a proper role for this body.

Furthermore, I am concerned about the potential sweeping reach of the majority's decision and have grave concerns about its application to future cases. While the majority purports to limit its public policy exception to situations in which an insured engages in illegal activity regarding Schedule I controlled substances, its underlying rationale for creating that limited exception could easily be extended to create exceptions for other illegal acts. Indeed, the majority suggests in a footnote that this court should not require an insurance company to reimburse a policyholder for damages arising from any "conduct . . . that our legislature has defined as illegal." I am uneasy about this court issuing such a broad and amorphous pronouncement. . . . Mr. Justice Nigro joins this dissenting opinion.

NOTES AND QUESTIONS

(1) Can the *Cook* and *Greenfield* opinions be reconciled? Is it odd that in one case, the policyholder is allowed to affirmatively shoot and kill but retain coverage while in the other case, the policyholder is denied coverage because his irresponsible behavior lead to another's death? (We assume it was an unexpected death in that Angela Smith was not trying to commit suicide by heroin and Greenfield was not trying to kill a customer.) Does the comparative "worthiness" of the two policyholders or their status as "mainstream" or "deviant" citizens explain the decisions? Are courts impermissibly making value judgments about "bad" policyholders and "good" policyholders—or at least understandable policyholders?

(2) *Minnesota Fire v. Greenfield*, is arguably too pro-insurer. It engages in two judicial pronouncements that should make even the most activist judge wince a bit. One, the court seems to find that heroin sale makes death by the user an "expected occurrence," concluding in effect that death to a third party was practically certain to occur from sale by the insured. Two, the court finds a public policy bar to insuring against liability from illicit drug sales. The first rationale is at odds with basic insurance principles in that liability insurance normally provides coverage even where the liability-creating conduct was foolish, socially undesirable, or even callous. The usual inquiry focuses on whether the insured had a subjective intent to inflict injury or cause the harm in question. Drug use is not a wise thing for the health conscious. But it is not inevitably fatal. If it were, the Rolling Stones, Aerosmith, and numerous other rock bands would no longer be with us. Although heroin does kill on occasion (e.g., Jimi Hendrix, Janice Joplin), so too does alcohol (e.g., Jim Morrison). If Greenfield gave a visitor too much to drink and she died by falling down the front steps of the house, no serious court would find the death uncovered absent a clear and specific alcohol or intoxication exclusion.

(3) Drug dealers tend not to be nice people and Michael Greenfield seems particularly unlikeable. After his customer used the heroin he sold, he neglected her and then attempted to cover up the death out of fear that he would be busted. As the court noted with some understatement, "there is not one scintilla of evidence to suggest that Greenfield felt remorse or

personal responsibility for the death of Smith. He seems to have little conscience or regret for what transpired." From this, the court concluded that his indifference combined with the dangers of heroin to make Smith's death a sufficient certainty to preclude coverage. But this is strained reasoning. Greenfield was no prince, but what was the court expecting, the Mr. Rogers of drug dealers? If Greenfield were a well-adjusted, emphathetic human being, perhaps he would be engaged in more socially useful activity. But the fact remains that Minnesota Fire sold him an insurance policy that provided coverage for his negligent, reckless, stupid, callous, and even sociopathic and remorseless acts—so long as he did not subjectively intend to injure anyone or the activity was not otherwise specifically excluded by the policy language. If one could look into Greenfield's presumably dark soul, one would probably find a drug seller who did not want Smith to die and did not expect Smith to die. Rather, he almost certainly expected Smith to live to purchase and shoot up again, all to Greenfield's profit. The question is not whether Greenfield is a good guy or bad guy. The question is whether Greenfield intended to injure or kill Smith. Also, Greenfield pled guilty to involuntary manslaughter and lesser crimes. As the name of the crime implies—and as the *Cook* decision implicitly found—"involuntary" manslaughter is not expected or intended. The "accident" or occurrence in question is not the sale of the heroin, which of course was volitional, but its impact on the victim. Angela Smith took the heroin to get high, not to die. Her adverse reaction to the drug and death was the accident.

(4) The second reason for the decision—a public policy against illegal drugs — is understandable but overreaching. Although insurance should not encourage misconduct, neither should insurance coverage litigation be a podium for the court's expression of moral outrage. Sure, drugs are a bad thing. But if the insurer wanted nothing to do with drug-related injury, it could have included specific language in the policy. If the court in fact fears that insurance coverage for drug-related death creates problems of moral hazard or adverse selection, the court would presumably want to encourage the use of clear and specific exclusions of this type in liability policies. A judicially created unwritten exclusion does not properly put policyholders on notice and does not encourage insurers to write clearer policies that adequately inform policyholders of the contours of coverage.

(5) In reaching its decision barring coverage and its enthusiasm for a public policy against drug abuse, the Pennsylvania Supreme Court also gave insufficient consideration to the important insurance public policy of compensation and misassessed the deterrence issues in the case. First, the matter of compensation: Angela Smith is dead and no amount of money will bring her back. But her parents are entitled to whatever compensation the law of wrongful death provides. Why should they be deprived of a source of funds when facing a perhaps judgment proof defendant who had insurance? More particularly, why should the state supreme court rewrite the defendant's insurance policy to absolve the insurer from keeping its contract commitment? Then there is the matter of deterrence. Greenfield will presumably pay his debt to society through the criminal justice system. Will

Greenfield (when he gets out of prison) and others like him be deterred from selling drugs because they cannot get insurance for the liability? Not likely. The Greenfields of the world run on a different motivational matrix than manufacturers or professionals that might reasonably be expected to adjust their behavior in response to these sorts of economic incentives. He may, however, shy away from drug dealing because of the deterrent prospect of a second prison term. But denying insurance to his victim hardly serves any reasonable deterrence goal in cases like this.

[3] Loss-in-Progress

Page 70: [Add immediately prior to § 1.04[A][4]:]

Because the known loss and loss-in-progress concepts are so similar, courts tend to conflate or even confuse them, or at least to talk about them with less clarity than precedent-loving attorneys would prefer. In addition, perhaps courts invoke these doctrines when other would provide a more effective or intellectually precise means of resolving coverage questions. *American & Foreign Insurance Company v. Sequatchie Concrete Services, Inc.*, 441 F.3d 341 (6th Cir. 2006) perhaps provides an example of this even though correctly decided. In the *Sequatchie Concrete* case, the policyholder was a subcontractor (Knoxville Cast Stone, a subsidiary of Sequatchie), which was hired by a general contractor (Frizzeli) building a hotel in Gatlinburg, Tennessee. Frizzeli contracted with Knoxville/Sequtchie to provide concrete block for the exterior of the hotel. Due to a communication breakdown, Knoxville/Sequatchie delivered concrete that was not water-proof. Sure enough, water was observed penetrating the concrete while the building was being constructed. Frizzeli had inquired about the water penetration in 1995 and 1996, during the construction phase of the hotel, but was assured by Knoxville/ Sequatchie that this was normal and the problem would be resolved when the building was sealed upon completion. Sure enough, the problem did not resolve itself even after the roof and gutters were in place and the hotel was substantially complete. In Fall 1996, Frizzeli memorialized its concerns to Knoxville-Sequatchie, which argued that it was not responsible because the contractor's purchase order had failed to specify waterproof concrete.

Frizzeli was understandably resistant to this excuse since Knoxville-Sequatchie knew that the concrete would be on the outside of a building exposed to the elements. Litigation ensued as Frizzeli sued its concrete subcontractor over the water damage to the hotel. The case was settled for $950,000, for which Knoxville-Sequatchie sought coverage from its general liability insurers—New Hampshire (which issued a policy for 1996) and American & Foreign (which issued a policy for 1997). Both insurers initially provided a defense of the Frizzeli claims but then denied coverage, with both insurers claiming that the water damage had taken place in the other insurer's policy period and that the damages stemmed from what the trial court and the U.S. Court of Appeals referred to as a "loss-in-progress."

The courts' terminology may seem a little misleading to insurers and lawyers. As discussed above, the term "loss-in-progress" normally is used in the context of first-party property insurance, not a liability insurance matter such as that in the *Sequatchie Concrete* case. In the context of liability insurance, insurers and counsel have tended more often to refer to this type of situation a "known loss" scenario rather than a loss-in-progress situation. But, as the *Sequatchie Concrete* decision shows, courts may use the terms interchangeably. Although this can be confusing and less accurate at the margin (loss-in-progress more accurately connotes the typical property insurance problems of acute deterioration already under-way while known loss more accurately describes a policyholder's knowledge that it has a legal liability time bomb on its hands), both terms focus on the same concept—lack of fortuity in that a policyholder's claim does not arise by chance and it is known at the time insurance is purchased that a claim will be presented. Although loss judicial verbiage may create confusion, the terms "known loss" and "loss-in-progress" are essentially synonyms in this regard.

In *Sequatchie Concrete*, the Court determined that Knoxville-Sequatchie knew that it had provided non-waterproof concrete, that water was coming through the concrete and causing physical injury to other tangible parts of the hotel (meeting the definition of "property damage" under the standard Commercial General Liability (CGL) insurance policy and making the "damage to your work" exclusion inapplicable). It further knew that Frizzeli knew about the situation and regarded this as the concrete subcontractor's fault and that a claim by Frizzeli was likely. The known/loss-in-progress situation gets more complicated when a hypothetical policyholder is genu-inely unaware of a liability-creating event or an unusually threatening deterioration of property. On one hand, the policyholder in such a situation is blameless and not purchasing insurance because of the adverse selection motivation. On the other hand, the situation arguably presents a greater-than-ordinary risk to the insurer because the impending loss is already "in the pipeline." Courts are divided on the issue. *Compare Inland Waters Pollution Control, Inc. v. National Union Fire Ins. Co.*, 997 F.2d 172, 176 (6th Cir. 1993) (applying Michigan law) (loss-in-progress/known loss doc-trine applicable either where policyholder is actually aware of loss or when there is "immediate threat of loss" sufficient to be "tantamount to fore-knowledge" by the policyholder) *with Montrose Chem. Corp. of Calif. v. Admiral Ins. Co.*, 35 Cal App. 4th 335, 5 Cal. Rptr. 2d 358 (1992) (policy-holder must be subjectively aware of substantial certainty of liability claim rather than merely potential for liability claims). In practice, most cases will satisfy both standards. But in some circumstances, an innocent but unobservant or undiscerning policyholder may simply have failed to appre-ciate the loss potential of a situation. In ensuing litigation, the availability of coverage may differ among courts. In general, however, the known loss or loss-in-progress concepts, like the general concept of fortuity and the intentional injury concept all express the same theme: insurance is only available where there is a risk of loss rather than when the loss is certainty.

Now, if the courts could only stick to a consistent terminology for the concept.

One possible means of improving judicial assessments in this area is to focus on the application and underwriting process as the gatekeeper rather than having coverage turn on post-hoc attempts to discern a policyholder's subjective anticipation of claims on the basis of often conflicting, usually circumstantial evidence. Regarding direct evidence, a policyholder will almost always testify that although it may have known it had significant exposure, it was not subjectively certain that its actions would cause injury, or that it would be sued or that it did not know that a claimant was practically certain to win. Insurers will then marshal available circumstantial evidence to suggest that the policyholder must have known that claims or losses of particular magnitude were practically certain to take place. This type of "swearing match" can result in extensive litigation and debatable outcomes depending on whether one thinks a court or jury has correctly assessed credibility and weighed the evidence. However, if these issues are addressed primarily as misrepresentation and concealment matters, the judicial inquiry may be more clearcut and the results more consistent. For example, if the insurer in *Sequatchie Concrete* had properly asked whether the applicant was aware of any disputes over past business and sought additional details, the insurer would be able to find out about the leaky concrete of Gatlinburg and could then determine whether to accept the risk (or perhaps charge a higher premium). If in the face of a properly posed question the applicant had falsely denied the presence of the leaky concrete dispute, the insurer would appear to have an almost "watertight" misrepresentation defense to coverage.

Chapter 2

CONTRACT LAW, LEGAL THEORY, AND THE CONSTRUCTION OF THE INSURANCE CONTRACT

§ 2.01 A BRIEF REVIEW OF CONTRACT LAW

Page 90: [Add at the end of § 2.01:]

Despite the long-standing rule that party intent is the touchstone of contract meaning, attorneys and courts sometimes focus so intently on the words of the writing that they lose sight of this larger picture. But the words on paper are more properly viewed as "contract documents" than the "contract" itself. Although the text of a written contract is of course important for determining contract meaning, the words on a piece of paper" and certainly not a few isolated words in one part of the policy form" are not themselves "the contract." Rather, the written document functions as a memorialization of the parties" intent and agreement. That agreement is "the contract." As one contract law casebook observes:

> People often use the work (contract" to refer to the writing that embodies an agreement or deal . . . . But the piece of paper is not a contract. . . . At most, that piece of paper is a memorialization of the contract . . . . [A] contract is a promise or set of promises that the law will enforce. That is the contract.

* * *

> [T]here is a tendency to confuse the written paper signed by the parties with the contract that binds them. It is an easy mistake to make; everyone calls the signed paper (the contract." But that paper is, at best, only *evidence* of the contract. That is, the contract is represented by that paper; it is not that paper.

See DAVID G. EPSTEIN, BRUCE A. MARKELL & LAWRENCE PONOROFF, MAKING AND DOING DEALS: CONTRACTS IN CONTEXT 1, 502 (2d ed. 2006) (emphasis in original).

§ 2.05 THE AMBIGUITY FACTOR

Page 99: [Add to § 2.05, footnote 14:]

See also Goldman v. Metropolitan Life Ins. Co., 5 N.Y.3d 561, 841 N.E.2d 742 (N.Y. 2005) (no ambiguity in use of word "annual" to describe premium payments).

21

Page 100: [Add to § 2.05, footnote 19:]

Examples of ambiguity of syntax abound. Common sources are toy or other assembly instructions and the *Federal Registrar*. Even well-edited newspapers and periodicals can produce some passages where, quite literally, one guess is as good as another regarding meaning. Consider the following example from the front-page news summary of the *Wall Street Journal*:

> **Women run** a higher risk of breast cancer after taking estrogen-only pills for at least 15 years, says a study overseen by Harvard-affiliated researchers.

See What's News, Wall St. J., May 9, 2006 at A1, col. 3. Do women who take estrogen pills face an increased risk of breast cancer for 15 years thereafter or do women only face this increased risk should they consume the estrogen pills for some 15 years? The bare text quoted above would permit either interpretation. Or, put another way, either interpretation would seem reasonable. A reader may have a preferred interpretation. For example, we think the news item more likely was intended to mean that women must be taking the estrogen pill for 15 years or more to face the increased risk. But although this is our preferred interpretation, we would be hard-pressed to refute the contrary construction of the new item. The text supports either interpretation and it cannot be definitively said that one interpretation is clearly correct or that the other is unreasonable.

Fortunately, there are usually means of resolving such a dispute rather than reflexively ruling against the drafter of the problematic language. For example, a look at the full Harvard study would probably reveal quite quickly the study's actual posited relationship between breast cancer and estrogen pills. Applied to contract disputes and insurance coverage questions, this usually means that the information other than simply the specific written term in dispute can be used to resolve the dispute. However, as discussed below, if there are no additional indicia of meaning, the ambiguity is resolved against the drafter of the problematic language.

§ 2.08   THE KINSHIP BETWEEN CONTRACT INTERPRETATION AND STATUTORY INTERPRETATION

Page 104: [Add at the end of § 2.08:]

See generally Jonathan T. Molot, *The Rise and Fall of Textualism*, 106 COLUM. L. REV. 1 (2006); John F. Manning, *What Divides Textualists from Purposivists*, 106 COLUM. L. REV. 70 (2006).

§ 2.09   THE ROLE OF REASONABLE EXPECTATIONS AND THE SEMI-CONTROVERSIAL REASONABLE EXPECTATIONS "DOCTRINE"

Page 108: [Add at the end of § 2.09:]

GESCHKE v. AIR FORCE ASSOCIATION

425 F.3d 337 (7th Cir. 2005)

SYKES, *Circuit Judge.* Clarence Geschke purchased a defined-benefit supplemental cancer insurance policy that promised to reimburse him for "incurred expenses for the cost of blood or blood plasma." Geschke developed leukemia and required numerous blood transfusions. He later died, and his widow, Irene Geschke, filed an insurance claim that included $33,689.81 in expenses for blood and transfusion-related charges such as laboratory testing, equipment, drugs, administrative fees, and other transfusion expenses. The insurer paid only the cost of the blood product itself, or $1,245.10, and denied coverage for the related charges. Mrs. Geschke filed suit in state court against the insurer and the association that marketed the policy to her late husband, alleging breach of contract, common law fraud, and violation of the Illinois Consumer Fraud Act ("ICFA"). The defendants removed the case to federal district court.

The district court granted summary judgment to the defendants, holding that the unambiguous policy language covered only the cost of the blood itself and not other costs associated with its delivery and administration. We agree with this conclusion. The insurance policy expressly covers only "incurred expenses for the cost of blood or plasma," not related transfusion charges. This coverage language is clear and unambiguous. Accordingly, the insurer did not breach its contract by paying only that portion of the transfusion-related claim that consisted of the cost of the blood. Summary judgment in favor of the defendants on the common law and statutory fraud claims was also appropriate, as there is no evidence of any false statement or deceptive act by the defendants in connection with the sale of the policy.

I. Background

In May 1997 Clarence Geschke enrolled in the Air Force Association's ("AFA") CancerCare Plan, a supplemental cancer insurance policy under-written by Monumental Life Insurance Company ("Monumental" or "the insurer"). The policy and its associated riders provided defined benefits for certain expenses incurred in the treatment of cancer, such as hospitaliza-tion, hospice care, ambulance services, anesthesia, and blood and plasma. As is relevant here, the "Blood and Plasma Benefit Rider" included in Mr. Geschke's policy provided as follows:

> Upon receipt of due proof that the Covered Person incurred ex-
> penses for the cost of blood or blood plasma, we will pay a benefit
> for these expenses not to exceed the Maximum Benefit shown on
> the Schedule. The expense of blood or blood plasma incurred while
> Hospital Confined, as an outpatient or in a free standing facility
> is eligible for this benefit.

The rider's maximum benefit per Illness Period was $500, but the Schedule
of Benefits also indicated that there was no maximum for leukemia. Mr.
Geschke paid a quarterly premium of $31.50 for "Member & Family"
coverage under the policy and its associated riders.

Mr. Geschke was diagnosed with leukemia in March 1999. On or about
April 14, 1999, he sent Monumental a claim form seeking benefits for inpa-
tient and outpatient services provided by Sherman Hospital in 1998 and
early 1999. The parties dispute exactly when Mr. or Mrs. Geschke provided
Monumental with documentation sufficient to establish Mr. Geschke's
cancer diagnosis, as required by the policy, but the issue is no longer
material. Sadly, Mr. Geschke died on June 21, 1999.

On October 18, 1999, Mrs. Geschke submitted an updated claim to
Monumental for $7,622.37. Of that amount, $33,689.81 related to Mr.
Geschke's blood transfusions. In December 1999 Monumental paid
$2,114.61 to Mrs. Geschke for hospitalization, surgical, and anesthesia
charges. Later, on March 31, 2000, Monumental paid $1,245.10 under the
Blood and Plasma Benefit Rider. In a follow-up letter to Mrs. Geschke dated
June 23, 2000, Monumental explained that the Blood and Plasma Benefit
Rider did not cover processing or administrative fees, supplies, drugs, or
laboratory charges associated with the blood transfusions, and that Monumental was declining to cover the remaining $32,444.71 of the transfusion-
related claim.

Mrs. Geschke never cashed Monumental's checks. Instead, she filed suit
against Monumental and the AFA, alleging breach of contract and seeking
recovery of benefits under the Blood and Plasma Benefit Rider. She also
alleged common law fraud and [statutory] fraud. The gravamen of both
fraud claims is that by failing to explain that the Blood and Plasma Benefit
Rider covered only the cost of blood products and not related tranfusion
expenses, the defendants fraudulently induced Mr. Geschke to purchase the
policy and pay premiums. For each of the three claims, compensatory
damages were alleged to be "in excess of $20,000 and not more than
$50,000." In addition, the two fraud claims included demands for punitive
damages. The district court concluded that although the terms "blood" and
"plasma" are not defined in the policy, a reasonable person would understand that the phrase "cost of blood or blood plasma" refers to the cost of
the blood product itself and not to other costs associated with the administration of the blood product to a sick person. As such, the court held that
Monumental did not breach its contract with Geschke. The court also held
that Mrs. Geschke could not carry her burden on the common law and
statutory fraud claims because no misrepresentation could be inferred from

policy language that was unambiguous, and no other evidence of false statements or deception by the defendants had been presented.

[Court's discussion of subject matter jurisdiction eliminated]

* * *

In Illinois, an insurance policy is treated as any other contract and is
subject to the same rules of construction. Policy language that is clear and
unambiguous is accorded its plain, ordinary, and popular meaning. Ambiguities should be construed in favor of the insured. But "a court should
not search for an ambiguity where there is none." The determination of
whether the terms of an insurance policy are ambiguous is made by
reference to a reasonable person standard; "the test is . . . what a reasonable person in the position of the insured would understand [the terms]
to mean." . . . . "All the provisions of an insurance contract, rather than an
isolated part, should be read together to interpret it and to determine
whether an ambiguity exists." The policy language at issue in this case is
contained in the Blood and Plasma Benefit Rider, which by its terms
provides benefits for "incurred expenses for the cost of blood or blood
plasma." The question here is whether the phrase "expenses for the cost
of blood or blood plasma" confers coverage for blood or plasma costs only,
or includes additional expenses associated with the transfusion of the blood
product. The policy does not define either "blood" or "plasma," but under
Illinois law "[a] policy term is not ambiguous because the term is not defined
within the policy or because the parties can suggest creative possibilities
for its meaning."

Monumental argues that the "blood or blood plasma" language in the
policy is clear and unambiguous and that a reasonable person would understand that the phrase refers only to the cost of the blood product itself and
not the various additional charges for equipment and services involved in
providing the blood to a medical patient undergoing treatment. Mrs.
Geschke argues that it is unreasonable to interpret the rider to cover the
cost of blood product but not the services essential for it to be useful. A
cancer patient in need of a blood transfusion, she argues, "is not merely
handed some blood and told to take it himself as if it were aspirin."

Mrs. Geschke is undoubtedly correct that no cancer patient expects to
be handed a pint of blood by medical staff and told to transfuse it himself.
But the way medical services are delivered is not the issue here. The issue
is whether Monumental contracted with Mr. Geschke to pay not only for
the pints of blood or plasma he received but for the various additional costs
associated with the delivery of blood to him. We agree with the insurer and
the district court that the "blood or plasma" language is clear on its face
and covers only the cost of blood or plasma.

Although it is true that blood and blood plasma are of no practical use
to a patient without being transfused, it does not follow that the Blood and
Plasma Benefit Rider covers more than the cost of the blood or plasma itself,

as only the blood products are specifically mentioned in the rider. "Blood" and "blood transfusion" are not synonyms, nor is the latter term subsumed within the former. The dictionary definition of "blood" is "the fluid that circulates in the principal vascular system of vertebrate animals carrying nourishment and oxygen to all parts of the body and bringing away waste products for excretion . . . ." WEBSTER'S THIRD NEW INTERNATIONAL DICTIONARY 236-37 (1981). "Plasma" is defined as "the fluid part of blood, or lymph, or milk that is distinguishable from suspended material . . . and that in blood differs from serum." Nothing in these definitions suggests anything other than what we colloquially refer to as "a pint of blood," nor do they encompass the medical process of transfusion.

The CancerCare Plan at issue here distinguishes the defined benefits included within the policy's coverages from general "treatment" and "cancer treatment." The policy itself does not generally cover cancer treatment, or any treatment at all; according to the "Cancer Insurance Benefit" provision, the policy pays "benefits according to the Schedule of Benefits for Cancer that manifests itself while the Covered Person is insured under this Policy." A special rider was available that did, under limited circumstances, provide coverage for cancer treatment. Mr. Geschke purchased this rider, called the "Extended Hospital Expenses Benefit Rider." It offered policyholders who purchased the rider a choice: the Plan would pay "Hospital charges for Cancer treatment while a Covered Person is Confined in the Hospital," beginning with the ninety-first day of hospitalization, but only in lieu of all the other benefits provided under the policy. Thus, for policyholders like Mr. Geschke who purchased the Extended Hospital Expenses rider, "cancer treatment" was considered a benefit distinct from all the other defined benefits included in the plan and the other riders. None of the other defined benefits were denominated "treatment" by the policy. This supports the conclusion that the phrase "cost of blood or blood plasma" means the cost of blood or plasma only and not the additional costs associated with treatment-related services such as laboratory testing and transfusion.

Furthermore, if Mr. Geschke's medical bills are any guide at all, the total cost of testing and transfusing the blood products dwarfs the cost of the blood itself by a ratio of roughly 27:1. We must therefore consider whether a reasonable purchaser of this policy would have thought that by paying $31.50 per quarter for "Member & Family" coverage he or she was obtaining coverage not only for blood products but for the full range of services necessary to the transfusion process. Under the Blood and Plasma Rider, the maximum benefit per illness period is $500. However, there is no limit on the benefit for leukemia patients. The parties agree that leukemia treatment generally requires numerous blood transfusions, and the rider's no-limit benefit for leukemia reflects that reality. But not every purchaser of the rider expects to develop leukemia; some are concerned about other forms of cancer. Given the great disproportion between the cost of blood itself and the costs associated with transfusions, it would be unreasonable for a purchaser of this policy to believe that the $500 maximum in nonleukemia cases covers transfusions as well as blood, for $500 will not pay for the transfusion of a single pint. [in footnote 2, the Court noted that "According to Geschke's October 18, 1999, claim, Geschke incurred the following expenses for blood and plasma on November 5-6, 1998: $82.70 for "IV Drugs," $225.75 for "Med/Sur Supplies," $1,660.36 for "Laboratory," $165.60 for "Lab/Immunology," $45.95 for "OR Services," and $112.65 for "Blood/Store-Proc." The same itemized charges, and others, were broken out in Sherman Hospital's other billings for blood and plasma. (Apparently $112.65 is the hospital's price for one pint of blood, as other "Blood/Store-Proc" charges were often exact multiples of that amount.) Accordingly, the total cost of transfusing one pint of blood on that particular day was $2,263.06."]

* * *

We agree with the district court that the phrase "cost of blood or blood plasma" in the insurance rider is unambiguous and includes only the cost of the blood product itself. Monumental did not breach its contract by declining to pay the administrative, testing, transfusion, and other charges associated with the administration of the blood products.

QUESTIONS

Does the *Geschke* opinion correctly interpret the textual trees at the expense of viewing the "forest" of the purpose and nature of the insurance product? Consider whether the reasonable expectations approach discussed in this chapter (§ 2.12[A]) would auger in favor of a different result. Does the Court's "low premium" argument persuade you of the limited scope of the policy? If so, was Mr. Geschke sold a policy that was inadequate and inappropriate for his needs? Why or why not? If so, is this a problem that should be addressed by courts, legislators, or regulators?

§ 2.10 GENERAL CANONS OF CONSTRUCTION AND OTHER GROUND RULES OF CONTRACT INTERPRETATION

Page 111: [Add at the end of § 2.10:]

Two relatively recent state supreme court cases reflect the degree to which courts tend to both emphasize text and read broad language broadly. In *BP America, Inc. v. State Auto Property & Casualty*, 2005 Okla Lexis 65 (Oklahoma Supreme Court, Sept. 20, 2005), the Oklahoma Supreme Court of answered certified questions from the Northern District of Oklahoma concerning the meaning of the phrase "any insured" contained in the Auto Exclusion of a commercial general liability policy. The exclusion at issue provided that the insurance did not apply to "'Bodily injury' or 'property damage' arising out of the ownership, maintenance, use or entrustment to others of any . . . 'auto' . . . owned or operated by or rented or loaned to **any** insured. Use includes operation and 'loading or unloading'. . . ." (emphasis added). The liability insurer apparently declined to provide coverage on the basis of the policy's Auto Exclusion and argued for a literal reading of the term "any" while the policyholder argued that the term "any insured" should be interpreted to mean "the named insured." The Oklahoma Supreme Court sided with the insurer, observing that:

> The overwhelming number of courts, addressing policy language similar to that at issue here, determines, as a matter of law, that the term "any insured" in an exclusionary clause is unambiguous and expresses a definite and certain intent to deny coverage to all insureds—even to innocent parties. These jurisdictions recognize that to impose liability on the insurer would raise coverage where none was intended and no premium was collected.

> Furthermore, adopting the position advanced by the insured would require that we unilaterally convert a general liability policy—without motor vehicle coverage—into an automotive liability policy. This we will not do.

Cases that address the distinction between the phrases "any insured" or "an insured" and "the insured," as used in a policy exclusion, are not unique, as evidenced by the *BP America* opinion citing nearly 60 of them from around the country in reaching its decision. The phrase "any insured" is seen in a variety of policy exclusions. As a result, the question whether an exclusion containing this phrase applies to so-called "innocent insureds" arises with regularity.

The Florida Supreme Court took a similar approach to the interpreting the term "arising under" in a liability insurance exclusion. In *Taurus Holdings, Inc. v. United States Fidelity and Guaranty Co.*, 913 So. 2d 528 (Fla. 2005), the court addressed a certified question from the Eleventh Circuit: Whether the products—completed operations exclusion contained in several insurers' commercial general liability policies issued to a gun manufacturer precluded coverage for suits brought by municipalities seeking to recover the cost of medical and other services incurred as a result of gun violence in their communities. On one hand, *Taurus Holdings* is a case about guns and presents a very narrow, but significant, coverage issue. On the other hand, the Florida high court's interpretation of the commonly used insurance policy phrase "arising out of" potentially gives it wider precedential influence.

Taurus Holdings argued that the phrase "arising out of" contained in an exclusion in the policy was ambiguous. The Florida Supreme Court, after an extensive review of case law, concluded that the majority position nationally is to interpret the phrase "arising out of" more broadly than mere proximate cause. "The general consensus [is] that the phrase 'arising out of' should be given a broad reading such as 'originating from' or 'growing out of' or 'flowing from' or 'done in connection with'—that is, it requires some causal connection to the injuries suffered, but does not require proximate cause in the legal sense." *Taurus Holdings* cited decisions from ten other jurisdictions and two insurance treatises. On the minority side, the court cited six opinions. Following this analysis, the court stated:

[W]e agree with the majority of states and conclude that the phrase 'arising out of your product' in the products-completed operations hazard exclusions at issue is unambiguous. "The term 'arising out of' is broader in meaning than the term 'caused by' and means 'originating from,' 'having its origin in,' 'growing out of,' 'flowing from,' 'incident to' or 'having a connection with.' " [T]his requires more than a mere coincidence between the conduct (or, in this case, the product) and the injury. It requires "some causal connection, or relationship." But it does not require proximate cause.

Consequently, the court held that coverage was excluded because "[t]he bodily injuries alleged all originated from Taurus's products—that is, the discharge of their manufactured guns."

A New York case takes a less textual and more contextual view of the term "arising out of in a vender's endorsement to a of a manufacturer's liability policy. However, the effect of this less textual approach was to limit insurance coverage to situations where a claim stemmed from a defect in the product rather than from vendor negligence. *See Raymond Corp. v. National Union Fire Ins. Co.*, 5 N.Y.3d 157, 833 N.E.2d 232 (N.Y. 2005). This less textual approach makes sense regarding a vendor's endorsement, which makes a retailer or other vendor an additional insured under a manufacturer's liability policy. The intent of such a provision is for the manufacturer's insurance to protect the vendor from claims arising due to problems with the manufacturer's product. In this way, the manufacturer, by providing such protection, can more effectively market its products by lowering the vendor's risk that it will be pulled into a lawsuit through the fault of the manufacturer's mis-designed or poorly manufactured product. The vendor's endorsement is not intended to provide free liability insurance to the vendor for all of the vendor's operations or for its own negligence. Consequently, a more restricted reading of the "arising under" endorsement makes sense in such a case.

Conversely, a broader reading of the arising under language in the *Taurus Holdings* gun liability coverage case makes perfect sense in that the insurer's intent was clearly to avoid gun litigation coverage as a part of the design of the liability policy. A broad construction of the term "any insured" as in *BP America* is closer question. The intent of this language is to avoid coverage whenever any covered person creates liability in ways the insurer considers outside the scope of the insurance product at issue. But giving this type of exclusion broad interpretative breadth tends to leave "innocent" co-insureds with no coverage, perhaps in derogation of their objectively reasonable expectations. It also may create public policy problems by shrinking available coverage and leaving victims uncompensated even though insurance was purchased that arguably covered the risk at issue. In addition, reading even relatively plain language too broadly runs counter to the traditional axiom that exclusions are to be strictly construed against the insurer, who must shoulder the burden of persuasion to demonstrate the applicability of an exclusion.

§ 2.12   CONTRACT CONSTRUCTION THEORY AND DOCTRINE IN PRACTICE

Page 122: [In the first full paragraph, update for citation in § 2.12:]

Hazel Beh's article, *Reassessing the Sophisticated Insured Exception* has been published at 39 TORT, TRIAL & INS. PRAC. L.J. 85 (2003).

§ 2.13   MORE ON THE ROLE OF UNCONSCIONABILITY AND PUBLIC POLICY IN CONSTRUING INSURANCE POLICIES

Page 161: [Add to § 2.13, Note (1):]

For a recent non-insurance decision reviewing the unconscionability concept in general and in connection with arbitration agreements in particular, see *Wisconsin Auto Title Loans, Inc. v. Jones*, 714 N.W.2d 155 (Wis. 2006).

Chapter 3
GOVERNMENT REGULATION OF INSURANCE

§ 3.01 GENERAL PRINCIPLES

[A] Introduction

Page 188: [Add at the conclusion of § 3.01[A]:]

One need only look at the newspaper to see the importance of insurance regulation and regulators, both "direct" regulators such as a state insurance commissioner and "indirect" regulators such as a state attorney general or local prosecutor. *See, e.g.,* Mark E. Ruquet & Michael Ha, *New York Sues AIG, Greenberg For Improper Accounting Practices*, NAT'L UNDERWRITER (Prop. & Cas. ed.), May 30, 2005 at 6; Karen Richardson & Gregory Zuckerman, *Gen Re Official to Plead Guilty and Cooperate*, WALL ST. J., June 7, 2005 at C1, col. 6. The "Greenberg" sued by New York Attorney General Eliot Spitzer is Maurice "Hank" Greenberg, former CEO of AIG, the world's largest insurance company, and the man generally credited with the company's growth and profitability over the past 40 years. *See* Daniel Hays & Michael Ha, *The Greenberg ERA Ends Abruptly*, NAT'L UNDERWRITER (Life & Health ed.), Mar. 21, 2005 at 6 (summarizing history of AIG and Greenberg career).

[B] The Power of the State to Regulate

Page 189: [Add the following to § 3.01[B], Note (1):]

Notwithstanding the *Silver* holding, Puerto Rico has continued to attempt to impose unconstitutional restrictions on nonresidents working in the insurance industry. *See, e.g., Council of Insurance Agents & Brokers v. Juarbe-Jimenez*, 443 F.3d 103 (1st Cir. 2006) (striking down as unconstitutional statutes prohibiting nonresident agents and brokers from soliciting insurance and inspecting risks in Puerto Rico). Although the *Silver* opinion is now 20 years old and lawmakers and litigants of course have a right to revisit even decided doctrine, we are a little surprised that the Puerto Rican legislature would have done this in light of the clear correctness of *Silver* and the clear unconstitutionality of such laws.

§ 3.02   Administrative Powers

[F] Regulation Seeking to Effect Public Policy — The Limits of Intervention?

Page 229: [Add to the note on page 229 in § 3.02[F]:]

California Insurance Commissioner John Garamendi is a particularly prominent and active regulator, with an overall track record that is quite good in spite of the loss on the issue of holocaust insurance denial disclosures. *See, e.g., State Farm Mut. Auto. Ins. Co. v. Garamendi*, 12 Cal. Rptr. 3d 343, 88 P.3d 71 (Cal. 2004) (unanimously upholding regulation that insurers may their "community service statements" available for public inspection even if some portions of the statement contained arguable "trade secrets" of the insurer; state Insurance Commissioner has broad discretion to adopt rules and regulations to promote public welfare). The community service statements are not, as the name may imply, brochures about the insurer's charitable activities but instead are required to contain statistical information regarding the insurer's activities in the state, including distribution of business by zip code (so the trade secret claim of the insurers was not as strained as it might appear from the title of the documents at issue).

§ 3.03   SPECIFIC INSURANCE PROGRAMS

[E] Other Programs

[3] Federal Flood Insurance

Page 259: [Add at the conclusion of § 3.03[E][3]:]

Because they so directly puts federal dollars at risk, flood insurance policies involve certain special protections in the law. *See, e.g., Palmieri v. Allstate Ins. Co.*, 445 F.3d 179 (2d Cir. 2006) (applying federal law) (flood insurance act precludes prejudgment interest on amounts recovered and preempts any contrary state law); *Gallup v. Omaha Prop. & Cas. Ins. Co.*, 434 F.3d 341 (5th Cir. 2005) (applying federal law) (Flood Act preempts state tort actions based on insurer's handling of claim under flood policy); *Studio Frames Ltd v. Standard Fire Ins. Co.*, 397 F.Supp. 2d 685 (M.D.N.C. 2005) (interest not available on judgments against flood insurers or NFIP). Similar state-supported insurance programs may have similar protection. *See, e.g., Jonathan Neil & Assocs., Inc. v. Jones*, 33 Cal. 4th 917, 94 P.3d 1055, 16 Cal. Rptr. 3d 849 (Cal. 2004) (bad faith tort remedy not available against insurers in connection with coverage issued due to participation in California Automobile Assigned Risk Plan).

§ 3.04   THE INSURANCE SUB-LAW OF ERISA

Page 288: [Add to § 3.04 on prior to the Notes and Questions:]

AETNA HEALTH INC. v. DAVILA

542 U.S. 200; 124 S. Ct. 2488; 159 L. Ed. 2d 312 (2004)

Justice **Thomas** delivered the opinion of the Court.

In these consolidated cases, two individuals sued their respective health maintenance organizations (HMOs) for alleged failures to exercise ordinary care in the handling of coverage decisions, in violation of a duty imposed by the Texas Health Care Liability Act (THCLA). We granted certiorari to decide whether the individuals' causes of action are completely pre-empted by the "interlocking, interrelated, and interdependent remedial scheme" We hold that the causes of action are completely pre-empted and hence removable from state to federal court. The Court of Appeals, having reached a contrary conclusion, is reversed.

Respondent Juan Davila is a participant, and respondent Ruby Calad is a beneficiary, in ERISA-regulated employee benefit plans. Their respective plan sponsors had entered into agreements with petitioners, Aetna Health Inc. and CIGNA Healthcare of Texas, Inc., to administer the plans. Under Davila's plan, for instance, Aetna reviews requests for coverage and pays providers, such as doctors, hospitals, and nursing homes, which perform covered services for members; under Calad's plan sponsor's agreement, CIGNA is responsible for plan benefits and coverage decisions.

Respondents both suffered injuries allegedly arising from Aetna's and CIGNA's decisions not to provide coverage for certain treatment and services recommended by respondents' treating physicians. Davila's treating physician prescribed Vioxx to remedy Davila's arthritis pain, but Aetna refused to pay for it. Davila did not appeal or contest this decision, nor did he purchase Vioxx with his own resources and seek reimbursement. Instead, Davila began taking Naprosyn, from which he allegedly suffered a severe reaction that required extensive treatment and hospitalization. Calad underwent surgery, and although her treating physician recommended an extended hospital stay, a CIGNA discharge nurse determined that Calad did not meet the plan's criteria for a continued hospital stay. CIGNA consequently denied coverage for the extended hospital stay. Calad experienced postsurgery complications forcing her to return to the hospital. She alleges that these complications would not have occurred had CIGNA approved coverage for a longer hospital stay.

Respondents brought separate suits in Texas state court against petitioners. Invoking THCLA, respondents argued that petitioners' refusal to cover the requested services violated their "duty to exercise ordinary care when making health care treatment decisions," and that these refusals "proximately caused" their injuries. *Ibid.* Petitioners removed the cases to Federal District Courts, arguing that respondents' causes of action fit within the scope of, and were therefore completely pre-empted by, ERISA § 502(a). The respective District Courts agreed, and declined to remand the cases to state court. Because respondents refused to amend their complaints to bring explicit ERISA claims, the District Courts dismissed the complaints with prejudice.

Both Davila and Calad appealed the refusals to remand to state court. The United States Court of Appeals for the Fifth Circuit consolidated their cases with several others raising similar issues. The Court of Appeals recognized that state causes of action that "duplicat[e] or fal[l] within the scope of an ERISA § 502(a) remedy" are completely pre-empted and hence removable to federal court. After examining the causes of action available under § 502(a), the Court of Appeals determined that respondents' claims could possibly fall under only two: § 502(a)(1)(B), which provides a cause of action for the recovery of wrongfully denied benefits, and § 502(a) (2), which allows suit against a plan fiduciary for breaches of fiduciary duty to the plan.

Congress enacted ERISA to "protect . . . the interests of participants in employee benefit plans and their beneficiaries" by setting out substantive regulatory requirements for employee benefit plans and to "provid[e] for appropriate remedies, sanctions, and ready access to the Federal courts." The purpose of ERISA is to provide a uniform regulatory regime over employee benefit plans. To this end, ERISA includes expansive pre-emption provisions, which are intended to ensure that employee benefit plan regulation would be "exclusively a federal concern."

ERISA's "comprehensive legislative scheme" includes "an integrated system of procedures for enforcement." This integrated enforcement mechanism, ERISA § 502(a), is a distinctive feature of ERISA, and essential to accomplish Congress' purpose of creating a comprehensive statute for the regulation of employee benefit plans. As the Court said in *Pilot Life Ins. Co. v. Dedeaux* (1987):

> "[T]he detailed provisions of § 502(a) set forth a comprehensive civil enforcement scheme that represents a careful balancing of the need for prompt and fair claims settlement procedures against the public interest in encouraging the formation of employee benefit plans. The policy choices reflected in the inclusion of certain remedies and the exclusion of others under the federal scheme would be completely undermined if ERISA-plan participants and beneficiaries were free to obtain remedies under state law that Congress rejected in ERISA. 'The six carefully integrated civil enforcement provisions found in § 502(a) of the statute as finally enacted . . . provide strong evidence that Congress did *not* intend to authorize other remedies that it simply forgot to incorporate expressly.' "

Therefore, any state-law cause of action that duplicates, supplements, or supplants the ERISA civil enforcement remedy conflicts with the clear congressional intent to make the ERISA remedy exclusive and is therefore pre-empted.

The pre-emptive force of ERISA § 502(a) is still stronger. In *Metropolitan Life Ins. Co. v. Taylor* the Court determined that the similarity of the language used in the Labor Management Relations Act, 1947 (LMRA), and ERISA, combined with the "clear intention" of Congress "to make § 502(a)(1)(B) suits brought by participants or beneficiaries federal questions for the purposes of federal court jurisdiction in like manner as § 301 of the LMRA," established that ERISA § 502(a)(1)(B)'s pre-emptive force mirrored the pre-emptive force of LMRA § 301. Since LMRA § 301 converts state causes of action into federal ones for purposes of determining the propriety of removal, so too does ERISA § 502(a)(1)(B). Thus, the ERISA civil enforcement mechanism is one of those provisions with such "extraordinary pre-emptive power" that it "converts an ordinary state common law complaint into one stating a federal claim for purposes of the well-pleaded complaint rule." Hence, "causes of action within the scope of the civil enforcement provisions of § 502(a) [are] removable to federal court." ERISA § 502(a)(1)(B) provides:

> "A civil action may be brought—(1) by a participant or beneficiary—. . . (B) to recover benefits due to him under the terms of his plan, to enforce his rights under the terms of the plan, or to clarify his rights to future benefits under the terms of the plan."

This provision is relatively straightforward. If a participant or beneficiary believes that benefits promised to him under the terms of the plan are not provided, he can bring suit seeking provision of those benefits. A participant or beneficiary can also bring suit generically to "enforce his rights" under the plan, or to clarify any of his rights to future benefits. Any dispute over the precise terms of the plan is resolved by a court under a *de novo* review standard, unless the terms of the plan "giv[e] the administrator or fiduciary discretionary authority to determine eligibility for benefits or to construe the terms of the plan."

It follows that if an individual brings suit complaining of a denial of coverage for medical care, where the individual is entitled to such coverage only because of the terms of an ERISA-regulated employee benefit plan, and where no legal duty (state or federal) independent of ERISA or the plan terms is violated, then the suit falls "within the scope of" ERISA § 502(a)(1)(B). In other words, if an individual, at some point in time, could have brought his claim under ERISA § 502(a)(1)(B), and where there is no other independent legal duty that is implicated by a defendant's actions, then the individual's cause of action is completely pre-empted by ERISA § 502(a)(1)(B).

To determine whether respondents' causes of action fall "within the scope" of ERISA § 502(a)(1)(B), we must examine respondents' complaints, the statute on which their claims are based (the THCLA), and the various plan documents. Davila alleges that Aetna provides health coverage under his employer's health benefits plan. Davila also alleges that after his primary care physician prescribed Vioxx, Aetna refused to pay for it. The only action complained of was Aetna's refusal to approve payment for Davila's Vioxx prescription. Further, the only relationship Aetna had with Davila was its partial administration of Davila's employer's benefit plan.

Similarly, Calad alleges that she receives, as her husband's beneficiary under an ERISA-regulated benefit plan, health coverage from CIGNA. She alleges that she was informed by CIGNA, upon admittance into a hospital for major surgery, that she would be authorized to stay for only one day. She also alleges that CIGNA, acting through a discharge nurse, refused to authorize more than a single day despite the advice and recommendation of her treating physician. Calad contests only CIGNA's decision to refuse coverage for her hospital stay. And, as in Davila's case, the only connection between Calad and CIGNA is CIGNA's administration of portions of Calad's ERISA-regulated benefit plan.

It is clear, then, that respondents complain only about denials of coverage promised under the terms of ERISA-regulated employee benefit plans. Upon the denial of benefits, respondents could have paid for the treatment themselves and then sought reimbursement through a § 502(a)(1)(B) action, or sought a preliminary injunction. . . . Respondents contend, however, that the complained-of actions violate legal duties that arise independently of ERISA or the terms of the employee benefit plans at issue in these cases. Both respondents brought suit specifically under the THCLA, alleging that petitioners "controlled, influenced, participated in and made decisions which affected the quality of the diagnosis, care, and treatment provided" in a manner that violated "the duty of ordinary care set forth in §§ 88.001 and 88.002." Respondents contend that this duty of ordinary care is an independent legal duty. They analogize to this Court's decisions interpreting LMRA § 301. Because this duty of ordinary care arises independently of any duty imposed by ERISA or the plan terms, the argument goes, any civil action to enforce this duty is not within the scope of the ERISA civil enforcement mechanism.

The duties imposed by the THCLA in the context of these cases, however, do not arise independently of ERISA or the plan terms. The THCLA does impose a duty on managed care entities to "exercise ordinary care when making health care treatment decisions," and makes them liable for damages proximately caused by failures to abide by that duty. However, if a managed care entity correctly concluded that, under the terms of the relevant plan, a particular treatment was not covered, the managed care entity's denial of coverage would not be a proximate cause of any injuries arising from the denial. Rather, the failure of the plan itself to cover the requested treatment would be the proximate cause. More significantly, the THCLA clearly states that "[t]he standards in Subsections (a) and (b) create no obligation on the part of the health insurance carrier, health mainte-nance organization, or other managed care entity to provide to an insured or enrollee treatment which is not covered by the health care plan of the entity." Hence, a managed care entity could not be subject to liability under the THCLA if it denied coverage for any treatment not covered by the health care plan that it was administering.

Thus, interpretation of the terms of respondents' benefit plans forms an essential part of their THCLA claim, and THCLA liability would exist here only because of petitioners' administration of ERISA-regulated benefit plans. Petitioners' potential liability under the THCLA in these cases, then, derives entirely from the particular rights and obligations established by the benefit plans. So, unlike the state-law claims in *Caterpillar, supra,* respondents' THCLA causes of action are not entirely independent of the federally regulated contract itself. * * * Hence, respondents bring suit only to rectify a wrongful denial of benefits promised under ERISA-regulated plans, and do not attempt to remedy any violation of a legal duty independent of ERISA. We hold that respondents' state causes of action fall "within the scope of" ERISA § 502(a)(1)(B), *Metropolitan Life* [1985] and are therefore completely pre-empted by ERISA § 502 and removable to federal district court.

* * *

Ultimately, the Court of Appeals [which ruled in favor of Davila and Casad] rested its decision on one line from *Rush Prudential.* There, we described our holding in *Ingersoll-Rand* as follows: "[W]hile state law duplicated the elements of a claim available under ERISA, it converted the remedy from an equitable one under § 1132(a)(3) (available exclusively in federal district courts) into a legal one for money damages (available in a state tribunal)." The point of this sentence was to describe why the state cause of action in *Ingersoll-Rand* was pre-empted by ERISA § 502(a): It was pre-empted because it attempted to convert an equitable remedy into a legal remedy. Nowhere in *Rush Prudential* did we suggest that the preemptive force of ERISA § 502(a) is limited to the situation in which a state cause of action precisely duplicates a cause of action under ERISA § 502(a).

Nor would it be consistent with our precedent to conclude that only strictly duplicative state causes of action are pre-empted. Frequently, in order to receive exemplary damages on a state claim, a plaintiff must prove facts beyond the bare minimum necessary to establish entitlement to an award. In order to recover for mental anguish, for instance, the plaintiffs in *Ingersoll-Rand* and *Metropolitan Life* would presumably have had to prove the existence of mental anguish; there is no such element in an ordinary suit brought under ERISA § 502(a)(1)(B). This did not save these state causes of action from pre-emption. Congress' intent to make the ERISA civil enforcement mechanism exclusive would be undermined if state causes of action that supplement the ERISA § 502(a) remedies were permitted, even if the elements of the state cause of action did not precisely duplicate the elements of an ERISA claim.

Respondents also argue-for the first time in their brief to this Court-that the THCLA is a law that regulates insurance, and hence that ERISA § 514(b)(2)(A) saves their causes of action from pre-emption (and thereby from complete pre-emption). This argument is unavailing. The existence of a comprehensive remedial scheme can demonstrate an "overpowering federal policy" that determines the interpretation of a statutory provision designed to save state law from being pre-empted. * * * As this Court stated in *Pilot Life*, "our understanding of [§ 514(b)(2)(A)] must be informed by the legislative intent concerning the civil enforcement provisions provided by ERISA § 502(a), 29 U.S.C. § 1132(a) [29 USCS § 1132(a)]." The Court concluded that "[t]he policy choices reflected in the inclusion of certain remedies and the exclusion of others under the federal scheme would be completely undermined if ERISA-plan participants and beneficiaries were free to obtain remedies under state law that Congress rejected in ERISA." The Court then held, based on

> "the common-sense understanding of the saving clause, the McCarran-Ferguson Act factors defining the business of insurance, and, *most importantly*, the clear expression of congressional intent that ERISA's civil enforcement scheme be exclusive, . . . that [the plaintiff's] state law suit asserting improper processing of a claim for benefits under an ERISA-regulated plan is not saved by § 514(b)(2)(A)."

Pilot Life's reasoning applies here with full force. Allowing respondents to proceed with their state-law suits would "pose an obstacle to the purposes and objectives of Congress." As this Court has recognized in both *Rush Prudential* and *Pilot Life*, ERISA § 514(b)(2)(A) must be interpreted in light of the congressional intent to create an exclusive federal remedy in ERISA § 502(a). Under ordinary principles of conflict pre-emption, then, even a state law that can arguably be characterized as "regulating insurance" will be pre-empted if it provides a separate vehicle to assert a claim for benefits outside of, or in addition to, ERISA's remedial scheme.

Respondents, their *amici*, and some Courts of Appeals have relied heavily upon *Pegram v. Herdrich*, in arguing that ERISA does not pre-empt or completely pre-empt state suits such as respondents'. They contend that *Pegram* makes it clear that causes of action such as respondents' do not "relate to [an] employee benefit plan," * * * *Pegram* cannot be read so broadly. In *Pegram*, the plaintiff sued her physician-owned-and-operated HMO (which provided medical coverage through plaintiff's employer pursuant to an ERISA-regulated benefit plan) and her treating physician, both for medical malpractice and for a breach of an ERISA fiduciary duty. The plaintiff's treating physician was also the person charged with administering plaintiff's benefits; it was she who decided whether certain treatments were covered. We reasoned that the physician's "eligibility decision and the treatment decision were inextricably mixed." We concluded that "Congress did not intend [the defendant HMO] or any other HMO to be treated as a fiduciary to the extent that it makes mixed eligibility decisions acting through its physicians."

A benefit determination under ERISA, though, is generally a fiduciary act. "At common law, fiduciary duties characteristically attach to decisions about managing assets and distributing property to beneficiaries." Hence, a benefit determination is part and parcel of the ordinary fiduciary responsibilities connected to the administration of a plan. The fact that a benefits determination is infused with medical judgments does not alter this result. * * * *Pegram* itself recognized this principle. *Pegram*, in highlighting its conclusion that "mixed eligibility decisions" were not fiduciary in nature, contrasted the operation of "[t]raditional trustees administer[ing] a medical trust" and "physicians through whom HMOs act." A traditional medical trust is administered by "paying out money to buy medical care, whereas physicians making mixed eligibility decisions consume the money as well." And, significantly, the Court stated that "[p]rivate trustees do not make treatment judgments." But a trustee managing a medical trust undoubtedly must make administrative decisions that require the exercise of medical judgment. Petitioners are not the employers of respondents' treating physicians and are therefore in a somewhat analogous position to that of a trustee for a traditional medical trust.

ERRISA itself and its implementing regulations confirm this interpretation. ERISA defines a fiduciary as any person "to the extent . . . he has any discretionary authority or discretionary responsibility in the administration of [an employee benefit] plan." When administering employee benefit plans, HMOs must make discretionary decisions regarding eligibility for plan benefits, and, in this regard, must be treated as plan fiduciaries. Also, ERISA § 503, which specifies minimum requirements for a plan's claim procedure, requires plans to "afford a reasonable opportunity to any participant whose claim for benefits has been denied for a full and fair review by the appropriate named fiduciary of the decision denying the claim." This strongly suggests that the ultimate decisionmaker in a plan regarding an award of benefits must be a fiduciary and must be acting as a fiduciary when determining a participant's or beneficiary's claim. The relevant regulations also establish extensive requirements to ensure full and fair review of benefit denials. These regulations, on their face, apply equally to health benefit plans and other plans, and do not draw distinctions between medical and nonmedical benefits determinations. Indeed, the regulations strongly imply that benefits determinations involving medical judgments are, just as much as any other benefits determinations, actions by plan fiduciaries. Classifying any entity with discretionary authority over benefits determinations as anything but a plan fiduciary would thus conflict with ERISA's statutory and regulatory scheme.

Since administrators making benefits determinations, even determinations based extensively on medical judgments, are ordinarily acting as plan fiduciaries, it was essential to *Pegram*'s conclusion that the decisions challenged there were truly "mixed eligibility and treatment decisions," *i.e.*, medical necessity decisions made by the plaintiff's treating physician *qua* treating physician and *qua* benefits administrator. Put another way, the reasoning of *Pegram* "only make[s] sense where the underlying negligence also plausibly constitutes medical maltreatment by a party who can be deemed to be a treating physician or such a physician's employer." Here, however, petitioners are neither respondents' treating physicians nor the employers of respondents' treating physicians. Petitioners' coverage decisions, then, are pure eligibility decisions, and *Pegram* is not implicated.

* * *

Justice **Ginsburg,** with whom Justice **Breyer** joins, concurring.

The Court today holds that the claims respondents asserted under Texas law are totally preempted by § 502(a) of the Employee Retirement Income Security Act of 1974 (ERISA or Act). That decision is consistent with our governing case law on ERISA's preemptive scope. I therefore join the Court's opinion. But, with greater enthusiasm, as indicated by my dissenting opinion in *Great-West Life & Annuity Ins. Co. v. Knudson* (2002), I also join "the rising judicial chorus urging that Congress and [this] Court revisit what is an unjust and increasingly tangled ERISA regime." Because the Court has coupled an encompassing interpretation of ERISA's preemptive force with a cramped construction of the "equitable relief" allowable under § 502(a)(3), a "regulatory vacuum" exists: "[V]irtually all state law remedies are preempted but very few federal substitutes are provided." * * * A series of the Court's decisions has yielded a host of situations in which persons adversely affected by ERISA-proscribed wrongdoing cannot gain make-whole relief. * * * * "[T]here is a stark absence-in [ERISA] itself and in its legislative history-of any reference to an intention to authorize the recovery of extracontractual damages" for consequential injuries. * * * As the array of lower court cases and opinions documents, fresh consideration of the availability of consequential damages under § 502(a)(3) is plainly in order.

The Government notes a potential amelioration. Recognizing that "this Court has construed Section 502(a)(3) not to authorize an award of money damages against a *non-fiduciary*," the Government suggests that the Act, as currently written and interpreted, may "allo[w] at least some forms of 'make-whole' relief against a breaching *fiduciary* in light of the general availability of such relief in equity at the time of the divided bench." As the Court points out, respondents here declined the opportunity to amend their complaints to state claims for relief under § 502(a); the District Court, therefore, properly dismissed their suits with prejudice. But the Government's suggestion may indicate an effective remedy others similarly circumstanced might fruitfully pursue. * * * "Congress . . . intended ERISA to replicate the core principles of trust remedy law, including the make-whole standard of relief." I anticipate that Congress, or this Court, will one day so confirm.

SEREBOFF v. MID ATLANTIC MEDICAL SERVICES, INC.

126 S. Ct. 1869 (2006)

Roberts, C. J., delivered the opinion for a unanimous Court.

In this case we consider again the circumstances in which a fiduciary under the Employee Retirement Income Security Act of 1974 (ERISA) may sue a beneficiary for reimbursement of medical expenses paid by the ERISA plan, when the beneficiary has recovered for its injuries from a third party. Marlene Sereboff's employer sponsors a health insurance plan administered by respondent Mid Atlantic Medical Services, Inc., and covered by ERISA. Marlene Sereboff and her husband Joel are beneficiaries under the plan. The plan provides for payment of certain covered medical expenses and contains an "Acts of Third Parties" provision. This provision "applies when [a beneficiary is] sick or injured as a result of the act or omission of another person or party," and requires a beneficiary who "receives benefits" under the plan for such injuries to "reimburse [Mid Atlantic]" for those benefits from "[a]ll recoveries from a third party (whether by lawsuit, settlement, or otherwise)." The provision states that "[Mid Atlantic's] share of the recovery will not be reduced because [the beneficiary] has not received the full damages claimed, unless [Mid Atlantic] agrees in writing to a reduction."

The Sereboffs were involved in an automobile accident in California and suffered injuries. Pursuant to the plan's coverage provisions, the plan paid the couple's medical expenses. The Sereboffs filed a tort action in state court against several third parties, seeking compensatory damages for injuries suffered as a result of the accident. Soon after the suit was commenced, Mid Atlantic sent the Sereboffs' attorney a letter asserting a lien on the anticipated proceeds from the suit, for the medical expenses Mid Atlantic paid on the Sereboffs' behalf. On several occasions over the next 21/2 years, Mid Atlantic sent similar correspondence to the attorney and to the Sereboffs, repeating its claim to a lien on a portion of the Sereboffs' recovery, and detailing the medical expenses as they accrued and were paid by the plan. * * * The Sereboffs' tort suit eventually settled for $750,000. Neither the Sereboffs nor their attorney sent any money to Mid Atlantic in satisfaction of its claimed lien which, after Mid Atlantic completed its payments on the Sereboffs' behalf, totaled $74,869.37.

Mid Atlantic filed suit in District Court under § 502(a)(3) of ERISA, seeking to collect from the Sereboffs the medical expenses it had paid on their behalf. Since the Sereboffs' attorney had already distributed the settlement proceeds to them, Mid Atlantic sought a temporary restraining order and preliminary injunction requiring the couple to retain and set aside at least $74,869.37 from the proceeds. The District Court approved a stipulation by the parties, under which the Sereboffs agreed to "preserve $74,869.37 of the settlement funds" in an investment account, "until the [District] Court rules on the merits of this case and all appeals, if any, are exhausted."

On the merits, the District Court found in Mid Atlantic's favor and ordered the Sereboffs to pay Mid Atlantic the $74,869.37, plus interest, with a deduction for Mid Atlantic's share of the attorney's fees and court costs the Sereboffs had incurred in state court. The Sereboffs appealed and the

Fourth Circuit affirmed in relevant part. The Fourth Circuit observed that the Courts of Appeal are divided on the question whether § 502(a)(3) authorizes recovery in these circumstances. We granted certiorari to resolve the disagreement.

A fiduciary may bring a civil action under § 502(a)(3) of ERISA "(A) to enjoin any act or practice which violates any provision of this subchapter or the terms of the plan, or (B) to obtain other appropriate equitable relief (i) to redress such violations or (ii) to enforce any provisions of this subchapter or the terms of the plan." There is no dispute that Mid Atlantic is a fiduciary under ERISA and that its suit in District Court was to "enforce . . . the terms of" the "Acts of Third Parties" provision in the Sereboffs' plan. The only question is whether the relief Mid Atlantic requested from the District Court was "equitable" under § 502(a)(3)(B).

This is not the first time we have had occasion to clarify the scope of the remedial power conferred on district courts by § 502(a)(3)(B). In *Mertens v. Hewitt Associates*, 508 U.S. 248 (1993), we construed the provision to authorize only "those categories of relief that were *typically* available in equity," and thus rejected a claim that we found sought "nothing other than compensatory *damages*." We elaborated on this construction of § 502(a)(3)(B) in *Great-West Life & Annuity Ins. Co. v. Knudson*, 122 S. Ct. 708 (2002), which involved facts similar to those in this case. Much like the "Acts of Third Parties" provision in the Sereboffs' plan, the plan in *Knudson* reserved "'a first lien upon any recovery, whether by settlement, judgment or otherwise,' that the beneficiary receives from [a] third party." After Knudson was involved in a car accident, Great-West paid medical bills on her behalf and, when she recovered in tort from a third party for her injuries, Great-West sought to collect from her for the medical bills it had paid.

In response to the argument that Great-West's claim in *Knudson* was for "restitution" and thus equitable under § 502(a)(3)(B) and *Mertens*, we noted that "not all relief falling under the rubric of restitution [was] available in equity." To decide whether the restitutionary relief sought by Great-West was equitable or legal, we examined cases and secondary legal materials to determine if the relief would have been equitable "[i]n the days of the divided bench." We explained that one feature of equitable restitution was that it sought to impose a constructive trust or equitable lien on "particular funds or property in the defendant's possession." That requirement was not met in *Knudson*, because "the funds to which petitioners claim[ed] an entitlement" were not in Knudson's possession, but had instead been placed in a "Special Needs Trust" under California law. The kind of relief Great-West sought, therefore, was "not equitable-the imposition of a constructive trust or equitable lien on particular property-but legal-the imposition of personal liability for the benefits that [Great-West] conferred upon [Knudson]." We accordingly determined that the suit could not proceed under § 502(a)(3).

That impediment to characterizing the relief in *Knudson* as equitable is not present here. As the Fourth Circuit explained below, in this case Mid

Atlantic sought "specifically identifiable" funds that were "within the possession and control of the Sereboffs"—that portion of the tort settlement due Mid Atlantic under the terms of the ERISA plan, set aside and "preserved [in the Sereboffs'] investment accounts." Unlike Great-West, Mid Atlantic did not simply seek "to impose personal liability . . . for a contractual obligation to pay money." It alleged breach of contract and sought money, to be sure, but it sought its recovery through a constructive trust or equitable lien on a specifically identified fund, not from the Sereboffs' assets generally, as would be the case with a contract action at law. ERISA provides for equitable remedies *to enforce plan terms*, so the fact that the action involves a breach of contract can hardly be enough to prove relief is not equitable; that would make § 502(a)(3)(B)(ii) an empty promise. This Court in *Knudson* did not reject Great-West's suit out of hand because it alleged a breach of contract and sought money, but because Great-West did not seek to recover a particular fund from the defendant. Mid Atlantic does.

While Mid Atlantic's case for characterizing its relief as equitable thus does not falter because of the nature of the recovery it seeks, Mid Atlantic must still establish that the basis for its claim is equitable. Our case law from the days of the divided bench confirms that Mid Atlantic's claim is equitable. * * * Much like Barnes' promise to Street and Alexander, the "Acts of Third Parties" provision in the Sereboffs' plan specifically identified a particular fund, distinct from the Sereboffs' general assets-"[a]ll recoveries from a third party (whether by lawsuit, settlement, or otherwise)"-and a particular share of that fund to which Mid Atlantic was entitled-"that portion of the total recovery which is due [Mid Atlantic] for benefits paid." Like Street and Alexander in *Barnes*, therefore, Mid Atlantic could rely on a "familiar rul[e] of equity" to collect for the medical bills it had paid on the Sereboffs' behalf. This rule allowed them to "follow" a portion of the recovery "into the [Sereboffs'] hands" "as soon as [the settlement fund] was identified," and impose on that portion a constructive trust or equitable lien.

The Sereboffs object that Mid Atlantic's suit would not have satisfied the conditions for "equitable restitution" at common law, particularly the "strict tracing rules" that allegedly accompanied this form of relief. When an equitable lien was imposed as restitutionary relief, it was often the case that an asset belonging to the plaintiff had been improperly acquired [***17] by the defendant and exchanged by him for other property. A central requirement of equitable relief in these circumstances, the Sereboffs argue, was the plaintiff's ability to "'trac[e]' the asset into its products or substitutes," or "trace his money or property to some particular funds or assets." 1 D. Dobbs, Law of Remedies § 4.3(2), (2d ed. 1993).

But as the Sereboffs themselves recognize, an equitable lien sought as a matter of restitution, and an equitable lien "by agreement," * * * see also 1 Dobbs, *supra*, § 4.3(3; 1 G. Palmer, Law of Restitution § 1.5(1978). *Barnes* confirms that no tracing requirement of the sort asserted by the Sereboffs applies to equitable liens by agreement or assignment: The plaintiffs in

Barnes could not identify an asset they originally possessed, which was improperly acquired and converted into property the defendant held, yet that did not preclude them from securing an equitable lien. To the extent Mid Atlantic's action is proper * * * its asserted inability to satisfy the "strict tracing rules" for "equitable restitution" is of no consequence.

The Sereboffs concede as much, stating that they "do not contend-and have never suggested-that any tracing was historically required when an equitable lien was imposed *by agreement.*" Their argument is that such tracing was required when an equitable lien was "predicated on a theory of *equitable restitution.*" The Sereboffs appear to assume that *Knudson* endorsed application of all the restitutionary conditions-including restitutionary tracing rules-to every action for an equitable lien under § 502(a)(3). This assumption is inaccurate. *Knudson* simply described in general terms the conditions under which a fiduciary might recover when it was seeking equitable restitution under a provision like that at issue in this case. There was no need in *Knudson* to catalog all the circumstances in which equitable liens were available in equity; Great-West claimed a right to recover in restitution, and the Court concluded only that equitable restitution was unavailable because the funds sought were not in Knudson's possession.

* * *

[T]he Sereboffs offer little to undermine the plain indication in [prior precedent] that the fund over which a lien is asserted need not be in existence when the contract containing the lien provision is executed. * * * Shifting gears, the Sereboffs contend that the lower courts erred in allowing enforcement of the "Acts of Third Parties" provision, without imposing various limitations that they say would apply to "truly equitable relief grounded in principles of subrogation." According to the Sereboffs, they would in an equitable *subrogation* action be able to assert certain equitable defenses, such as the defense that subrogation may be pursued only after a victim had been made whole for his injuries. Such defenses should be available against Mid Atlantic's action, the Sereboffs claim, despite the plan provision that "[Mid Atlantic's] share of the recovery will not be reduced because [the beneficiary] has not received the full damages claimed, unless [Mid Atlantic] agrees in writing to a reduction."

But Mid Atlantic's claim is not considered equitable because it is a subrogation claim. As explained, Mid Atlantic's action to enforce the "Acts of Third Parties" provision qualifies as an equitable remedy because it is indistinguishable from an action to enforce an equitable lien established by agreement, of the sort epitomized by our decision in *Barnes*. Mid Atlantic need not characterize its claim as a freestanding action for equitable subrogation. Accordingly, the parcel of equitable defenses the Sereboffs claim accompany any such action are beside the point. * * * * Mid Atlantic's action in the District Court properly sought "equitable relief" under § 502(a)(3); the judgment of the Fourth Circuit is affirmed in relevant part.

Page 289: [Add to § 3.04 at the conclusion of the Notes and Questions:]

See also Barber v. UNUM Life Ins. Co., 383 F.3d 134 (3d Cir. 2004) (Pennsylvania bad faith statute preempted by ERISA); *Hollaway v. UNUM Life Ins. Co.*, 89 P.3d 1022 (Okla. 2004) (following *Pilot Life* analysis; holding that states common law bad faith cause of action does not regulate insurance and is therefore not saved from ERISA preemption) (answering certified question from 10th Circuit). *See generally* Russell Korobkin, *The Failed Jurisprudence of Managed Care, and How to Fix It: Reinterpreting ERISA Preemption*, 51 UCLA L. Rev. 457 (2003); Donald T. Bogan, *ERISA: State Regulation of Insured Plans After* Davila, 38 J. MARSHALL L. REV. 693 (2005).

(8) The involvement of an ERISA plan also has significant implications regarding litigation procedure and jurisdiction. *See, e.g. Peralta v. Hispanic Business, Inc., 419 F.3d 1064 (9th Cir. 2005) (finding existence of federal subject matter jurisdiction where interpretation of ERISA is "at heart" of dispute; also discussing nature and scope of fiduciary duties under ERISA); Hawaii Management Alliance Assoc. v. Insurance Commissioner, 100 P.3d 952 (Haw. 2004) (state external review statutes directed toward health insurers impliedly preempted by ERISA).*

(9) Regarding actual questions of coverage for claims made under an ERISA plan, the standard of review for denial of claims is highly deferential to the plan administrator (or its agent, an insurer). *See, e.g., Sisto v. Ameritech Sickness and Accident Disability Benefit Plan*, 429 F.3d 698 (7th Cir. 2005) (upholding plan administrator's decision that employee injured in bathroom was not eligible for work-related accident benefits on ground that worker's job did not involve bathroom and incident therefore was not "during and in direct connection with" her employment duties; Sisto did receive sickness benefits which were limited to one year in duration while accident benefits would have continued throughout the period of disability). Cynics might ask whether company workers are supposed to go off premises when nature calls; one suspects the employer would then very much consider use of the company's bathroom to be part of the job. *But see King v. Hartford Life & Accident Ins. Co.*, 414 F.3d 994 (8th Cir. 2005) ((refusing to accept plan administrator's determination that motorcycle crash injuries were insufficiently "accidental" where victim had been intoxicated at the time of the event).

Chapter 4

THE FORMATION, OPERATION, AND TERMINATION OF THE INSURANCE CONTRACT

§ 4.05 CONTRACTUAL POWERS OF INSURANCE AGENTS

Page 312: [Add to § 4.05 at the end of the carryover paragraph on top of page 312:]

Agents of both types are generally compensated on a commission basis, although some may have a base salary as well. The commission is typically based on a percentage of the premiums collected, with the amount varying according to the type of policy sold. For insurance products with low turnover, such as life insurance (where consumers are less likely to change insurers), the agent's commission can be quite high, perhaps more than 100 percent of the first-year premium (because once sold, the policy is likely to be kept in effect, generating premiums for years to come). For insurance products with higher turnover, such as auto insurance (where consumers are more likely to switch in search of lower rates or because of a move to another state), the percentage of commission is usually lower.

For purposes of assessing the existence of insurance and resolving coverage questions, the crucial point to remember is that the agent represents the insurer and her conduct may bind or be imputed to the insurer. The broker represents the applicant/policyholder and her conduct may bind or be imputed to the policyholder. Frequently, there are some mixed aspects of the intermediary's role. For example, a broker may primarily be the agent of the policyholder but is the agent of the insurer for purposes of collecting premiums. The agent may primarily be an insurance company employee but still may have duties to the applicant that require the agent to respond appropriately in a given situation. For example, if an applicant wants to insure his ice rink, it would be negligent for the agent to sell a policy that expressly excludes coverage for liability claims arising out of ice-skating injuries (unless, perhaps, if this is openly discussed with the applicant and acceptance of the exclusion results in a lower premium). Whether the agent is individually liable apart from the insurer (which may have to pay for a skating injury because of the reasonable expectations of the policyholder) depends on the facts and applicable state law of agency. An insurance agent owes a very limited duty to assess the adequacy of coverage and/or to suggest additional coverage. This body of law, however, may be contrary to commercial trends in much of the insurance brokerage business today, which are driving agents to foster an increasingly professional image. The gap between the current trend and the legal precedent does not show signs of closing soon. . .

The general rule adopted by most courts is that an insurance agent's obligation to procure insurance is defined by the specific request made to the agent by the insured. Absent a specific request for coverage, the agent is under no common law duty to guide, advise, or direct an insured to obtain coverage beyond that requested.

Courts have found, however, that an advisory duty may exist where a 'special relationship' exists: a set of circumstances between the parties that makes it reasonable to impose additional legal duties upon the agent beyond those imposed by the common law.

See Robert M. Sullivan and David H. Paige, *The Insurance Broker: Order Taker or Professional?*, TORTSOURCE, Vol. 6, No. 3 (Spring 2004) at 3.

Brokers by contrast are expected not only to respond reasonably to specific requests by policyholder but also to act as fiduciaries toward policyholders and to act reasonably on behalf of the policyholder even in the absence of specific direction. This does not, however, mean that brokers are expected to be omniscient in anticipating policyholder needs or possible claims. For example, a policyholder that purchases a reasonable amount of insurance but later is hit with an unanticipatedly large claim will be unlikely to persuade the court that the broker is liable for failing to recommend higher policy limits. In extreme cases, however, the broker may be responsible. For example, if the broker sells a drug manufacturer a $1 million package of insurance without any warning that this amount is likely to be inadequate if the product becomes the target of litigation, this could be found to be professionally negligent in view of the possibility that drug product liability lawsuits could easily far exceed this amount of coverage. *See also* Todd A. Schoenhaus & Adam M. Share, *Liability of the Insurance Broker for Breach of Duty to Advise*, RISK MGMT. MAG. (Feb. 2006) at 39. *See, e.g., AYH Holdings, Inc. v. AVRECO, Inc.*, 826 N.E.2d 1111 (Ill. Ct. App. 2005) (surplus lines exchange broker had duty to inform policyholder of insurer's financial condition).

For commercial policyholders, large brokers such as Marsh & McLennan, Aon, or Willis Group do not sell individual policies so much as they help the policyholder put together an insurance program or package of policies on a variety of coverages, with both primary insurance and multiple levels of excess insurance lest the company be saddled with a large liability claims. This part of the insurance world, of course, is quite distinct from that of most consumer policyholders, who simply buy auto, home, and perhaps life insurance from their friendly neighborhood agent with a storefront office in the local strip shopping center next to the grocery store.

Brokers, even large commercial insurance brokers, however, are similar to agents in that the primary means of compensation is through commissions based on the amount of insurance placed and the commissions are usually paid by insurers even though it is the policyholders who are the "clients" of the commercial brokerage firm. In 2004, a related part of this relatively common aspect of insurance broker compensation came under fire. *See* Theo Francis, *Spitzer Studies New Conflicts On Insurance*, WALL ST. J., May 5, 2004 at C1; Gretchen Morgenson, *Hat Trick: A 3rd Unit of Marsh Under Fire*, N.Y. TIMES, Sun., May 2, 2004 at Sec. 3, p. 1; Douglas McLeod, *N.Y. investigating brokers: Contingent commissions under fire as attorney general issues subpoenas*, BUS. INS., April 26, 2004 at 1. New York Attorney General Eliot Spitzer, who has made a name for himself as a foe of business fraud, began an investigation of broker compensation, with particular attention to the practice of not only having brokers (who agents of the policyholder) compensated by commissions from insurers but also that commissions increased according to the amount of business a broker provides to a particular insurer (so-called "contingent commissions").

Common 'fee payments, known as placement service agreements, range from 5 percent to 7.5 percent of the insurance that is underwritten' as a result of the broker's procurement of coverage for a client from a particular insurer. These fees "are typically paid above the regular commission of 15 percent that insurance brokers charge when they match an insurer with a corporation that needs coverage." *See* Morgenson, supra, at p. 4.

> Because contingency fees to not require a broker to perform any additional service or make additional expenditures, they are extremely profitable. By one analyst's estimate, contingent commissions account for roughly 5 percent of the brokerage industry's revenue but can total more than 30 percent of a broker's net income.

See Morgenson, supra, at p. 4. However, because brokers "have fiduciary duty to find the best coverage at the best price for their clients [the issue arises as to] whether the fees encourage insurance brokers to put their own interests ahead of their clients." *See* Morgenson, *supra*, at p. 4.

What is perhaps most surprising about Spitzer investigation is that it did not happen earlier. Although the extra contingent bonus provided by the "placement service agreements" may be particularly lucrative and thus more likely to skew a broker's judgment, the long-standing practice of having brokers compensated by insurer-paid commissions when the broker is the policyholder's fiduciary is inherently suspect, as is the similar practice of having investment advisors paid by commissions from mutual funds selected for the investor by the advisor. Regulators would certainly think it odd if estate planning attorneys made their money from commissions by the banks or stock companies used by the client at the behest of the attorney.

So why has there been no similar outcry about investment advisor or (more important for our purposes) insurance broker compensation? The answer is part simply habit and tradition. What has been (normal" for decades is unlikely to be questioned so long as the system appears to work reasonably well. In addition, many brokers appear to have thought that the practice was adequately disclosed to customers. On a more functional level, the commission practice can be defended to a degree by the (everybody does it" rationale. If all insurers pay roughly the same commission, the broker still arguably has plenty of incentive to serve the policyholder well. Failure will result in a lost client and compensation will be roughly the same regardless of which insurer is tapped by the broker. In addition, when seeking coverage for a large commercial entity with special needs, the broker may have relatively little choice (particularly in a (hard" market) and thus has little realistic chance to steer clients in search of a higher commission even if that is the less scrupulous broker's goal. But the bonus fees awarded when a given broker does a lot of business with a particular insurer arguably raise greater conflict of interest questions that cannot be refuted by the standard defense.

Page 315: [Add to § 4.05 prior to the Notes and Questions:]

MURPHY v. KUHN

90 N.Y.2d 266, 682 N.E.2d 972; 660 N.Y.S.2d 371 (N.Y. 1997)

Bellacosa, J.

The question for this case is whether an insurance agent should be liable to a former customer for tortious misrepresentation and breach of implied contract. The alleged wrongdoing is a failure of the defendant insurance agent to advise plaintiff Thomas Murphy as to possible additional insurance coverage needs. The theory of the lawsuit and the asserted duty is a special relationship and special level of advisory responsibility. The Appellate Division affirmed an order of Supreme Court, which granted defendants' motion for summary judgment and dismissed the complaint. Plaintiffs appeal pursuant to leave granted by this Court. We affirm the order of the Appellate Division because no special relationship was established on this record.

Plaintiffs Thomas Murphy and Webster Golf Course, Inc. sued defendants Donald C. Kuhn, Kuhn & Pedulla Agency, Inc., and its predecessor Roman A. Kuhn Agency, alleging professional negligence and breach of implied contract. This dispute originates in a 1991 automobile accident in Florida involving Murphy's son. One person died and several others suffered serious injuries as a result of the accident. At that time, the title to the son's car was in his father's name and the personal insurance was placed under the commercial automobile policy covering Murphy's business, Webster Golf Course, Inc. After exhausting the $500,000 policy limit to settle the car accident claims, Thomas Murphy assertedly paid an additional $194,429.50 plus $7,500 in attorneys' fees. Then, he sued these defendants to recover the additional sums he had to pay personally.

Defendants began providing the property, casualty and liability insurance to plaintiffs in 1973 in connection with their golf business. Beginning in 1977, defendant Donald Kuhn also handled all of Murphy's personal insurance needs, providing him with both homeowners insurance and personal automobile coverage. In 1979, plaintiff Thomas Murphy and his partner, Edward Rieflin, completed their purchase of the Happy Acres Golf Course and formed Webster Golf Course, Inc. Happy Acres had been a client of the Roman A. Kuhn Agency since 1957.

In 1990, Kuhn placed personal automobile coverage for Murphy with The Hartford, as insurer. Later that year, Hartford notified Murphy that his coverage was in danger of cancellation due to the poor driving records of his children. Murphy then transferred the insurance covering his son's car, which was registered and titled in Murphy's name, from Murphy's personal policy to Webster Golf Course's commercial automobile insurance policy. Murphy testified at his deposition that it was his standard arrangement to place title and register his children's cars in his name. From 1984 until the time of the accident, the liability limits on the commercial policy were $250,000 per person and $500,000 total per accident. Murphy never requested higher liability coverage for his personal and family automobile insurance needs, which were subsumed within the commercial automobile liability policy.

[The trial court] concluded that, absent a request by the customer, an insurance agent "owes no continuing duty to advise, guide or direct the customer to obtain additional coverage." Therefore, acknowledging that on this record plaintiffs never specifically requested defendants to increase the liability limits on the commercial automobile policy, the court held that defendants owed no special duty of affirmative advisement to plaintiffs. The court also declined to adopt plaintiffs' "special relationship" theory.

Plaintiffs propose that insurance agents can assume or acquire legal duties not existing at common law by entering into a special relationship of trust and confidence with their customers. Specifically, plaintiffs contend that a special relationship developed from a long, continuing course of business between plaintiffs and defendant insurance agent, generating special reliance and an affirmative duty to advise with regard to appropriate or additional coverage.

Generally, the law is reasonably settled on initial principles that insurance agents have a common-law duty to obtain requested coverage for their clients within a reasonable time or inform the client of the inability to do so; however, they have no continuing duty to advise, guide or direct a client to obtain additional coverage. Notably, no New York court has applied plaintiffs' proffered "special relationship" analysis to add such continuing duties to the agent-insured relationship.

Recently, however, this Court recognized a special relationship in a commercial controversy, involving no generally recognized professional relationship. We held that the relationship between the parties "under the circumstances [there] required defendant to speak with care." [However,] "liability for negligent misrepresentation has been imposed only on those persons who possess unique or specialized expertise, or who are in a special position of confidence and trust with the injured party such that reliance on the negligent misrepresentation is justified." For example, "[p]rofessionals, such as lawyers and engineers, by virtue of their training and expertise, may have special relationships of confidence and trust with their clients, and in certain situations we have imposed liability for negligent misrepresentation when they have failed to speak with care." [*See, e.g.,*] *Ossining Union Free School Dist. v Anderson LaRocca Anderson*, 73 NY2d 417 [engineering consultants]; *White v Guarente*, 43 NY2d 356 [accountants]; *Ultramares Corp. v Touche*, 255 NY 170 [accountants]; *Glanzer v Shepard*, 233 NY 236 [public weighers]).

The Court concluded that given "the absence of obligations arising from the speaker's professional status" in the commercial context, "there must be some identifiable source of a special duty of care" in order to impose tort liability. "The existence of such a special relationship may give rise to an exceptional duty regarding commercial speech and justifiable reliance on such speech" (*id.*). We determined, to be sure, that "[w]hether the nature and caliber of the relationship between the parties is such that the injured party's reliance on a negligent misrepresentation is justified generally raises an issue of fact". * * *

Even assuming the general applicability of the "special relationship" theory in the customer-agent automobile insurance coverage setting, we conclude that the relationship between these parties was insufficiently established to warrant or justify this case surviving a defense summary judgment motion. As a matter of law, this record does not rise to the high level required to recognize the special relationship threshold that might superimpose on defendants the initiatory advisement duty, beyond the ordinary placement of requested insurance responsibilities. Rather, the record in the instant case presents only the standard consumer-agent insurance placement relationship, albeit over an extended period of time. Plaintiffs' plight does not warrant transforming his difficulty into a new, expanded tort opportunity for peripheral redress. The record does not support plaintiffs' effort in this manner to shift to defendant insurance agent the customer's personal responsibility for initiating, seeking and obtaining appropriate coverage, without something more than is presented here.

We note in this respect that Murphy never asked Kuhn to increase the liability limits on the Webster Golf Course commercial automobile policy. In fact, there is no indication that Murphy ever inquired or discussed with Kuhn any issues involving the liability limits of the automobile policy. Such lack of initiative or personal indifference cannot qualify as legally recognizable or justifiable reliance. Therefore, there was no evidence of reliance on the defendant agent's expertise . . . . The absence of reliance is further reflected in Murphy's deposition testimony that it was his standard procedure to simply register his children's cars in his name. Additionally, Murphy's deposition description of his relationship with Kuhn concerning the golf course's general insurance matters shows that he had not met personally with Kuhn to discuss the insurance needs of Webster Golf Course, Inc. for approximately 12 years preceding the accident in question.

Rather, his partner Rieflin was the one actively and personally involved in handling the insurance needs of the golf course.

We also note that Murphy's contention that he mistakenly believed that the commercial policy had a $1,000,000 liability limit on all covered vehicles can be given no weight in resolving this dispute on this theory. The liability coverage had remained the same since 1984 and Murphy's deposition testimony failed to establish the basis for his plainly unfounded assumption. Therefore, plaintiffs are not entitled to advance beyond the summary judgment stage of this lawsuit because they failed to establish the existence of a legally cognizable special relationship with their insurance agent in this standard set of circumstances.

Plaintiffs-appellants urge this Court to avoid generally absolving insurance agents from legal principles which subject other individuals to duties beyond those rooted in the common law. They overstate the concern and effect of this decision and the principle that emanates from it. Our decision today does not break any new ground and does not immunize insurance brokers and agents from appropriately assigned duties and responsibilities. Exceptional and particularized situations may arise in which insurance agents, through their conduct or by express or implied contract with customers and clients, may assume or acquire duties in addition to those fixed at common law.

Notably, other jurisdictions have recognized such an additional duty of advisement in exceptional situations where, for example, (1) the agent receives compensation for consultation apart from payment of the premiums, (2) there was some interaction regarding a question of coverage, with the insured relying on the expertise of the agent); or (3) there is a course of dealing over an extended period of time which would have put objectively reasonable insurance agents on notice that their advice was being sought and specially relied on. In these circumstances, insureds bear the burden of proving the specific undertaking. The relationship established in the instant case does not rise to the level of these exceptional situations and we refrain from determining when the special relationship analysis may apply in the insurance context.

We do, however, take note that the uniqueness of customary and ordinary insurance relationships and transactions is manifested by "the absence of obligations arising from the speaker's professional status" with regard to the procurement of additional coverage. As stated, it is well settled that agents have no continuing duty to advise, guide, or direct a client to obtain additional coverage. No doubt, therefore, public policy considerations will have to be weighed on the question of whether to override this settled principle by recognizing additional advisement duties on insurance agents and brokers. But we do not reach that question here.

Insurance agents or brokers are not personal financial counselors and risk managers, approaching guarantor status. Insureds are in a better position to know their personal assets and abilities to protect themselves more so than general insurance agents or brokers, unless the latter are informed and asked to advise and act. Furthermore, permitting insureds to add such parties to the liability chain might well open flood gates to even more complicated and undesirable litigation. Notably, in a different context, but with resonant relevance, it has been observed that "[u]nlike a recipient of the services of a doctor, attorney or architect . . . the recipient of the services of an insurance broker is not at a substantial disadvantage to question the actions of the provider of services." * * * Order affirmed, with costs.

HARRIS v. ALBRECHT

86 P.3d 728 (Utah 2006)

DURHAM, Chief Justice:

The instant case is one of first impression in which we determine when an insurance agent creates a contract to procure insurance or when a duty to procure insurance arises. Petitioner Rick Albrecht seeks review of the Utah Court of Appeals' reversal of the trial court's grant of summary judgment in Albrecht's favor. Albrecht is a Utah-licensed insurance agent employed by Rick Albrecht Insurance Agency, Inc. He sells policies exclusively for co-petitioner, State Farm Fire & Casualty Company (State Farm). Ken Harris earned his architecture license in 1981, formed Harris and Olsen Architects in 1987, changing the firm's name to Ken Harris Architects in 1990. Harris' business grew considerably after 1990, and he made substantial investments in equipment and office furnishings from 1995 to 1997. By the summer of 1997, the scope of the improvements prompted an interest in acquiring business insurance.

In 1989, Albrecht and Harris commenced a business relationship when Harris obtained an auto insurance policy from State Farm through Albrecht. Albrecht continued procuring various insurance policies for Harris, including an umbrella policy and coverage for his home, boat and Recreational Vehicle. They conducted most of their business over the telephone, talking every couple of months. A conversation generally consisted of requests from Harris for insurance coverage, followed by fulfillment of each request by Albrecht, without detailed discussion of different types of coverages.

In mid-summer 1997, Harris contacted Albrecht to obtain business insurance for his architectural firm. He told Albrecht "to place business and fire coverage on [his] equipment and the contents [of his office]." Harris alleged that Albrecht responded by saying that "he would take care of [it]," and "he would come out and look at [the] equipment." On December 31, 1997, a fire destroyed the building housing Harris' architectural firm. The losses totaled $1,143,855.50. Harris attributed $940,000 to the loss of architectural plans and other valuable papers. While watching the building burn, Harris called Albrecht and asked: "You placed that [business] coverage we talked about, didn't you?" Albrecht replied: "We talked about it Ken, but we never did anything about it."

Harris brought claims against Albrecht, Rick Albrecht Insurance Agency and State Farm for breach of a contract to procure insurance and negligent failure to procure insurance. The trial court granted Albrecht's motion for summary judgment, and the Court of Appeals reversed.

* * *

Whether an insurance agent breached a contract to procure insurance or whether the agent had a duty to procure insurance are matters of first impression for this court. The Court of Appeals erred when it concluded that "whether a contract to procure insurance or a duty to procure insurance ultimately exists [are] questions of fact best left to the trier of fact." This court's precedent establishes that whether a contract or duty exists is a matter of law.

The formation of a contract requires a meeting of the minds. "Where a person seeks to enter into a contract of insurance with an insurance company or its agent it is understood that the negotiations will not ripen into a contract until the parties arrive at an agreement as to all of the elements which are essential to an insurance contract, including the subject matter to be covered, the risk insured against, the amount of the indemnity, the duration of the coverage and the premium." We conclude that no contract of insurance existed between Harris and Albrecht. They did not discuss any of the elements essential to an insurance contract except that Harris "wanted business and fire coverage on [the] equipment and the contents" of his architectural business. There was no mention, except fire, of the types of risks Harris wanted covered, the amount of indemnity, the duration of coverage, or the premium. Therefore, there was no meeting of the minds on which to base a contract of insurance.

However, the issue here is not whether an oral contract of insurance existed but rather whether an oral contract to procure insurance existed. * * * In entering into a contract to procure insurance, obviously the owner is seeking the same ultimate objective, that is, a contract of insurance, but the performance for which he bargains is the services of the insurance agent in obtaining the best possible terms consistent with the owner's insurance needs. Such a contract could arise even though the agent was given the authority to ascertain some of the facts essential to the creation of the ultimate contract of insurance, such as the appraised value of the property to be covered or the most advantageous premium. * * * "Obviously, liability for failure to procure insurance could not arise unless the agent had sufficiently definite directions from his principal to enable him to consummate the final insurance contract . . . . An express agreement is not necessary; the scope of the risk, the subject matter to be covered, the duration of the insurance, and other elements can be found by implication." * * * Therefore, a contract to procure insurance may arise when the agent has definite directions from the insured to consummate a final contract, when the scope, subject matter, duration, and other elements can be found by implication, and when the insured gives the agent authority to ascertain some of the essential facts.

In the present case, Albrecht did not have sufficiently definite directions from Harris to consummate the final insurance contract. Harris requested fire coverage for the contents and equipment of his business and also asked for business insurance. In order for Albrecht to procure business insurance, he needed to know the type of coverage Harris desired, such as loss of income, earthquake, employee dishonesty, money and securities, and theft. Depending on the types of coverage desired, Albrecht potentially needed to know the value of all furniture and equipment, accounts receivable, and building improvements, as well as the amount of deductible Harris wanted, why Harris' business had never been insured, when Harris wanted the policy to go into effect, whether there had been any prior losses, and, crucially, the value of architectural documents and other valuable papers. Albrecht had none of this information because all of Harris' previous policies were personal. Furthermore, Harris has not cited any instance where a court has held that an insurance agent must procure part of an insurance policy while waiting for the remaining sections to be sufficiently identified.

For similar reasons, Albrecht could not identify "the scope of the risk, the subject matter to be covered, the duration of the insurance, and other elements . . . by implication." Although Harris requested fire insurance for the contents and equipment in his business, too many variables remained. The auto, home, boat and RV policies offered no information from which Albrecht could determine the missing terms of the contract.

Additionally, Harris failed to give authority for Albrecht to ascertain some of the essential facts. He merely made a general request for insurance, which falls short of giving Albrecht authority. Harris was required to give explicit instructions to Albrecht rather than make a blanket request for insurance. Giving authority to the agent requires more than such a blanket request. * * * Albrecht lacked sufficient information from which the terms of a contract of insurance or a contract to procure insurance could be implied. The expression of a desire to procure business insurance followed by an oral affirmation of that desire is not enough to create a contract to procure insurance. Creation of a contract to procure insurance requires that the agent know or have ready access to the information needed to procure the insurance or be able to imply the terms from prior dealings. If the insured gives authority to the agent to obtain some information, he must do so explicitly.

The second issue before us is whether Albrecht assumed a duty to procure insurance when he allegedly told Harris "he would take care of that," and that he would come out and look at the equipment" after Harris called Albrecht and told him that he "wanted business and fire coverage on [the] equipment and the contents" of his architectural business. * * * One standard for determining whether an insurance agent has assumed a duty to procure has been stated as follows:

> [A] court must look to the conduct of the parties and the communications between them, and more specifically to the extent to which

they indicate that the agent has acknowledged an obligation to secure a policy. Where an insurance agent or broker promises, or gives some affirmative assurance, that he will procure or renew a policy of insurance under circumstances which lull the insured into the belief that such insurance has been effected, the law will impose upon the broker or agent the obligation to perform the duty which he has thus assumed. Further, if the parties have had prior dealings where the agent customarily has taken care of the customer's needs without consultation, then a legal duty to procure additional insurance may arise without express and detailed orders from the customer and acceptance by the agent . . . . An application from the customer is sufficient to support a duty to procure insurance. A bare acknowledgment of a contract to protect the insured against casualty of a specified kind until a formal policy can be issued is enough . . . .

* * *

Factors that indicate a duty include (1) whether Harris gave Albrecht an application, (2) whether Albrecht made a bare acknowledgment of a contract covering a specific kind of casualty even though all the terms had not been settled, (3) whether Albrecht made promises to procure insurance that lulled Harris into believing a policy had been procured, and (4) whether there were prior dealings where Albrecht took care of Harris' needs without consultation.

The final three factors are relevant to the instant case, requiring a close look at the language used during Albrecht's and Harris' telephone call. Albrecht said "he would take care of that, he would come out and look at the equipment." This statement is not a bare acknowledgment of an obligation to procure insurance because the statement that "he would come out and look at the equipment" indicated that Albrecht needed to gather more information or do other work before procuring a policy. A bare acknowledgment occurs when an agent confirms coverage pending the issuance of a formal policy.

Albrecht's comments failed to rise to the level of a promise to procure insurance and were insufficient to lull Harris into believing a policy had been procured because they lacked the requisite specificity. An agent must affirmatively assure the insured that a policy will be procured or has been procured. Harris argues that their prior dealings lulled him into believing Albrecht would procure insurance. Rather, Harris lulled himself into believing he had an insurance policy. No reasonable and experienced businessperson would believe the conversation here gave rise to a duty to procure insurance when considered in light of its brevity and the lack of any specificity for such a complex and customized type of policy. Even if Albrecht's comments lulled Harris into believing Albrecht would procure a policy, the fact that Harris never completed an application, never received a bill or policy, and was never contacted by Albrecht in the five months after the conversation should have put Harris on notice that he did not yet have a policy. Failing to examine one's mail is not a defense.

* * *

A significant distinction exists between business insurance policies and personal insurance policies. The ease of procuring an auto or homeowner's policy contrasts sharply with the customization required for a business policy. The information available to Albrecht at the time of the telephone conversation provides the essential elements needed to create an insurance contract. A policy for an architectural business requires more customization than one for a simple retail business. Valuable papers, for which Harris now seeks to recover damages, were beyond Albrecht's authority to bind State Farm, and State Farm would likely have required Harris to take certain loss-reduction measures regarding the safe-keeping of those papers before binding them. It was impossible for Albrecht to provide Harris with a "standard business policy."

Albrecht did not acknowledge an obligation to secure an insurance policy for Harris because Albrecht did not: (1) take an application for insurance; (2) make a bare acknowledgment against casualty of a specific kind; (3) lull Harris into believing he would procure insurance or that a policy had been procured; or (4) have a pattern of prior dealings of the type sufficient to impose a duty to procure insurance. At most, Albrecht lulled Harris into believing that he would come out and look at his business.

The court of appeals cited several cases supporting its decision. We agree with Judge Davis' dissent, however, finding those cases distinguishable from the instant case because in each the agent had all the information needed to procure a policy. * * * Here, Harris merely requested insurance and expressed a desire to procure insurance. [In footnote 2, the Court observed that "The nature of the losses here underscores the reason summary judgment was appropriate. The most basic business policy includes $5,000 of protection for valuable papers. Albrecht only had binding authority up to $25,000 for valuable papers, and Harris could not have received such coverage without taking loss-reduction measures. It is also possible that State Farm would not have bound the policy or that Harris would not have insured his valuable papers for as much as he now claims. The latter is of particular importance because Harris offered his investment in new equipment as the reason for obtaining business insurance, as opposed to protecting valuable papers, which presumably increased in value throughout his career in contrast to the recent equipment purchases. In light of these unknowns, a jury determination of damages would be purely speculative."]

A contract to procure insurance may arise when the agent has definite directions from the insured to consummate a final contract; when the scope, subject matter, duration, and other elements can be found by implication; and when the insured gives the agent authority to ascertain some of the essential facts. A duty to procure insurance may arise when an agent accepts an application; makes a bare acknowledgment of a contract covering a specific kind of casualty; lulls the other party into believing a contract has been effected through promises; and has taken care of the insured's needs without consultation in the past. * * * The court of appeals erred when it failed to determine that the telephone conversation between Albrecht and Harris created neither a contract nor a duty to procure insurance. We reverse.

NOTES AND QUESTIONS

(1) Are these Court decisions too forgiving to agents? Or do they simply reflect practical realities in light of the agent's limited role? Would it be unfairly impossible to hold agents accountable for every phone call? But even if an agent is the employee of an insurer, does the applicant not rely on the agent's expertise? Does the applicant not have an objectively reasonable expectation that the policy purchased from the agent will be appropriate to the applicant's needs?

(2) Alternatively, would it be reasonable for the applicant to at least reasonable expect that he or she is being sold a consumer insurance policy that is at least provides the industry standard minimum of coverage?" Or that if the actual policyholder is not at least this comprehensive, the agent will point this out to the applicant? Or does this simply revisit the issue about the agent's obligation (or lack of obligation) to explain coverage provisions. For the most part, agents do not have a duty to explain. But as a counterweight, an agent's lack of explanation will make it more likely that ambiguous, hidden, or unfairly surprising language is construed against the insurer.

(3) *See also President v. Jenkins*, 180 N.J. 550, 853 A.2d 247 (N.J. 2004) (broker not liable for failing to explain gap in coverage for doctor switching medical malpractice coverages where doctor did not advise broker that former coverage that would have eliminated gap was being allowed to lapse). This holding makes sense for agents. But does it make sense for brokers? Should the broker have been required to at least inquire as to whether the doctor was planning to keep the prior coverage in force?

(4) *See also Canales v. Wilson Southland Insurance Agency*, 261 Ga. App. 529, 583 S.E.2d 203 (2003) (agent not liable for selling policy with US/ Canada coverage but no coverage for Mexico when accident takes place while van driven in Mexico). The court held that even though the policyholder had been going to the agent for some time for insurance needs, this alone did not create the requisite (special relationship" that would require more of an agent. So far, the decision seem unobjectionable if a bit harsh. But would it affect your view to know that the policyholder spoke Spanish and did not read or write English? Should the agent selling the policy have foreseen that this particular policyholder might be likely to drive from Georgia to Mexico?

5. *See also DeHayes Group v. Pretzels, Inc.*, 786 N.E.2d 779 (Ind. App. 2003) (no special relationship and no broker liability to insurer where

insurer is forced to pay commercial property claim because of fire). The insurer contended that the broker should have recognized that the policyholder's sprinkler system was not adequate to protect the property. Was the insurer asking the broker to do its job?

§ 4.08   CANCELLATION AND RENEWAL OF THE INSURANCE CONTRACT

[A]   Introduction

Page 328: [Add at the end of § 4.08[A] on p. 328:]

Cancellation of a policy can also of course be done by the policyholder. A common example takes place when a policyholder decides to sign up with a new insurer and then directs the old insurer to cancel his or her old policy, refunding the "unearned" premium (premium for future coverage through the policy period).

[D]   Policy Renewal

Page 336: [Add at the end of § 4.08[D] prior to the Problem on p. 336:]

Insurers also commonly revise or amend their policies in order to refine language, broaden coverage in response to demand, or restrict coverage due to unwanted new loss exposures. A policyholder that stays with the same insurer for decades may find the policy's scope changing in significant ways even though the policyholder thinks it has had essentially the "same" policy since the inception of the relationship. Normally, insurers cannot alter policy provisions during a given policy period. They must wait until the policy is up for renewal and then may amend the policy language in the course of charging a renewal premium for the ensuing policy period. As a matter of formal contract law, the insurer offers a slightly different insurance policy to the policyholder, who accepts by sending in a premium payment.

Both parties assume the policy is in force and rely on it, although policyholders may be at best only dimly aware of changes in coverage, which are usually outlined in a brochure-like insert to the billing sent for the renewal premium. The insert often states that it is an "Important Notice Regarding Changes To Your Policy" but the common belief is that policyholders do not bother to read it and are unlikely to seek to change insurers even if they notice that coverage has contracted to some degree. Why? Because most laypersons are busy thinking about and doing other things. In addition, they probably assume that most other insurers are making similar changes in their renewal policies, making it unlikely the policyholder could obtain broader coverage from a competing insurer.

Further, the changes may be the type of thing that is unlikely to lead to a coverage problem. For example, a major auto insurer's notice of policy revisions sent to one of the authors informs the policyholder

> If you buy or lease a new or used care, your car policy will provide coverage for that car as a "newly acquired car" for up to 14 days after you take possession of that car. Previously, the policy provided for up to 30 days of coverage. This change applies to your new or used car whether it replaces an existing car or is an additional car in your household.

The brochure/notice also informs the policyholder that the changes are effective on the renewal date or a set future date, whichever arrives first.

Clearly, the new change gives the policyholder less protection in that it provides a shorter period of "automatic" coverage for a newly purchased vehicle. But is this change worth getting upset about? Not if the policyholder is reasonably diligent in contacting his or her insurance agent within two weeks of the purchase, which seems a reasonable course of conduct even if the car purchase itself was the result of impulse buying. Although fictional movie star Vincent Chase and the rest of his posse in *Entourage* are given to this sort of spur-of-the-moment acquisitions, two weeks is still plenty of time for business manager Eric or agent Ari to arrange the insurance. The insurer undoubtedly shortened the time of automatic coverage in order to encourage swifter contact with the agent and swifter payment of the premium on a new policy, which is likely to be larger than the premium paid on the old policy covering the old car.

Regulators and courts generally permit this type one-sided amendment of policies without much discussion. Rolling changes of this sort in standardized policies are perceived as efficient and unlikely to harm the policyholder except in rare circumstances. But rare circumstances are what makes for litigation. What if, for example, if the policyholder receiving the language above buys a new car, forgets to call his agent, and is involved in a multiple fatality crash 16 days later? Can the policyholder validly claim that he had an objectively reasonable expectation that his policy provided a month's worth of insurance? Or that the renewal policy was unchanged from the previous year's policy? Does it matter if the automobile purchase and accident straddle the renewal date rather than taking place after the renewal date? Who would likely win this coverage dispute: the policyholder or the insurer?

Although most insurers cannot ordinarily change policy provisions during the midst of the policy period and must wait for renewal, this is not a particularly significant impediment to the insurer. As we have seen, all that is needed by the insurer is a little planning, a printing press, and a renewal premium billing in order to accomplish even substantial changes in policy scope, all usually without any significant risk of losing customers. The conventional wisdom holds that most policyholders do not shop for insurance based on the scope of coverage but instead shop by price. If narrowing coverage keeps premiums in check, the insurer is unlikely to encounter policyholder resistance or flight because the policyholder will ordinarily not appreciate the consequences of a change restricting coverage until after an loss has taken place.

Some insurers have even more latitude and may amend their policies in the midst of a coverage period. *See* Theo Francis, *Some Life Insurers Play by Different Rules: State Laws Allow Unilateral, Retroactive Changes in Policies Issued by Fraternal Societies*, WALL ST. J., May 30, 2006 at D1, col. 4.

§ 4.09   POLICY FORM AND CONTENTS VERSUS STATE REGULATION

Page 340: [Add at the conclusion of § 4.09:]

§ 4.10   LOST POLICIES

How many insurance policies do you have in force? Do you have any idea where they are? Could you produce them? What if the insurer claimed never to have issued the policy you claim you have? In most personal lines of insurance, the policyholder deals somewhat regularly with an agent (or at least an 800 number operator) and presumably expects the agent or company to come up with a copy of the policy if necessary to resolve a coverage question. But what if the agent acts like she's never heard of you or produces a policy that you think is different from what was promised? What would you do (after getting nauseous or belting the agent)?

For personal lines insurance, where we tend to know the agent or have palpable losses that are contemporaneous with the policy period, the sort of scenario described above seems like something out of the Twilight Zone. But it's less farfetched for commercial insurance, where claims may arise years after the time (and policy period) during which the injury to a third party first took place. In addition, there may have been changes in corporate form by both the commercial policyholder and the insurer. The former Ma & Pa Grocery Store Fraternal Liability Association is now part of InsuranceGiantCo, which has no record of a 1963 policy held by Jack's CornerMart, which has since become part of the national A&P/Albertson's/Giant/ Pathmark/ Publix/Smith's/SuperValue/Winn-Dixie chain that cannot locate a copy of the old Jack's CornerMart policy. But Jack, who retired in 1980 and is still sharp as the metaphorical tack (he knew when to get out of the grocery business, right?) distinctly remembers purchasing general liability insurance every year he ran the store. Is this enough to prove coverage? What else is necessary? Does the following case provide some guidance?

CITY OF SHARONVILLE v. AMERICAN EMPLOYERS INSURANCE CO.

109 Ohio St. 3d 186, 846 N.E.2d 833 (Ohio 2006)

LANZINGER, J.

This case, involving the question of an insurer's duty to defend law-enforcement officers in a civil rights action, is accepted upon a discretionary appeal. * * * A federal action was filed against the city of Sharonville, Ohio and three of its current or former police officers. The officers were sued in their official capacity over an alleged ongoing conspiracy to cover up evidence relating to the murders of Marie Wright Schuholz and Starla Burns on May 8, 1981. The third amended complaint alleges that James Cramer, William Nuss, Mike Schappa, and other unknown officers ("John Doe(s)") have destroyed evidence of a murder and conspired for over 20 years to cover up facts crucial to solving the murder. Four claims are asserted in the third federal amended complaint: a civil rights action under Section 1983, Title 42, U.S. Code, conspiracy under state law, spoliation of evidence, and intentional infliction of emotional distress.

To obtain a defense in the federal suit, Sharonville and the named police officers filed a declaratory judgment action in the Hamilton County Court of Common Pleas against the various insurance companies that had provided coverage to the city from 1979 to 2002, alleging that the policies imposed a duty to defend. Each insurance company denied the allegations, and the trial court granted summary judgment to all insurers on the issues of defense and indemnity. Sharonville and the officers appealed.

The Court of Appeals for Hamilton County affirmed in part and reversed in part. Summary judgment was found to have been proper for the general liability insurers, as they had no duty to defend either the city or the police officers. Nevertheless, the appellate court reversed and granted judgment in favor of Sharonville and against the law-enforcement liability insurers (appellants North East Insurance Company, United National Insurance Company, Folksamerica Reinsurance Company, Scottsdale Insurance Company, and Ohio Governmental Risk Management Plan). * * * This cause is now before the court on a discretionary appeal. We review the granting of summary judgment de novo.

Lost Insurance Policy

North East Insurance Company ("North East") has refused to defend Sharonville for the year September 16, 1980, through September 16, 1981, because Sharonville has not been able to locate that particular insurance policy. "It is undisputed that one seeking to recover on an insurance policy generally has the burden of proving a loss and demonstrating coverage under the policy." Thus, an insured seeking benefits must prove the existence of a policy covering the relevant period. When the document of insurance has been lost or destroyed, the existence of coverage may be proved by evidence other than the policy itself when the loss or destruction was not occasioned by bad faith on the part of the proponent of the document. Evid. R. 1004. "The coverage provided by destroyed or lost policies can be proven through use of circumstantial evidence (i.e. payment records, renewal letters, miscellaneous correspondence, or prior claims files)." We hold that when an insurance policy is missing, lost, or destroyed, its terms may be proved by secondary evidence, unless the record contains evidence that the policy was lost or destroyed in bad faith.

The appellate court accurately determined that Sharonville presented sufficient evidence to establish the relevant contents of the missing insurance policy. The parties stipulated that North East did have a policy with Sharonville that covered the previous year, September 16, 1979, through September 16, 1980. On an application for liability coverage filed by the Sharonville Police Department sometime in 1981, James Darland, the Sharonville Safety and Service Director, stated that the city's present insurer was North East and listed the policy (with its disputed number, GL56-20-665) as expiring on September 16, 1981. Darland's May 5, 2003 affidavit stated that in filling out that application, he got his information from the city's insurance files, that to the best of his recollection, the city was insured by North East from September 16, 1980, through September 16, 1981, and that the city was continuously insured by North East with law-enforcement liability insurance from September 16, 1979, through September 16, 1981.

Additional evidence supported the existence of a North East policy covering the period in question. Sharonville produced several documents from an unrelated suit against the city of Sharonville and members of its police department involving an incident alleged to have occurred on November 23, 1980, within the coverage period of the lost policy. The suit alleged violations of Section 1983, Title 42, U.S. Code. In its attempt to prove that a North East law-enforcement liability policy existed during 1980-1981, Sharonville has produced the following documents from that suit: (1) a letter from North East, dated February 3, 1981, to the city of Sharonville, that expressly refers to Policy No. GL56-20-665 and admits that the policy entitled the city to defense and indemnity for the November 1980 incident, (2) a January 3, 1981 letter from attorney H. Louis Sirkin to North East, in which Sirkin inquires whether he should proceed to defend the suit, (3) a North East letter to Sharonville confirming that Sirkin had been retained, and (4) an answer filed on February 9 on behalf of the Sharonville defendants, signed by Sirkin.

In short, there was sufficient evidence to show that North East policy number GL56-20-665 existed and nothing to show that it was lost due to bad faith. A law-enforcement liability policy insured appellants during the time in question, and that policy included the duty to defend a Section 1983 claim. Thus, the Court of Appeals for Hamilton County acted properly when it held that North East policy No. GL56-20-665 existed and that it provided coverage for Sharonville.

QUESTIONS

How else might a modern policyholder prove the existence of insurance in the absence of being able to produce the policy itself? What type of cyber trail might be available (at least for modern claims)? What about bank records or similar documents? Does the widespread standardization of insurance policies make the task easier?

§ 4.11 TRANSFER OF POLICIES AND POLICY RIGHTS

THE GLIDDEN COMPANY vs. LUMBERMENS MUTUAL CASUALTY CO.

2004 Ohio App. LEXIS 6468 (Ohio Ct. App. 8th Dist. December 17, 2004)

SEAN C. GALLAGHER, J.:

Appellant The Glidden Company ("Glidden III") appeals from the trial court's decision granting judgment in favor of appellees. "Appellees" are insurance companies that sold comprehensive general liability insurance policies under which Glidden III is seeking coverage. For the reasons discussed below, we reverse the decision of the trial court and remand the matter for further proceedings.

Overview

Glidden III filed this action seeking a declaratory judgment that appellees are required to defend and indemnify Glidden III with respect to a series of underlying lead-based paint actions ("underlying actions"). The underlying actions assert liability against Glidden III for bodily injury and/or property damage arising from the manufacture and sale of lead paint products nationwide over many years prior to 1974. Glidden III had acquired the paints business in 1986, following an extensive history of corporate transactions. * * * The intricate corporate history is set forth in detail in the trial court's memorandum opinion entered May 8, 2002. In the interest of judicial economy, we adopt that portion of the trial court's statement of the facts which follows.

"A. Undisputed Corporate History and Relevant Facts

"1. Pre-1987 Background

"The original SCM Corporation (SCM (NY)) was a New York corporation from 1924 to 1986. SCM is the sobriquet for Smith/Corona/Marchant. SCM (NY) is a named insured on the CGL policies at issue covering the period from April 1, 1967 to January 1, 1987. "The original 'The Glidden Company' ('Glidden I') was an Ohio corporation with its principal place of business in Cleveland, Ohio from 1917 to 1967. Glidden I was a manufacturer and seller of lead based paints and lead pigments used in paints. Glidden I was insured by London for property damage (1959-1967). Glidden I merged into SCM (NY) on September 22, 1967, which succeeded to the London policies previously issued to Glidden I. The former business operations of Glidden

I were carried on through SCM (NY)'s subsidiaries or divisions. Thus, in 1968 Glidden I's acquired paint business became part of SCM (NY)'s Glidden-Durkee Division until 1976 when it was transferred to the Coatings & Resins Division, where it remained until 1986. In 1976, the former pigments part of the business was placed in the Chemical/Metallurgical Division of SCM (NY) where it remained until 1985. On September 6, 1985, SCM (NY) incorporated ABC Chemicals, Inc. as a wholly owned subsidiary and transferred to it the assets of the domestic pigments business. "Glidden I was a named insured on certain London policies for the period from 1959 to September 22, 1967 when it merged into SCM (NY). Upon the merger the London policy was endorsed to change the named insured to the Glidden-Durkee Division of SCM (NY) and coverage continued until January 1, 1970.

"2. The Hanson Take-Over in 1986 and Sale to ICI

"In January, 1986 HSCM Industries, Inc., a Delaware corporation and an indirect subsidiary of a British company known as Hanson Trust Plc, acquired control of SCM (NY) by a stock tender offer and implemented a plan of reorganization in order to sell off certain SCM (NY) businesses piecemeal. Thus, in May, 1986 HSCM Industries, Inc. was liquidated and stock ownership of SCM (NY) was transferred to certain indirect subsidiaries of Hanson known as the 'fan companies' (HSCM-1, Inc. through HSCM-20, Inc.).

"In May, 1986 SCM (NY) adopted a Plan of Liquidation and Dissolution pursuant to which SCM (NY) transferred specified assets and liabilities of its business units to the various fan companies which held its stock. On August 12, 1986, pursuant to the liquidation, SCM (NY) transferred its paints, resins, coatings, caulking and adhesives business (essentially the Coatings & Resins Division) to HSCM-6, Inc. Then on August 14, 1986, Hanson agreed to sell HSCM-6, Inc. to ICI American Holdings, Inc. ('ICI'). On August 22, 1986 HSCM-6 Inc.'s name was changed to The Glidden Company ('Glidden II').

"The Purchase and Sale Agreement between Hanson and ICI called for a sharing of pre-closing (October 31, 1986) liabilities of the paint business. Hanson and ICI agreed that Hanson would retain ownership of all insurance policies, i.e. including the ones at issue herein. However, a side Letter Agreement of the same date provided that 'Hanson shall give ICI and its subsidiaries the benefit of any policy of insurance to the extent the same would provide cover for liability in respect of occurrences relating to the Business prior to Closing giving rise to loss, injury, or damage thereafter subject to indemnity on costs.'

"Before the October 31, 1986 closing, ICI assigned its rights under the Purchase and Sale Agreement to two of its wholly owned subsidiaries, Atkemix Seven, Inc. and Atkemix Eight, Inc. On December 30, 1986, Glidden II, (formerly named HSCM-6, Inc.) was liquidated and its assets distributed to Atkemix Seven and Atkemix Eight, after which Atkemix

Eight was renamed 'The Glidden Company' ('Glidden III'). Glidden III acquired Atkemix Seven (then known as the Macco Company) in 1987.

"3. SCM (NY) Since the Hanson Take-Over

"On October 30, 1986 as part of the liquidation and dissolution of SCM (NY), the name of its subsidiary, ABC Chemicals, was changed to SCM Chemicals, Inc. ("SCM Chemicals"). On November 14, 1986, minus the assets and liabilities that [**10] had been transferred to the fan companies, SCM (NY) was merged into HSCM-20, Inc., a Delaware corporation, which was then renamed SCM Corporation ("SCM II"). On November 17, 1986 SCM II was merged into HSCM Holdings, Inc., another Hanson-controlled Delaware corporation, which then was renamed SCM Corporation ("SCM III").

"On October 14, 1988 SCM III was merged into HM Holdings, Inc., another Hanson-controlled Delaware corporation. Thus SCM Chemicals became a subsidiary of HM Holdings, Inc. Almost eight years later, on September 30, 1996, Hanson sold HM Holdings, Inc.'s indirect parent, Hanson Overseas Holdings Limited, to a newly formed corporation, Millennium Chemicals, Inc. HM Holdings, Inc., the survivor, after merger with Millennium Holdings, Inc. was renamed Millennium Holdings, Inc. SCM Chemicals, which had been a subsidiary of Millennium Holdings, Inc. then changed its name to Millennium Inorganic Chemicals, Inc. in 1997.

"On June 11, 2001 Millennium Chemicals incorporated a Delaware limited liability company named MHI 2, LLC. Two days later, on June 13, 2001, Millennium Holdings was merged into MHI 2, LLC which was renamed Millennium Holdings LLC, plaintiff herein."

Based on the foregoing corporate history outlined by the trial court, Glidden III and the Millennium plaintiffs brought actions, which were consolidated, claiming coverage under policies sold to Glidden I, SCM (NY), and the Glidden-Durkee Division of SCM (NY). Glidden III has brought this appeal challenging the trial court's rulings pertaining to its rights to coverage under the policies.

The Insurance Policies

The various insurance policies involved in this action were issued prior to the existence of Glidden III and before its acquisition of the paints business. The policies were issued during policy periods in which the risk of liability asserted in the underlying actions against Glidden III arose.

Prior to Glidden I's 1967 merger with SCM (NY), Glidden I purchased policies from London covering the period from April 27, 1959 to April 27, 1968. Upon the merger, SCM (NY) acquired the former business operations of Glidden I, including the paints business. When Glidden I merged into SCM (NY), the existing London policy was endorsed to change the named insured to the "Glidden-Durkee Division of SCM Corporation," the division in which Glidden I's paints business had been placed. The Glidden-Durkee

Division continued as the named insured under the London policies at issue until January 1, 1970.

SCM (NY) is the named insured on the policies issued by Lumbermens, AMICO, Century (as successor to INA), and Hartford, covering the collective period of April 1, 1967 to January 1, 1987. None of these insured companies has engaged in the production or sale of lead-based paints since 1973. The risk of lead-paint liability that Glidden III faces is a result of the pre-1974 operations of the paints business.

C. The Trial Court's Decision

Glidden III and appellees filed cross-motions for partial summary judgment. The trial court denied Glidden III's motion for partial summary judgment, granted certain defendant insurers' cross-motion for summary judgment, granted final judgment in favor of the insurers, and dismissed Glidden III's second amended complaint as to all defendants with prejudice. The trial court issued a memorandum opinion, which was later amended, and a final order. In its final order, the trial court ruled that (1) collateral estoppel did not apply to an order of partial summary judgment entered in a prior Ohio action entitled *The Glidden Company and HM Holdings, Inc. v. Lumbermen's Mut. Cas. Co.*, (2) Glidden III was not entitled to claim rights under insurance policies issued to SCM Corporation (or any division thereof) or issued to The Glidden Company (as the corporation existed prior to its 1967 merger with SCM Corporation); and (3) Glidden III was not an insured under any of the policies at issue. Glidden III has brought this appeal, raising nine assignments of error for our review.

* * *

Analysis of Assigned Errors

* * *

Glidden's first, second, third and fourth assignments of error provide:

"I. The trial court erred in concluding that Glidden III did not retain the beneficial rights to insurance coverage pursuant to the 1986 corporate transactions."

"II. The trial court erred in concluding that Hanson could not transfer the paints business' rights to insurance coverage to ICI."

"III. The trial court erred in concluding that Hanson, as the ultimate parent of SCM (NY), did not have the authority to bind SCM (NY) with respect to insurance."

"IV. The trial court erred in concluding that the anti-assignment clause in the policies prohibited the assignment of the policies without the consent of appellees after a loss has occurred."

Under these assignments of error, Glidden III argues, among other issues, that (1) the paints business was independently insured under the policies, (2) the policies provide specific beneficial rights to coverage to the paints business and that these rights remained with the paints business when it was acquired by Glidden III, and (3) the rights to coverage were available to Glidden III after the 1986 corporate transactions.

Appellees state that the "paints business" was actually paint-related assets and operations that once belonged to Glidden I and after they were acquired by SCM (NY) were housed in the Glidden-Durkee Division and then the Coatings and Resins Division, which were unincorporated operating divisions. Appellees claim that the paint-related assets and operations, even as part of a division of SCM (NY), had no legal identity apart from SCM (NY) and therefore had no rights independent of SCM (NY). We agree with appellees that an unincorporated division has no separate legal identity from the corporation of which it is a part. However, this does not mean an unincorporated division is not entitled to the benefits of coverage.

In the absence of a policy exclusion, a corporation's insurance policy extends rights to coverage, including the duty to defend, to unincorporated divisions. *Container Supply Co. v. Fireman's Fund Ins. Co.* (1989), 712 F. Supp. 871 (finding insurance company owed a duty to defend an unincorporated division that was merely a name used for marketing plastic containers produced by the insured corporation). Moreover, an insurance company is obligated to extend coverage for operations of such divisions. See *Id.* The reason for extending coverage to corporate divisions and subdivisions was explained in *Container Supply:*

> **"First, a corporation is 'a single entity in contemplation of law, and, although it may have many departments, or subdivisions, being a corporation, it is an indivisible unit.' Consequently, insurance applicable to the corporation as a whole naturally extends to an indivisible part of the whole."**

In this case, the paints business was initially part of Glidden I and, following the merger, became part of SCM (NY)'s Glidden-Durkee Division and then the Coatings and Resins Division. These divisions were owned, controlled and managed by SCM (NY).

Because the policies do not contain any exclusions with respect to the paints business or the divisions in which it was housed, coverage was extended to the paints business. The policies covered risks associated with the paints business. To the extent that the paints business was covered by the policies while operating as part of the insured corporation, benefits of insurance coverage extended to liabilities of the paints business.

The main issue before this court is whether the insurance benefits covering pre-acquisition risks of the paints business were assigned to or acquired by Glidden III. In considering this issue, we find it unnecessary to determine whether the paints business was an independent insured under the policies or whether it could possess rights independent of SCM as a non-legal entity. Instead, we can resolve this issue by considering whether the insurance rights and benefits passed through the 1986 corporate transactions or as a matter of law.

In 1986, Hanson acquired control of SCM (NY) by a stock tender offer. Glidden III claims that Hanson, as the ultimate parent of SCM (NY), owned the benefits of the policies and had the right to sell the benefits under the policies to ICI. Glidden III further asserts that the fact that SCM (NY) held legal title to the policies is inapposite to Hanson's conveyance of the benefits through the side letter agreement. Glidden III also argues that a parent company's actions can bind its subsidiaries.

We do not agree with Glidden III's logic. As a general rule, an insurance policy issued to a subsidiary does not automatically cover the parent company. Furthermore, a parent company that is not a named party cannot transfer the rights and duties under the policies. * * * "as a matter of contract law, because [the parent company] was not a party to the contract, it could not transfer the rights through an asset purchase agreement." Accordingly, since Hanson was not a party to the insurance policies, it could not transfer benefits of the policy through the side letter agreement.

The record reflects that SCM (NY), which was a party to the insurance policies, did not transfer the policies or the rights to insurance when it distributed the paints business to HSCM-6. SCM (NY) explicitly excluded all insurance policies from the distribution of the paints business to HSCM-6 (Glidden II) in the memorandum of distribution. The language used by the parties manifests a clear intent to exclude the policies and any rights and benefits thereunder.

We find that the rights and benefits of the policies did not transfer through the distribution or purchase agreement. However, we must still examine whether these rights transferred by operation of law. n8 [Footnote 8 reads: "Although the assignment issue is moot, we note that a majority of courts refuse to enforce anti-assignment provisions against claims for pre-assignment losses. See, e.g., *Northern Ins. Co. of N.Y. v. Allied Mutual Ins. Co.* (C.A.9, 1992); *B.S.B. Diversified Co. v. American Hardware Mutual Ins. Co.* (W.D.Wash. 1996), 947 F. Supp. 1476; *Texaco A/S, S.A. v. Commercial Ins. Co.* (S.D.NY Oct. 26, 1995), *Total Waste Management Co. v. Commercial Union Ins. Co.* (Dist.NH 1994). The majority rule recognizes that an insurer's risk does not increase where the loss or liability arose prior to the transfer."]

Glidden III is seeking to obtain coverage for liabilities it faces in connection with the manufacture and sale of paints containing lead pigment by Glidden I or SCM (NY) prior to 1974. The underlying litigation in which Glidden III is involved relates to pre-acquisition operations of the paints business. Glidden III claims that the benefits of insurance followed the liability by operation of law. Appellees argue that New York law should be applied to this determination. Before engaging in any choice of law analysis, a court must first determine whether any conflict exists. If the competing states would use the same rule of law or would otherwise reach the same result, it is unnecessary for a court to make a choice of law determination because there is no conflict. This court has not found any cases from either Ohio or New York that have squarely addressed the issue of whether insurance follows the liability for pre-acquisition occurrences. * * * [T]here is authority in New York which has applied the *Northern Insurance* decision and has determined that a surviving corporation is entitled to insurance coverage for claims arising out of pre-acquisition activities in a merger situation. Because of the lack of clear authority in Ohio and New York, we find no choice of law determination is necessary.

There is limited authority in other jurisdictions on the issue of whether insurance coverage follows liability by operation of law. This authority is split on the issue. Glidden III argues that this court should follow the *Northern Insurance* line of cases, which support the operation of law theory. Appellees claim this court should follow the *Henkel* line of cases, which have rejected the operation of law theory. See *Henkel Corp. v. Hartford Acc. and Indem. Co.* (Cal. 2003).

Courts have found that insurance coverage transfers by operation of law in various contexts. Coverage of a predecessor corporation has been held to transfer by operation of law to a surviving corporation after a merger that does not result in an increase in risk to the insurer. Coverage, including rights to indemnity and a defense, has been held to transfer by operation of law to a successor corporation in product-line successor cases for pre-sale occurrences.

In *Northern Insurance*, the Ninth Circuit court explained: **"This right to indemnity followed the liability rather than the policy itself.** As a result, even though the parties did not assign the [insurance company]'s policy in the agreement, the right to indemnity under the policy transferred to the [buying company] by operation of law." *Id.* at 1357 (emphasis added).

In the case at bar, the trial court defined the issue as whether the right to a defense follows the assets. The issue, rather, is whether this right **follows the liability.** * * * The product-line theory has been extended to a successor responsible for environmental cleanup where the events creating the liability occurred prior to the transfer of liability. It has also been found that coverage may transfer by operation of law to a corporation that purchases certain assets of a business under a more general theory of corporate succession. [In] *Total Waste Management Corp. v. Commercial Union Ins. Co.* (D.N.H. 1994) [the]lower court applied a "common sense" look at the corporate transfer and found that there was a material issue of fact as to whether the purchaser of assets was in substance, if not form, liable as the successor corporation. ["A successor corporation is defined as 'another corporation, which through amalgamation, consolidation, or other legal succession, becomes invested with rights and assumes burdens of [the] first corporation.'"]

Appellees cite certain cases which have rejected the operation of law theory. [*Henkel, Red Arrow Prods. Co., Inc. v. Employers Ins. of Wausau* (Wis. App. 2000); *General Accident Ins. Co. v. Western MacArthur Co.* (1997); *Quemetco, Inc. v. Pacific Auto Ins. Co.* (1994); *Koppers Industries, Inc. v. North River Ins. Co.* (W.D.Pa. Mar. 5, 1996).] Appellees claim that policy language restricts the insurer's obligations to insureds, not to the insured's "risks." According to appellees' argument, under principles of contract law, insurance rights may not be transferred by operation of law. Appellees argue that this court should reject the "operation of law" approach of the *Northern Insurance* line of cases, and follow the *Henkel* decision.

In *Henkel*, the Henkel Corporation acquired the metallic chemical product line of another company and assumed all related liabilities. The court found that liability was not being imposed upon Henkel by law, but rather by its assumption of liability by contract. As a result, the court found that Henkel's rights as a successor were defined and limited by the contract. The court further held that because the policy benefits were assigned without the insurer's consent, the assignment violated the anti-assignment clause. The court rejected the claim that under an occurrence-based policy, benefits can be assigned without consent once the event giving rise to the liability has occurred. Instead, the court found that the claims could not be assigned because they had not been reduced to a sum of money due or become due under the policy.

The dissenting judge in *Henkel* found the majority's decision was contrary to well-settled law and the general rule that after a loss has occurred, the policy benefits can be assigned without insurer consent or regard to the no-assignment clause. This rule applies to events or activities preceding assignment. We agree with the *Henkel* dissent and the cases which refuse to enforce anti-assignment provisions against claims that arise from pre-assignment occurrences. Further, because *Henkel* viewed the liabilities as arising after the acquisition, we do not adopt its rejection of the "operation of law" theory. * * * *

We believe the better-reasoned authority applies the operation of law theory. Courts applying this theory have continued to extend its application to more general successor liability situations. We find that a corporation which succeeds to liability for pre-acquisition operations of another entity acquires rights of coverage by operation of law. This theory applies even where the acquisition was a purchase of assets or only part of a predecessor corporation.

Appellees argue that transferring insurance rights by operation of law will result in increased risks because multiple entities will be able to claim coverage under the policies, namely, Glidden III and Millennium Holdings (the ultimate successor to SCM (NY)). We do not believe that this presents an increased risk. Risks of mergers, acquisitions, sale of assets, and other corporate restructures were present when the policies were written.

Further, several courts have recognized that insurers' risks have not increased when their duty to indemnify and defend relates to events occurring prior to transfer. When the activities giving rise to the damage or loss occur during the term of the policy and prior to any transfer of assets, the risk is no greater than when the policy was written. As stated in *Northern Ins. Co.*, "When the loss occurs before the transfer, however, the characteristics of the successor are of little importance: regardless of any transfer the insurer still covers only the risk it evaluated when it wrote the policy."

To find that an insurance company is not obligated to provide coverage to a party that is liable for a risk the insurance company promised to insure against and for which they were paid, an agreed premium would result in an unfair windfall to the insurance company. As stated in the *Henkel* dissent:

"The majority's holding allows insurers to secure [an] unfair windfall. The Lockheed plaintiffs alleged that their injuries were caused byexposure to metallic chemicals manufactured by Anchem and occurred during the time in which the policies issued by defendant insurers were in effect. The insurers in this case had received premiums to insure against these types of injuries. Yet under the majority's holding, the insurers will owe no coverage to *any* party for a risk they promised to insure against and for which they were paid an agreed premium.

"Moreover, the majority's conclusion could restrict corporate restructuring, reorganization, merger, or sale. * * *.

"A successor company would not be inclined to assume this risk of liability for the torts of a predecessor without also receiving the benefits of the predecessor's insurance coverage for presale occurrences. It is highly unlikely that a successor company would be able to obtain insurance coverage for injuries *that have already occurred* before the successor's acquisition of the business."

We agree with the *Northern Insurance* line of cases and the rule that insurance benefits follow the liability for losses arising from pre-acquisition activities by operation of law. We hold that Glidden III is entitled to insurance benefits under the insurance policies at issue for the pre-acquisition activities of the paints business, including the right to indemnification and the right to a defense.

Glidden III raises this assignment of error with respect to the allocation of insurance coverage among the multiple insurers. Allocation involves the apportionment of a covered loss across multiple triggered insurance policies. *Goodyear Tire & Rubber Co. v. Aetna Cas. & Sur. Co.*, (Ohio 2002). The parties contest whether defense costs should be prorated among the various carriers or whether Glidden III is entitled to recover "all sums" against any specific carrier. The trial court applied New York law and found that allocation of defense costs among insurers was to be pro rata. Glidden III argues that Ohio law should govern and that an "all sums" approach should be applied.

When Ohio law conflicts with that of another state, a court must engage in a choice of law analysis. When the parties to an insurance contract do not specify which state's law applies to the contract's interpretation, a court should consider the factors set forth in Section 188 of the Restatement (2nd) of Conflict of Laws. Section 188 provides that when the parties do not specify the choice of law, the parties' "rights and duties under the contract are determined by the law of the state that, with respect to that issue, has 'the most significant relationship to the transaction and the parties.'"

A court that considers which state has the most significant relationship to the transaction and to the parties should examine the following factors: (1) the place of contracting; (2) the place of negotiation; (3) the place of performance; (4) the location of the subject matter; and (5) the domicile, residence, nationality, place of incorporation, and place of business of the parties. The above factors "are keyed to the justifiable expectations of the parties to the contract, not to the ultimate benefit of one party over another."

In insurance cases, the most significant contact is considered to be the location of the subject matter, i.e., the location of the insured risk. [T]he rights created by an insurance contract should be determined "by the local law of the state which the parties understood was to be the principal location of the insured risk during the term of the policy, unless with respect to the particular issue, some other state has a more significant relationship * * * to the transaction and the parties."

The parties agree that the policies at issue do not provide which state's laws are to be applied. Since state laws are conflicting on the issue of allocation, we must engage in a choice of law analysis. * * * The London policies were issued to Glidden I. Glidden I was a stand-alone Ohio corporation before the merger; the policies were sent to Glidden I in Ohio where its executive offices and principal place of business were located; and the paints business operations were in Ohio. Although the Glidden-Durkee Division of SCM (NY) became the named insured under the London policy following the merger, the paints business remained in Ohio. * * * SCM (NY) was a New York corporation. The SCM (NY) insurance policies were negotiated, issued and delivered to SCM (NY) in New York. Premiums were also paid in New York. However, here again, the paints business remained in Ohio. * * * Appellees contend that because SCM (NY) had a wide range of operations in many states, its insured risks were spread across the country. Glidden III argues that the appellees which sold the policies to SCM (NY) were aware that they were insuring risks associated with the paints business operations located in Ohio.

We have previously recognized that "where nationwide coverage is provided, the policy's legitimate expectation is that the site of the insured risk is more significant than the insurer's residence or the place of negotiation. When a large insurer issues a policy designed to apply nationwide, it has no legitimate expectation that the law of its residence will apply in other states." * * * We find that although SCM (NY) may have purchased nationwide coverage, the risks at issue relate to liability arising from the paints business, and therefore the principal location of the insured risk was Ohio. Appellees should have been aware at the time of contracting that they could be required to indemnify and defend liability arising from the Ohio operations of the paints business. The allocation of costs for a covered loss arising from those Ohio operations should be determined by Ohio law. * * * We believe that with respect to the particular issue, Ohio has the most significant relationship to the transaction and the parties. We conclude that Ohio law should be applied to determine allocation issues.

Under Ohio law, when a continuous occurrence triggers claims under multiple primary insurance policies, "the insured is entitled to secure coverage from a single policy of its choice that covers 'all sums' incurred as damages 'during the policy period,' subject to that policy's limit of coverage. In such an instance, the insurers bear the burden of obtaining contribution from other applicable primary insurance policies as they deem necessary." Judgment reversed and remanded.

TIMOTHY E. MCMONAGLE, J., dissenting:

I decline to join the majority in concluding that a successor corporation such as Glidden III is entitled to the benefits of various insurance policies issued to its predecessor on the basis that these benefits transferred by operation of law. Instead, I concur with the well-reasoned opinion issued by Judge James Porter, the trial judge in this case. * * * In rejecting the rationale behind the *Northern Insurance* line of cases, Judge Porter based his decision, in part, on the contractual nature of insurance policies issued by the primary insurers to SCM(NY) or Glidden I.

"The coverage of liability insurance does not automatically follow the assets purchased by a stranger to the insurance policy. Furthermore, *Northern Insurance* and cases following it did not present the case, as here, where the insurance companies would have to potentially defend two or more parties rather than a single insured [that] once held the assets. The logical extension of [Glidden III's] theory, if accepted, would require the defendant insurers to defend the ten or more 'fan companies' to which Hanson spun-off SCM(NY)'s operating divisional assets. Although the risk for which coverage is now claimed may relate solely to pre-1987 activities of Glidden I and SCM(NY) the obligation to defend multiple parties emanating from those events is not the same. Furthermore, the Court cannot conclude on the record before it that the expense of defending multiple successor corporations is the same. * * * Accordingly, the Court rejects the 'operation of law' argument made by [Glidden III]."

This reasoning was recently adopted in *Century Indemn. Co. v. Aero-Motive Co.* (W.D.Mich 2003). After a thorough review of the split in authority on this issue, the *Century Indemnity* court declined to follow *Northern Insurance*. Instead, the court agreed with the reasoning of *Gen. Acc. Ins. Co. v. Superior Court* (Cal. 1997), when it stated that "the relationship between an insurer and an insured is determined under contract principles rather than upon public policy."

I agree with this reasoning. Whether one is entitled to the benefits of coverage under a policy of insurance is a matter of contract, not tort, law. "An insured-insurer relationship is a matter of contract. Successor liability is a matter of tort duty and liability. It is one thing to deem the successor corporation liable for the predecessor's torts; it is quite another to deem the successor corporation a party to insurance contracts it never signed, and for which it never paid a premium, and to deem the insurer to be in a contractual relationship with a stranger. Glidden III was neither a named insured under the various policies nor a valid assignee. It cannot now assume either status merely because it succeeded to the assets of a predecessor corporation that held that status. "The law can impose tort liability on a successor corporate entity; it cannot impose a contractual insurance relationship between an insurer and a stranger to the insurance contract. * * *

I also dissent from the majority's disposition of Glidden III's eighth assignment of error, which addresses the issue of choice of law for purposes of allocation under the various policies.

NOTES AND QUESTIONS

(1) As indicated in the *Glidden* opinion above, the largest state has a markedly different view of such situations. *See Henkel Corp. v. Hartford Accident & Indem. Co.*, 29 Cal 4th 934, 62 P.3d 69, 129 Cal. Rptr. 2d 828 (Cal. 2003). Although *Henkel*'s facts involved corporate acquisitions and a claim that the acquired company's liability policies came with the acquired company (an argument the California Supreme Court rejected), the *Henkel* majority (with only one dissent) went on to suggest that rights under a liability policy could not be assigned even if the events giving rise to any claims preceded the original policyholder's assignment.

(2) One of the authors finds this an astounding bit of misanalysis by the California high court that is at odds with decades of seemingly settled doctrine. *See Stempel on Insurance Contracts* § 3.15. For most courts, the crucial distinction is whether a policyholder is attempting to assign the policy's protections for future risks (in which case the insurer can justifiably complaint not only that this violates any anti-assignment clause in the policy but also may subject the insurer to risk beyond what it bargained for in selling the policy at a given premium) or whether the policyholder is assigning its rights under a policy after the potential liability event has already occurred. In this latter situation, the insurer is subjected to no additional risk of consequence. It sold a policy (and collected a premium) to a particular policyholder and it was that policyholder's actions (or inactions) that led to the claim and possible settlement or judgment. There is thus no logical harm to the insurer if it must defend and perhaps indemnify the policyholder's assignee. The time for underwriting and risk management to have any affect on the claim has long passed.

(3) But formalists and textualists would undoubtedly respond that if the policy has an anti-assignment clause, it should be enforced—right? The functionalist answer is that strict application of restrictions on assignment after the fact are economically inefficient and violate the widely accepted

public policy that contract rights (like other property rights) should generally be freely alienable so that assets can be transferred to the entity that places most value on the asset. Are you satisfied with the functionalist response? Why or why not?

(4) Are corporate acquisition cases without an express assignment different than cases where policy rights have been separately assigned as part of the transaction? Why or why not? Which situation presents a stronger case for insurers?

(5) Since *Henkel*, insurers have been more aggressive in contesting transfer of policy rights and the judicial scorecard is mixed. *Compare Century Indem. Co. v. Aero-Motive Co.*, 318 F. Supp. 530 (W.D. Mich. 2003) (agreeing with *Henkel*) *with P.R. Mallory & Co. v. American States Ins.*, 2004 WL 1737489 (Ind. Cir. Ct. July 29, 2004) (agreeing with *Glidden* and disapproving of *Henkel*). *See generally* Patricia A. Bronte & Jennifer A. Burke, *Inheriting Insurance Coverage for Successor Liabilities*, 19-12 MEALEY'S LITIG. REP. INS. 10 (Jan. 25, 2005).

Chapter 5

THE INSURABLE INTEREST REQUIREMENT

§ 5.02   LIFE INSURANCE

[A]   Who Has an Insurable Interest in a Life?

Page 374: [Add at the end of § 5.02[A]:]

Notwithstanding that murder-for-insurance proceeds is a genuine risk, life insurers tend to be willing to write coverage largely without much scrutiny of the net worth or future prospects of a proposed applicant or CQV. The general approach to insurable interest of both insurers and the courts is to look merely for a factual or legal benefit from the continued life of the person insured. Beyond this, courts seldom worry about whether the person's life was overinsured unless there are reasonable grounds for suspecting crime and fraud. The traditional rule is that "every person has an unlimited insurable interest in his or her own life." *See* Peter Nash Swisher, *The Insurable Interest Requirement for Life Insurance*, 53 DRAKE L. REV. 477, 485, n. 23, 541 (2005).

For example, everyone in the neighborhood may "know" that Ellie Mae's new husband Billy Ray is a shiftless no-account, that she will likely be the family's breadwinner, and that she is probably better off without him. But Ellie Mae (assuming her financial planning instincts are better than her taste in men) will normally have no problem insuring Billy Ray's life for $100,000 or more even if he is unemployed. Hope, and the insurer's desire for premium dollars, springs eternal. Billy Ray may be overpriced but most situations of this type result from undue optimism (to Ellie Mae, at least, he's a knight in shining armor) rather than planned spouse removal. If Billy Ray is himself seeking to purchase insurance on his own life, the insurable interest doctrine puts no limit on the amount he may purchase, although insurers may be reluctant to issue large policies to this type of applicant.

Where the face amounts of life insurance are large, insurers may take considerably more interest in having the policy limits be commensurate with the CQV's wealth or earning power so that he or she is not "worth more dead than alive" to the beneficiaries. But it appears that insurers do not do much if any financial investigation as part of the underwriting process until the policy limits approach the mid-six figures or even the million dollar mark, particularly if the person whose life is insured is also the person purchasing the insurance (and not appearing to be pushed into it by a spouse or business associate). The notion underlying the public policy behind the insurable interest in life insurance is that a well-insured person is not significantly more likely than an uninsured or underinsured person to take his own life (and there is the suicide exclusion in such cases; which is good for two years in most states or by express policy language) or conspire to have himself murdered.

In addition, because life insurance is a common financial planning tool, insurers traditionally give middle class policyholders substantial berth in determining how much life insurance is enough. A young couple may now not have much net worth or a huge salary, but if both are junior investment bankers or Wall Street lawyers, it is not absurd for them to be considering million-dollar policies. If they buy when younger, premiums are lower or leveled. Conversely, a rural farmer may not have much income but may purchase large amounts of life insurance to assist in estate planning as well as to protect his major asset of farm acreage. In addition, of course, a higher policy limit means higher premiums, giving agents little incentive to scrutinize policy amounts in relation to policyholder wealth or prospects.

As a result of these practical factors, insurers seldom show much interest in vetting proposed life insurance policy limits until after a suspicious loss has occurred. Thereafter, insurers may seek to argue that a policyholder had an insufficient insurable interest to purchase the amount of insurance at issue. Although such arguments may have superficial appeal to lay jurors, they are inconsistent with historical practices and the legal parameters of the insurable interest doctrine. An insurer can still, of course, defend a claim on grounds of fraud, misrepresentation or concealment (see §§ 6.02, 6.03) but should not be permitted to second guess its own decision as to policy limits. Of course, nothing is to prevent an insurer from simply refusing to write policies above certain limits for the CQV in question.

Chapter 6

INSURER'S LIMITATION OF RISK: WARRANTIES, REPRESENTATIONS, AND CONCEALMENT

§ 6.03   CONCEALMENT

[B]   Concealment Involving Different Types of Insurance

Page 446: [Add following § 6.03[B]:]

[C]   The Sometimes Blurred Lines of Misrepresentation and Concealment

(1) Courts are often lack precision in discussing misrepresentation and concealment defenses by an insurer. For example, in *O'Riordan v. Federal Kemper Life Assur. Co.*, 114.3d 753, 755, 30 Cal. Rptr. 753 (Cal. 2005), the court speaks of whether a life insurance applicant "concealed" a history of smoking, although the case could be analyzed as a misrepresentation problem, specifically whether the applicant answered truthfully when the insurer asked whether the applicant had "smoked cigarettes in the past 36 months." In *O'Riordan*, the Court concluded that the applicant's negative answer did not bar coverage as a matter of law even though a post-death examination of medical records reflected some more recent tobacco use, arguably making the applicant's statement false (although the insurer obtained blood and urine samples that "showed no traces of nicotine."). Summary judgment was not available to the insurer and trial was required as to the decedent applicant/policyholder's state of mind (i.e., whether the applicant had intentionally misrepresented the length of time as a non-smoker).

(2) Most policyholder lawyers, of course, regard surviving a summary judgment motion as a long step on the road to successful settlement or judgment due to the prevailing view that jurors are relatively unlikely to presume fraud by the decedent, who is represented in court by his or her widowed spouse who may desperately need the insurance policy proceeds to survive. But, at least under the formal law of misrepresentation, a misstatement of material fact need not be made with fraudulent intent. Even an innocent material misrepresentation makes the policy voidable, at least until the period of policy incontestability (usually two years), has passed.

(3) So why was applicant state of mind an issue in this case if the question was answered incorrectly? (Whether an applicant is a smoker is a material fact in life insurance because smokers on average die earlier than nonsmokers.) A complicating fact was that the insurer's agent had, in the course of taking the application by interview, discussed the question with the applicant. She "mentioned that she 'might have had a couple of cigarettes in the last couple of years,'" to which the agent replied: "That's not really what they're looking for. They're looking for smokers." The insurer was charged with the agent's assurances, with made the applicant's negative response to the question sufficiently true to bar a successful misrepresentation defense. In effect, the court saw the matter as converted into a concealment question, in which case an intent to mislead the insurer is required to void coverage. But this is not the typical concealment scenario, which usually has an insurer making no inquiry and the applicant intentionally withholding information the applicant subjectively knows is material to the insurer's underwriting decision.

(4) California Insurance Code § 330 states that "[n]eglect to communicate that which a party know, and ought to communicate, is concealment." While § 331 provides that "[c]oncealment, whether intentional or unintentional, entitles the injured party to rescind insurance." Section 332 further requires that "[e]ach party to a contract of insurance shall communicate to the other, in good faith, all facts within his knowledge which are or which he believes to be material to the contract and as to which he makes no warranty, and which the other has not the means of ascertaining." On its face, this portion of the Insurance Code can be read as a codification of the marine insurance duty of *uberimai fidei* (the "utmost good faith"), which imposes on an insurance applicant the affirmative duty of notifying the insurer of anything that the applicant reasonably should no might be material to the risk. These statutory provisions can also be read to remove the element of knowing intent to withhold material information (as opposed to mere failure to recognize that the insurer might be interested in certain data) that is an element of common law concealment.

(5) If this were the actual law of California, this would create a comparative rarity: state law imposing the heighten standard of marine insurance to more circumscribed land based risks and personal insurance policies purchased by individuals. On closer examination, the law of California, although perhaps less forgiving to applicants than some states, does not depart from the general rule of land-based insurance: if an insurer fails to ask a question, the applicant has no affirmative duty to volunteer information. This is reflected in as reflected in court decisions long before *O'Riordan. See, e.g., Thompson v. Occidental Life Ins. Co.*, 9 Cal. 3d 904, 513 P.2d 353, 109 Cal. Rptr. 473 (Cal. 1973); *Barrera v. State Farm Mutual Auto. Ins. Co.*, 71 Cal. 2d 659, 456 P.2d 674, 79 Cal. Rptr. 106 (Cal. 1969); *Harte v. United Benefit Life Ins. Co.*, 66 Cal. 2d 148, 424 P.2d 329, 56 Cal. Rptr. 889 (Cal. 1967); *Olson v. Standard Marine Ins. Co., Ltd.*, 109 Cal. App. 2d 130, 240 P.2d 379 (Cal. Ct. App. 1952). *See also Telford v. New York Life Ins. Co.*, 9 Cal. 2d 103, 69 P.2d 835 (Cal. 1937) (inaccurate answer

to specific question makes policy voidable even where insurer's medical examiner could observe that applicant had previously had left breast removed) (but not requiring voluntary disclosure of such information in the absence of a direct question from the insurer).

(6) Crazy activist judges refusing to follow legislation with which they may disagree? Probably not. Examination of the state insurance statutes as a whole suggests that the statutory provisions quoted above were not designed to dramatically alter the common law rule that an insurer must make inquiry and cannot depend on the applicant to determine what is relevant information that must be disclosed. Even § 332 does not require disclosure if the insurer has the "means of ascertaining" information. Insurers almost always have such means through asking questions, conducting physicals, obtaining medical records, and inspecting real property, automobiles, or business operations. Section 333 then provides that certain matters not be disclosed "except upon inquiry" by the insurer where the information (a) is known by the other; (b) can be obtained in the exercise of ordinary care; (c) is subject to waiver, (d) relate to an excluded, non-material risk.

(7) In addition, California Insurance Code § 1900 governing marine insurance that states that "[i]n marine insurance, each party is bound to communicate, in addition to what is required in the case of other insurance: (a) All the information which he possesses and which is material to the risk, except such as is exempt from such communication in the case of other insurance [and] (b) The exact and whole truth in relation to all matters that he represents or, upon inquiry assumes to disclose." If California disclosure law for nonmarine risks were the same as for marine insurance, this particular statute for marine insurance would seem to be superfluous. The presence of the particular statutory provision for marine insurance disclosure strongly suggests that non-marine insurance requires less disclosure by the applicant (although the applicant is of course required to answer questions truthfully when specific questions are propounded). This probably explains why in practice, California courts tend not to permit rescission of a nonmarine insurance policy merely because an applicant fails to voluntarily disclose information to the insurer. Ordinarily, rescission is permitted only where the insurer has affirmatively asked for information and received a materially inaccurate response from the applicant. If an applicant fails to appreciate the significance of undisclosed information in the absence of inquiry by the insurers, this type of nondisclosure is not tantamount to "concealment" and will not void coverage.

(7) Although there may be some room for debate, we see *O'Riordan* as a misrepresentation case rather than a concealment case. If *O'Riordan* were a true concealment case, there would be no need for the Court's discussion of precisely what was asked of Mrs. O'Riordan or what she understood was being sought by the insurer; she would be obligated to disclose material facts regarding whether she smoked irrespective of any inquiry by the insurer. Of course, *O'Riordan* could be characterized as a concealment case

akin to marine insurance and the policyholder could still prevail on the grounds that occasional backsliding by a former smoker was not in fact information that materially would affect a life insurer's underwriting decision. At the very least, the California Supreme Court seems indisputably correct in finding that the dispute was not appropriate for summary judgment because of contested questions of fact.

Chapter 7

THE INSURED'S DEFENSES: WAIVER, ESTOPPEL, ELECTION, AND CONTRACT REFORMATION

§ 7.01 WAIVER, ESTOPPEL, ELECTION, AND CONTRACT REFORMATION

[B] Definition and General Rules of Waiver and Estoppel

Page 452: [Add to § 7.01[B] at the end of the Notes and Questions:]

(6) An agent's conduct normally binds as a matter of contract and may create estoppel against the insurer as well. *See, e.g., Guerrier v. Commerce Ins. Co.*, 847 N.E.2d 1113 (Mass. Ct. App. 2006) (agent's misstatement in an application previously signed in blank by applicant estops insurer from rescinding policy on grounds of misrepresentation; agent's errors imputed to insurer rather than applicant). *See, e.g.*, Walker v. Employers Ins. of Wausau, 846 N.E.2d 1098 (Ind. Ct. App. 2006) (insurers admission that no policy exclusion applied estopped it from later asserting applicability of an exclusion).

Chapter 9

DUTIES OF THE POLICYHOLDER AND INSURER AFTER LOSS

§ 9.01   DUTIES OF THE INSURED

[A]   Requirement of Notice of Loss: Is Prejudice to the Insurer Necessary?

Page 521: [Add to § 9.01[A]:]

(6) Since the *Molyneaux* case, New Jersey has more clearly joined the majority of states requiring prejudice to the insurer to sustain a late notice defense to coverage. *See Gazis v. National Catholic Risk Retention Group, Inc.*, 186 N.J. 224, 892 A.2d 1277 (N.J. 2006). Although lower New Jersey state courts, as in *Molyneaux*, generally followed the majority rule, the state's Supreme Court had not previously issued a clear pronouncement on the issue. Nearby New York remains a tough jurisdiction regarding notice and adheres to its no-prejudice-required" rule but also one with nuanced exceptions to the traditional rule in cases involving statutorily mandated coverage (*see, e.g., Rekemeyer v. State Farm Mutual Automobile Ins. Co.* 4 N.Y.3d 468, 828 N.E.2d 970 (N.Y. 2005)) or where the policyholder had not reason to believe it a third party would seek to impose legal liability (see, e.g., *Great Canal Realty Corp. v. Seneca Ins. Co., Ins.*, 5 N.Y.3d 742, 833 N.E.2d 1196 (N.Y. 2005)). Two different notice rules in adjoining states with large populations can make choice of law important in coverage disputes emanating from the New York metropolitan area.

(7) In *Country Mutual Ins. Co. v. Livorsi Marine*, 2006 Ill. LEXIS 623 (Ill. May 18, 2006), the Illinois Supreme Court found no coverage—not even a duty to defend—due to the policyholder's late notice 20 months after it was hit with a lawsuit. Because the notice was so unreasonably late, the court found that the question of prejudice to the insurer need not be addressed. Whether this case reflects a special case of judicial frustration or whether it is the beginning of Illinois sliding in the direction of a New York rule remains to be seen. Certainly, the modern trend remains in favor of the notice-prejudice rule, even though some states still have old, New York-style notice cases that have never been formally overruled. The following case reflects one state's movement toward the modern rule but also reflects that even the notice-prejudice rule does not give policyholders carte blanche for late notice without consequences.

[C]   Requirement of Cooperation by the Insured

Page 529: [Add at the end of Note (2) in § 9.01[C]:]

But see Hartshorn v. State Farm Ins. Co., 838 N.E.2d 211 (Ill. App. 2005) (precluding coverage due to policyholder's "almost complete lack of cooperation" without regard to intent; but circumstances suggest failure to cooperate was knowing and intentional in that policyholder provided no documentation of claim and failed three times to appear for examination under oath; court also examines extent of prejudice to insurer but does not require showing of prejudice as condition to enforcing cooperation clause).

§ 9.02   DUTIES OF THE INSURER

[A]   Duty to Defend the Insured

Page 541: [Add to § 9.02[A] on p. 541]

Insurers frequently agree to defend a policyholder under a "reservation of rights," in which the insurer reserves its rights to contest coverage depending on the facts elucidated during discovery or trial of the matter. The question then arises as to whether an insurer's reservation creates a conflict of interest between insurer and policyholder. If so, the policyholder is generally permitted to select its own defense counsel, with the insurer paying reasonable legal fees commensurate with what the insurer would otherwise pay counsel selected by the insurer. However, a mere reservation of rights alone normally is not viewed as creating sufficient adversity to permit policyholder choice of counsel, although there are a few jurisdictions to the contrary. *See Twin City Fire Insurance Co. v. Ben Arnold Sunbelt Beverage Co.*, 433 F.3d 365 (4th Cir. 2005) (applying Virginia law) (collecting authorities from many states).

Assume a long-time client of yours has been sued and wants to tender defense of the matter to its liability insurer. However, the client also wants your law firm to defend it in the action. What information will you need to determine if this is possible? What will you tell your client? Should your client still tender the matter to the insurer or should you defend the case and then send the insurer the bill? *Compare Herbert A. Sullivan, Inc. v. Utica Mut. Ins. Co.*, 439 Mass 387, 788 N.E.2d 522, 539 (Mass. 2003); *Moeller v. Am. Guar. & Liability Ins. Co.*, 702 So.2d 1062, 1069 (Miss. 1996; *CHI of Alaska, Inc. v. Employers Reins. Corp.*, 844 P.2d 1113, 1118 (Alaska 1993) (reservation of rights creates conflict between insurer and policyholder that entitles policyholder to choice of counsel) *with Finley v. Home Ins. Co.*, 90 Haw. 25, 975 P.2d 1145, 1150-55 (Haw. 1998), *L & S Roofing Supply Co. v. St. Paul Fire & Marine Ins. Co.*, 521 So. 2d 1298, 1304 (Ala. 1987); *Tank v. State Farm Fire & Cas. Co.*, 715 P.2d 1133, 1137-38 (Wash. 1986) (defense of claim under reservation of rights does not create per se conflict or right to policyholder choice of counsel but may heighten insurer's already existing duties of good faith). *See also Nationwide Mut. Fire Ins.*

Co. v. Bourlon, 617 S.E.2d 40 (N.C. Ct. App. 2005) (even though applicable state law provides that insurer is a secondary client of attorney selected by insurer to defend claim, attorney's primary client is policyholder and it was a breach of the attorney-client relationship with policyholder for counsel to deliver his file to insurer after insurer had settled covered claims and refused to pay in connection with other claims against policyholder).

ABA Formal Opinion 05-435 (Dec. 8, 2004) touches on these issues and concludes that a law firm may under certain circumstances represent a plaintiff suing a policyholder and also represent the policyholder's liability insurer because the plaintiff and the defendant's liability insurer are not automatically "directly adverse." The rationale underlying this view is the important concept that a liability insurer is generally regarded as a third party responsible for obtaining a lawyer and resolving claims but is not itself a part to the litigation. "However, a concurrent conflict may arise if there is a significant risk the representation of the individual plaintiff will be materially limited by the lawyer's responsibilities to the insurer. . . ." The concern is that an insurer client may be so important to the law firm (because of the insurer's frequent need to hire lawyers for policyholders or its own legal work) that the law firm is compromised in its zeal for representing a plaintiff that, if it wins, will be paid at least in part by the insurer. But even then, the ABA Opinion concludes, it may be possible for the plaintiff and the insurer to waive the conflict if the attorney for the plaintiff has a reasonable belief that he or she "will be able to provide competent and diligent representation."

The standard answer to the question of whether to tender defense of a claim to the insurer is "always tender." Most liability insurers will not pay for any "pre-tender" defense expenditures even if the matter is eventually tendered to them. In addition, failure to tender can create defenses to coverage such as late notice and failure to cooperate. It also is not a great way to strengthen the client-policyholder's relationship with its insurers. Sometimes common sense and practicality are as important as the precise contours of legal right. But like almost any rule, there may be exceptions. For example, Illinois has a line of cases permitting "targeted tender," in which the policyholder covered by overlapping insurers can tender the defense of a claim to a single insurer rather than providing notice and tender of defense to all insurers. *See John Burns Construction Co. v. Indiana Insurance Co.*, 189 Ill. 2d 570, 727 N.E.2d 211 (Ill. 2000). Why would a rational policyholder do such a thing? What are the risks? What's the potential "reward" in asking only one insurer to defense when several insurance policies have arguably been "triggered" by a particular claim against the policyholder? What would you tend to advise to clients in this position? Does the following case give you any guidance? If you were practicing in a state other than Illinois that had no precedent on the issue, what would you advise the client?

NOTES AND QUESTIONS

(1) Where there are multiple insurers implicated by a claim, the question can also arise as to the relative responsibilities of the insurers in providing

a defense or paying defense costs. Sometimes insurers faced with the situation imitate "Alphonse and Gaston," two cartoon characters popular during the first half of the 20th Century (but at least dimly remembered by the authors). Alphonse and Gaston were not exactly a laugh-riot and would not threaten currently popular comedians like Jerry Seinfeld, Ray Romano, Jon Stewart or Lewis Black. Alphonse and Gaston's primary activity was continually deferring to one another about who should first go through a door. They regularly wasted countless hours with an "After you." "No, no, after you." Routine similar to the famous Laurel & Hardy seen where the two say good bye to friends for an interminable time before finally driving off. Insurers are accused of engaging in an Alphonse and Gaston routine when they delay mounting a policyholder's requested defense while hoping that another triggered insurer will rise to the occasion and defend the matter, saving the waiting insurer the time, effort, and money.

(2) Unfortunately, this Alphonse and Gaston routine sometimes works. For example, a "good" liability insurer may "step up to the plate" and provide a defense of the claim and resolve the matter economically while a "bad" insurer (or insurers) continues to sit on the sideline with money that it would have otherwise spent on defense safely in the bank earning interest. Worse yet, the sitting insurer is sometimes the insurer that had primary defense responsibility while the defending insurer may have been further from the risk or even a higher level excess insurer. For example, in *Iowa National Mut. Ins. Co. v. Universal Underwriters, Ins. Co.*, 276 Minn. 362, 150 N.W.2d 233 (Minn. 1967), a primary insurer with a duty to defend refused but the policyholder's excess insurer stepped into the void and defended. After the matter was concluded, the defending insurer sought to be reimbursed for half of the defense costs. Incredibly, the Minnesota Supreme Court held that no good deed goes unpunished and that the defending excess insurer (which should have been able to sit on the sideline) had no right to reimbursement from the primary insurer.

The formalist logic of the Court was that the duty to defend is not divisible, making pro-rated reimbursement inappropriate. The functional effect of the decision was to reward the insurer that acted improperly toward its policyholder. Notwithstanding that the decision is an embarrassment for even the most ardent formalist, *Iowa National* remains good law in Minnesota. *See, e.g. Home Ins. Co. v. National Union Fire Ins.*, 658 N.W.2d 522, 527 (Minn. 2003). Fortunately, most jurisdictions have adopted the reasonable view that the defending insurer in such cases is entitled to reimbursement. See, e.g., Church Mut. Ins. Co. v. Smith, 509 N.W.2d 274 (S.D. 1993); Farm & City Ins. Co. v. U.S. Fid. & Guar. Co., 323 N.W.2d 259 (Iowa 1982); Continental Cas. Co. v. Zurich Ins. Co., 57 Cal.2d 27, 366 P.2d 455, 17 Cal. Rptr. 12 (Cal. 1961); Farmers Ins. Group. v. Progressive Casaulty Ins. Co., 84 Mich. App. 474, 269 N.W.2d 647, 653 (Mich. Ct. App. 1978).

(3) As should perhaps go without saying, an insurer cannot escape duty to settle responsibilities by misleading a policyholder (or any insured under

the policy) into thinking that a claim is not available and that settlement is therefore not a possibility. *See, e.g., Roberts v. Printup*, 422 F.3d 1211 (10th Cir. 2005) (applying Kansas law) (where insurer initially misrepresented to mother than intra-family tort claim was not available against her son for negligent destruction of automobile registered in both names; insurer's duty to settle arises at time of loss and duty is triggered even absent formal pending claim).

Chapter 10

PROPERTY INSURANCE ISSUES

§ 10.01   AN OVERVIEW OF PROPERTY INSURANCE

Page 588: [Add to the Notes and Questions at the end of § 10.01:]

See also *BP America, Inc. v. State Auto Property & Casualty*, 2005 Okla. LEXIS 65 (Okla. 2005).

(4) For a recent scholarly review of the issue, see John F. Dobbyn, *Subrogation and the Innocent Spouse Dilemma*, 78 St. John's L. Rev. 1095 (2004).

§ 10.02   SCOPE OF PROPERTY COVERAGE

[E]   Theft and Mysterious Disappearance

Page 607: [Add the following at the end of § 10.02[E]:]

(5) The most common form of property insurance provides indemnity protection when tangible physical property is damaged "by the elements" so to speak, e.g., fire, wind, water, hail (frozen water), or other externally imposed physical injury such as vandalism. As discussed in this subsection, general property policies sometimes cover theft and sometimes exclude it. In addition to general property insurance, policyholders may purchase insurance against loss from crime or employee dishonesty. These policies typically cover only physical taking of property or money but may also cover losses from losses caused by more subtle crimes such as fraud, forgery, or securities law violations. As discussed in Chapter 11, Directors and Officers Insurance acts to protect companies from the liability consequences of wrongdoing that may lie at the boundary between misfeasance and outright intentional wrongdoing or crime. Even a fairly broad crime policy is relatively limited in its scope of coverage and should not be confused with an all-risk property policy insuring against damage from the elements or other external forces. Nor should it be confused with a general liability policy.

[J]   Business Interruption Insurance

Page 625: [Add to § 10.02[J] prior to the Omaha Paper case:]

The devastation of Hurricane Katrina in 2005, which followed a hurricane-heavy 2004, not only led to tight property insurance markets but also launched a rash of business interruption claims. These claims were often more problematic than usual because of both the magnitude and length of the "BI" claims (which made insurers less willing to pay in close cases and which presented expanded problems of valuation and concern that businesses were not doing all they could to resume operations) and because of uncertainty as to whether physical loss that interrupted commerce resulted from covered or uncovered causes. *See* Rhonda D. Orin, *Wind vs Water: Battle Royale Over Hurricane Claims*, RISK MGMT. MAG., May 2006 at p. 24; Andrew B. Downs, *Now What Do We Do?: Time Element Claims Following a Megaloss*, THE BRIEF, Winter 2005, at p. 37. *See also* Heath B. Monesmith, *Business Interruption Insurance Or Complete Cessation Insurance: Are Some Insurers Attempting to Rewrite Their Policies When Claims Are Asserted?*, 3-2 MEALEY'S BUS. INTERRUPTION INS. 11 (Jan. 2004).

Page 630: [Add the following new subsection following § 10.02[J]:]

[K] Hurricane Katrina and Property Coverage

In late August 2005, Hurricane Katrina brought devastation to New Orleans and the Gulf coast region. It exposed years of pennywise, poundfoolish decisions by state and local officials (e.g., insufficient maintenance of the levees around New Orleans), the incompetence of FEMA (the Federal Emergency Management Agency) since FEMA lost its cabinet post status and became part of the Department of Homeland Security (who can forget President Bush's "Heckava Job, Brownie" endorsement of the now-departed Agency head or the President's initial shocking disengagement on the matter?). However, it remains to be seen whether Katrina's devastation, much of it arguably preventable, will be the type of watershed event (and we hate the pun as much as you do) that realigns government programs, approaches to disaster, or political coalitions. It also remains to be seen whether Katrina will spur substantial changes in federal insurance programs or insurance law, although it clearly has spawned a significant amount of litigation over coverage and discussion about national property and disaster insurance reform.

It does appear that Katrina (along with the large hurricane losses of 2004) has already spurred changes in insurer behavior, with efforts to diversify the risk pool, a much harder market for insurance in the Southeastern United States, and a generally more adversarial claims environment as insurers attempt to minimize or recoup losses stemming from the tough 2004 and 2005 policy years. *See* Mark E. Ruquet, *Miss., La. Face Harder Property Markets*, NAT'L UNDERWRITER (Prop. & Cas. ed.), April 24, 2006 at 46; Mark E. Ruquet, *Gulf Agents Give Insurers Poor Grades*, NAT'L UNDERWRITER (Prop. & Cas. ed.), April 24, 2006 at 43. Unfortunately, the worst may be yet to come. *See Killer Hurricanes: No End in Sight*, NAT'L GEOGRAPHIC (Aug. 2006).

As of July 2006, there were more than reported 30 judicial decisions involving Katrina claims or at least discussing Katrina's effect on the litigation, nearly all at the trial level. Until these cases have all been resolved or run their appellate course, it is difficult to say whether Katrina claims will effect significant change in the law or merely apply prevailing legal doctrine to a particularly devastating loss. Many of the Katrina cases are not insurance coverage decisions although they may raise interesting or important legal issues. For example, several cases focus on the propriety of removal of state cases to federal court. *See, e.g., Wallace v. Louisiana Citizens Property Ins. Corp.*, 444 F.3d 697 (5th Cir. 2006) (applying federal procedural law) (reversing trial court's remanding of removed case and returning to trial court for further proceedings; Appeals Court suggests that removal and consolidation of Katrina-related claims may be appropriate under Multiparty, Multiform Trial Jurisdiction Act, 28 U.S.C. § 1441(e)(1)(B) in class action based on 28 U.S.C. § 1369, which seeks class action commonality on theory that claims arise from the "same accident"); *Koppel v. Eustis Ins. Co.*, 2006 U.S. Dis. LEXIS 31378 (E.D. La. May 19, 2006) (remanding removed Katrina-related claim of agent negligence in failing to procure contents flood coverage; federal establishment and regulation of flood insurance program did not establish complete federal preemption of state law-based tort claims against agent selling flood insurance); *Landry v. State Farm Fire & Cas. Co.*, 428 F. Supp. 2d 531, 534-36 (E.D. La. 2006) (rejecting insurer's Rule 59(a) motion to amend court's prior order of remand after removal). Strategically, policyholders tend to favor state court and particular venues within the affected states while insurers tend to prefer to remove Katrina coverage claims to federal court, which is thought to have a bench and jury venire more sympathetic to insurers and more willing to find that contested policy language defeats coverage.

One case sustained a default judgment against insurers that failed to defend policyholder claims. *See White v. North American Gen. Ins. Co.*, 2006 U.S. Dist. LEXIS 47503 (E.D. La. July 12, 2006). Another granted a policyholder's Rule 60(b) motion to vacate a judgment entered because the policyholder failed to respond to the insurer's Rule 12 motion. *See, e.g., Monticello Ins. Co. v. Dynabilt Mfg. Co., Inc.*, 2005 U.S. Dist. LEXIS 35249 (M.D. Fla., Oct. 13, 2005). A few cases simply reflect the powerful indirect effects of Katrina on dispute resolution. *See, e.g., Consolidate Brokers Ins. Serv., Inc. v. Enoch*, 427 F. Supp. 2d 1074 (Kan. 2006) (party seeking arbitration successfully argues that delay in pursuing arbitration was due to disruption caused by Katrina and hence should not be considered waiver);

Although perhaps just gaining momentum, Katrina's legal wake is apparent and growing. *See, e.g., Turk v. Louisiana Citizens Prop. Ins. Corp.*, 2006 U.S. Dist. LEXIS 41537 (W.D. La. June 7, 2006) (finding state valued policy statute, which requires payment of policy limits when damaged property is a "total loss," not to apply where sufficient portion of the property damage results from perils not covered under policy). To perhaps unwisely mix national disaster metaphors, it appears that the epicenter of Katrina coverage litigation has become the Southern District of Mississippi, particularly the courtroom of Senior Federal District Judge L.T. Senter, Jr., who as of July 2006 had issued nearly a fourth of the Hurricane

Katrina decisions. (Just to clarify: we consider an opinion reported if it is in the Lexis caselaw database) (and we're not taking that position because this is a LexisNexis casebook). Following are Judge Senter's most prominent rulings to date.

BUENTE v. ALLSTATE INSURANCE CO.

422 F. Supp. 2d 690 (S.D. Miss. March 24, 2006)

L. T. Senter, Jr., Senior Judge

The Court has before it Defendant Allstate Insurance Company's (Allstate) motion for judgment on the pleadings under F.R. Civ. P. 12(c). * * * The complaint alleges the following relevant facts: In June 2005, Plaintiffs purchased a residence in Gulfport, Mississippi. At the time this property was purchased, Plaintiffs also purchased a policy of homeowners insurance from Defendant Allstate. * * * The policy was in force during the policy period June 24, 2005, through June 24, 2006. * * * The Allstate policy was sold through Allstate agent Brenda Pace. Plaintiffs have alleged that ". . . Allstate and its agent Brenda Pace expressly represented to Plaintiffs that they would have full and comprehensive coverage for any and all hurricane damage, including any and all damage proximately, efficiently, and typically caused by hurricane wind and 'storm surge' proximately caused by hurricanes." * * * Plaintiffs have also alleged that they made an inquiry to Allstate representative Ms. Pace as to whether they needed to purchase additional flood insurance. This inquiry was apparently answered, according to the complaint, not by Ms. Pace, but by one of her employees. The plaintiffs allege that ". . . prior to purchasing the home, [Pace's office, Allstate's agent] told Plaintiffs they were required to have hurricane insurance on the residence. However, when Plaintiffs asked Allstate's agent Pace about whether they should also obtain optional 'flood coverage,' [they were told] they did not need additional flood coverage because they did not live in a flood plain. In this conversation, this same Allstate representative further affirmed that Plaintiffs' hurricane coverage would cover any damage caused by a hurricane." * * * Plaintiffs allege that they relied upon the representations set out in paragraphs 11 and 12 of the complaint. Specifically, the complaint alleges that "Plaintiffs . . . relied upon Allstate's agent's representations that their hurricane coverage would cover any damage caused by a hurricane and thus they did not need flood insurance." (Complaint, Paragraph 14). * * * Plaintiffs allege that they reasonably relied upon the representations made by Allstate's representatives and upon their own subjective expectations concerning the coverage provided by the insurance policy in making the decision not to purchase flood insurance coverage.

On August 29, 2005, the insured property was damaged during Hurricane Katrina. Plaintiffs allege that the damage was caused by "hurricane wind, rain, and/or storm surge from Hurricane Katrina." * * * Plaintiffs allege that "Plaintiffs also called the Allstate 'Natural Disaster Hotline' to inquire whether the damage to their residence would be covered under the subject policy. The Allstate representative they spoke to assured Plaintiffs that damage from 'storm surge' would be covered under the subject policy." * * * The adjuster Allstate sent to inspect the insured property after Hurricane Katrina told the plaintiffs that "Allstate only pays him for adjustment of damages caused by wind, not water." * * * Allstate tendered its check for $2,600.35, representing the amount of the covered loss (net of the applicable deductible) as determined by the Allstate adjuster. Plaintiffs contend that their covered losses are between $50,000 and $100,000. . . .

Allstate's insurance policy [labeled an "Allstate Property and Casualty Insurance Company Deluxe Homeowners Policy"] contains the following relevant provisions:

With respect to the insured dwelling (Section I, Coverage A) and other structures (Section I, Coverage B):

Losses We Cover. . .

We will cover sudden and accidental direct physical loss to [the insured property] : *. . . except as limited or excluded in this policy.* (Policy Pages 5 through 8.)

Losses We Do Not Cover. . .

We do not cover loss to the [insured] property consisting of or caused by:

1. Flood, including, but not limited to surface water, waves, tidal water or overflow of any body of water, or spray from any of these, whether or not driven by wind.

　　* * *

4. Water or any other substance on or below the surface of the ground, regardless of its source. This includes water or any other substance which exerts pressure on, or flows, seeps or leaks through any part of the residence premises.

　　* * *

21. Weather Conditions that contribute in any way with a cause of loss excluded in this section to produce a loss.

　　* * *

23. We do not cover loss to covered property . . . when:

　a) there are two or more causes of loss to the covered property; and

　b) the predominant cause(s) of loss is (are) excluded under Losses We Do Not Cover, items 1 through 22 above.

With respect to personal property (Section I, Coverage C, Personal Property Protection):

Losses We Cover. . .

We will cover sudden and accidental direct physical loss to the [insured personal] property . . . except as limited or excluded in this policy, caused by:

2. Windstorm or Hail.

We do not cover:

   a) loss to covered property insidea building structure, caused by rain, snow, sleet, sand or dust unless the wind or hail first damages the roof or walls and the wind forces rain, snow, sleet, sand or dust through the damaged roof or wall. . .

   * * *

16. Breakage of glass, meaning damage to covered personal property caused by breakage of glass constituting a part of any building structure on the residence premises. This does not include damage to the glass.

   Losses We Do Not Cover

We do not cover loss to [insured personal] property caused by or consisting of:

1. Flood, including, but not limited to surface water, waves, tidal water or overflow of any body of water, or spray from any of these, whether or not driven by wind.

   * * *

4. Water or any other substance on or below the surface of the ground, regardless of its source. This includes water or any other substance which exerts pressure on, or flows, seeps or leaks through any part of the residence premises.

   * * *

13. Weather conditions that contribute in any way with a cause of loss excluded in this section to produce a loss.

   * * *

15. We do not cover loss to [insured personal] property when:

   a) there are two or more causes of loss to the covered property; and

   b) the predominant cause(s) of loss is (are) excluded under Losses We Do Not Cover items 1 through 14 above.

Additional Protection

11. Collapse

   We will cover:

a) the entire collapse of a covered building structure;

b) the entire collapse of part of a covered building structure;

c) direct physical loss to covered property caused by (a) or (b) above.

   For coverage to apply, the collapse of a building structure specified in (a) or (b) above must be a sudden and accidental direct physical loss caused by one or more of the following:

   a) a loss we cover under Section I, Coverage C—Personal Property Protection;

* * *

When I apply these legal principles to the facts alleged in the complaint, it is apparent to me that Allstate's motion for judgment on the pleadings cannot be granted. Much depends on the evidence that may be adduced in support of the allegations of the complaint. But under the standards applicable to a motion for judgment on the pleadings under F.R. Civ. P. 12(c), i.e. accepting all of the material allegations of the complaint as true and granting the plaintiffs all reasonable inferences in support of their claims, I cannot say that there is no set of facts the plaintiffs may establish in support of their claim that would entitle them to relief.

I begin with the allegation of paragraph 18 of the complaint that the plaintiffs' property damage was caused by ". . . hurricane wind, rain, and/or storm surge from Hurricane Katrina. . . ." I accept this allegation as true, and I grant the plaintiffs the favorable inference that the destruction of their property was attributable in part to wind, in part to rain, and in part to storm surge.

As to the damage caused by wind and rain, there is apparently no dispute that these losses are covered by the policy. It is apparently undisputed that the winds generated during Hurricane Katrina were sufficient to do substantial damage to the roof of the plaintiffs' home. There is obviously a dispute about the extent of this covered loss. Allstate adjusted the plaintiffs' claim for wind damage and concluded that only $2,600.35 of the plaintiffs' damages were attributable to the effect of the hurricane winds. Allstate apparently acknowledges that its policy provides coverage for wind damage and for rain damage resulting from winds that breach the roof or walls of the insured premises.

The major dispute is whether losses attributable to "storm surge" are covered losses because the "storm surge" is wind driven or whether losses attributable to "storm surge" are excluded from coverage because such damages are caused by "water" (Exclusion 4) or by "flood, including but not limited to surface water, waves, tidal water or overflow of any body of water, or spray from any of these whether or not driven by wind" (Exclusion 1).

The exclusions found in the policy for water damage and for damages attributable to flooding are valid and enforceable policy provisions. Indeed, similar policy terms have been enforced with respect to damage caused by high water associated with hurricanes in many reported decisions. * * *

But because this is an exclusion from coverage in a comprehensive homeowners insurance policy, and because the exclusion constitutes an affirmative defense, Allstate would bear the burden of proving that the exclusion applies to the plaintiffs' claims. * * * If the evidence were to indicate that part of the plaintiffs' losses were attributable to wind and rain (making them covered losses under the "Windstorm" provisions of Coverage C and under the broader "sudden and accidental direct physical loss" provision applicable to Coverages A and B) and part of the losses were attributable to flooding (which is excluded from coverage), the determination which was the proximate cause of the damage to any given item of property (or the determination of the proportion of the damage to any given item of property was proximately caused by each phenomenon) would be a question of fact under applicable Mississippi law. * * * Likewise, if the evidence shows that the damage occurred over time, so that wind damage preceded damage from a "storm surge," the wind damage would be a covered loss even if subsequent damage from the "storm surge" that exacerbated the loss were properly excluded from coverage. *Litiz Mutual Insurance Co. v. Boatner* (Miss. 1971).

Because this policy carries a specific "Hurricane Deductible Endorsement," it is apparent to me that it was intended to cover damages sustained in a hurricane because of the effects of rain, hurricane winds, and objects that might be carried by those winds, whether or not there was also damage caused by high water. Thus, to the extent Allstate contends that the hurricane itself, i.e. the hurricane winds and rain, would constitute a weather condition that would relieve them of liability for damage to insured property (under Exclusion 21 in Coverages A and B and/or Exclusion 13 in Coverage C), I find that the policy is ambiguous and its weather exclusion therefore unenforceable in the context of losses attributable to wind and rain that occur during a hurricane. Under applicable Mississippi law, where there is damage caused by both wind and rain (covered losses) and water (losses excluded from coverage) the amount payable under the insurance policy becomes a question of which is the proximate cause of the loss. To the extent that the Allstate policy is inconsistent with this settled rule of Mississippi law, under Exclusion 21 of Coverages A and B and Exclusion 13 of Coverage C, the exclusionary language is invalid.

I find that Exclusion 23 under Coverages A and B and Exclusion 15 under coverage C create ambiguities in the context of damages sustained by the insured during a hurricane. These provisions purport to exclude coverage for wind and rain damage, both of which are covered losses under this policy, where any excluded cause of loss, e.g. water damage, is "the predominant cause of the loss." I find that these two exclusions are ambiguous in light of the other policy provisions granting coverage for wind and rain damage and in light of the inclusion of a "hurricane deductible" as part of the policy. To the extent that plaintiffs can prove their allegations that the hurricane winds (or objects driven by those winds) and rains entering the insured premises through openings caused by the hurricane winds proximately caused damage to their insured property, those losses will be covered under the policy, and this will be the case even if flood damage, which is not covered, subsequently occurred. Again, these are fact-specific inquiries that must be resolved on the basis of the evidence adduced at trial. For purposes of resolving Allstate's motion, I must give the plaintiffs the benefit of all reasonable inferences available to support their claim.

Of course, I cannot know at this juncture what the evidence will be. It is likely that both the plaintiffs and Allstate will present expert evidence on the issue of the cause or causes of the damage to the plaintiffs' property. But it is my opinion, upon a thorough review of the terms of the Allstate policy, that the damage attributable to wind and rain will be covered, regardless of whether a later inflow of water caused additional damage that would be excluded from coverage.

* * *

Allstate's agent was under no duty to advise the plaintiffs what coverages were necessary for the protection of their property. Yet if the plaintiffs made an inquiry of the agent and the agent (or one of her employees with actual or apparent authority to respond to the inquiry), in response, made the representations concerning coverage that the plaintiffs have alleged, All-state may have potential liability for all of the damage to the plaintiffs' property. Again, this is a fact-specific inquiry into exactly what the plain-tiffs asked and exactly what was said in response to their inquiry.

I cannot tell from the documents before me when the policy in question was actually delivered to the plaintiffs. The cover letter is undated. The policy took effect on June 24, 2005, and presumably the policy was delivered around this date. The date that the plaintiffs received the policy may be relevant to the question of whether it was reasonable to rely on the statements attributed to Allstate's agent in the complaint. At this juncture, plaintiffs are entitled to the inference that their reliance was reasonable.

BUENTE v. ALLSTATE PROPERTY & CASUALTY INS. CO.

2006 U.S. Dist. LEXIS 23742 (S.D. Miss. April 11, 2006)

L. T. Senter, Jr., Senior Judge.

The Court has before it Plaintiffs Elmer and Alexa Buente's motion for partial summary judgment. For the reasons discussed below, this motion will be denied. * * * The facts relevant to the resolution of this motion are not in dispute. Plaintiffs' home was severely damaged during Hurricane Katrina. Plaintiffs allege that the damage to their home was caused in part by wind and wind driven rain and in part by rising water during the hurricane. The home was insured under a Deluxe Homeowners Policy issued by Defendant Allstate * * * This policy insures the plaintiffs' home against *"sudden and accidental direct physical loss . . . except as limited or excluded by this policy."* Allstate Policy, Section I; Losses We Cover Under Coverages A and B. * * * The policy contains an exclusion for damage attributable to inundation: *"We do not cover loss to the [insured] property consisting of or caused by: 1. Flood, including, but not limited to surface water, waves, tidal water or overflow of any body of water, or spray from any of these, whether or not driven by wind. . . 4. Water or any other sub-stance on . . . the surface of the ground regardless of its source."* Allstate Policy, Section I; Losses We Do Not Cover Under Coverages A and B. * * * Plaintiffs assert that these exclusions, which I will refer to collectively as the policy's "flood exclusions," are ambiguous and are therefore unenforce-able in the context of property damage sustained in Hurricane Katrina. * * * Defendant contends that these policy provisions are clear and unambiguous, and that the provisions are enforceable as valid policy provisions forming part of the insurance contract.

Plaintiffs acknowledge that the insured property sustained damage as a result of water that entered their home during Hurricane Katrina. Plaintiffs contend that this damage should be covered because it is a result of "storm surge." Plaintiffs contend that because the phenomenon of "storm surge" is not specifically listed as a peril excluded by the Allstate policy the water damage they experienced should be a covered loss.

The critical issue in resolving this motion is whether the entry of water into the plaintiffs' home is within the terms of the "flood exclusions" in the Allstate policy. The exclusions are drawn quite broadly, and they have the clear purpose of excluding damage caused by inundation from coverage.

Hurricane Katrina moved tidal waters from the Mississippi Sound on shore and inundated thousands of homes, some within and some beyond the ordinary flood plane established by responsible agencies of the United States government. Since the water that entered and damaged the plaintiffs' home was tidal water, I find that the damage caused by this inundation is excluded from coverage under the Allstate policy.

The inundation that occurred during Hurricane Katrina was a flood, as that term is ordinarily understood, whether that term appears in a flood insurance policy or in a home owners insurance policy. The exclusions found in the policy for damages attributable to flooding are valid and enforceable policy provisions. Indeed, similar policy terms have been enforced with respect to damage caused by high water associated with hurricanes in many reported decisions. *Fireman's Ins. Co. v. Schulte* (Miss. 1967); *Lunday v. Lititz Mutual Insurance Co.* (Miss.1973); *Lititz Mutual Insurance Co. v. Buckley* (Miss. 1972); *Home Ins. Co. v. Sherrill*, (5th Cir.1949); *Grace v. Lititz Mutual Insurance Co.*, (Miss. 1972); *Commercial Union Ins. Co. v. Byrne*, (Miss. 1971); *Litiz Mut. Ins. Co. v. Boatner* (Miss. 1971).

The terms of an insurance policy are to be given their ordinary meaning unless some special usage must be implied from the policy itself. Where the terms of the policy are clear and unambiguous, the provisions must be enforced as written. *Shaw v. Burchfield* (Miss. 1985); *Farmland Mutual Ins. Co. v. Scruggs* (Miss. 2004). It is my opinion that the terms of [*5] the Allstate policy, specifically the "flood exclusions" set out above, are clear and unambiguous. Since the Court is not free to change or invalidate the unambiguous terms of an insurance contract (or any other contract), plaintiffs' motion for partial summary judgment will be **DENIED**.

COMER v. NATIONWIDE MUTUAL INSURANCE CO.

2006 U.S. Dist. LEXIS 33123 (S.D. Miss. February 23, 2006)

L. T. Senter, Jr., Senior Judge.

The Court has before it plaintiffs' motion for leave to file a second amended complaint. For the reasons set out below, I will deny the motion.

* * * This is an action brought by fourteen plaintiffs who are owners of properties damaged in Hurricane Katrina. Each of these individual plaintiffs is alleged to have had property insurance with one of the seven individual insurance companies specifically named as defendants or one of one hundred unidentified "Insurance Entities." Plaintiffs have asked the Court to certify, under Rule 23 F.R. Civ. P., an "Insurance Defendant Class" composed of the seven identified insurance company defendants and the one hundred unidentified "Insurance Entities."

Plaintiffs have asked the Court to certify them as representatives of a class composed of all "similarly situated" property owners in Mississippi who were insured with any of the defendants to be included in the "Insurance Defendant Class." In other words, these fourteen plaintiffs are seeking to represent all of the owners of insured property in Mississippi who suffered losses as a result of Hurricane Katrina against all of the insurance companies who have written policies that potentially cover these losses.

Plaintiffs have also asked the Court to certify a second defendant class composed of six identified and one hundred unidentified mortgage lenders. The members of this "Mortgage Lending Defendant Class" allegedly breached legal duties to maintain proper insurance coverage for the mortgaged property damaged in Hurricane Katrina. Plaintiffs have asked the Court to certify them as representatives of a class composed of all "similarly situated" property owners in Mississippi whose mortgage lenders breached the duties alleged to have been owed to the property owners with respect to maintaining insurance coverage on the mortgaged property.

Plaintiffs have also asked the Court to certify a third defendant class composed of three chemical companies and a trade association for the chemical industry as a "Chemical Manufacturer Defendant Class." This class has been sued because they are alleged to have caused damage to the plaintiffs' properties by actions that have contributed to global warming.

Plaintiffs have also asked the Court to certify a fourth defendant class composed of five major oil companies, a trade association, and one hundred unidentified oil companies as an "Oil Company Defendant Class." This class has been sued because they are alleged to have caused damage to the plaintiffs' properties through actions that have contributed to global warming.

Plaintiffs have asked the Court to certify them as representatives of a class composed of all "similarly situated" property owners in Mississippi who sustained property damage during Hurricane Katrina to the extent that the property damage sustained during Hurricane Katrina is attributable to the allegedly wrongful actions of the "Oil Company Defendant Class" and the "Chemical Company Defendant Class." * * * I perceive at least four problems with the approach the plaintiffs are asking the Court to permit in this action:

> 1. Each property owner in Mississippi who had real and personal property damaged in Hurricane Katrina is uniquely situated. No

two property owners will have experienced the same losses. The nature and extent of the property damage the owners sustain from the common cause, Hurricane Katrina, will vary greatly in its particulars, depending on the location and condition of the property before the storm struck and depending also on what combination of forces caused the damage. Thus, at least with respect to the issue of damages, each individual claim will require particular evidence to establish the cause of and the extent of the loss.

2. To the extent the property was insured, the particulars of coverage will vary from policy to policy and from one insurance company to the next. In order to adjudicate the rights and liabilities between the policy holder and his insurance company, the particular terms of each policy must be considered.

3. Likewise, the undertakings of the various mortgage holders and the undertakings of the owners of the mortgaged property will vary from one owner to the next, and from one mortgage holder to the next, depending on the particulars of the contracts that govern the legal relationships between the mortgage holders and the property owners. As I appreciate the allegations of the complaint with respect to the mortgage lenders, plaintiffs contend that the mortgage lenders owed and breached a duty to the plaintiffs to keep the mortgaged property "properly and sufficiently" insured. This duty must arise, if at all, under the terms of the agreements that govern the legal relationships between the individual plaintiffs and their mortgage holders. Thus, each of these agreements must be considered on its own terms.

4. The plaintiffs' basic theory of recovery against the insurance companies and the mortgage lenders is quite distinct from the plaintiffs' basic theory of recovery against the chemical companies and the oil companies named as defendants. The plaintiffs' claims against the insurance companies and the mortgage lenders are essentially contract claims under existing insurance policies or negligence claims related to the procurement of insurance policies. Neither the insurance companies nor the mortgage lenders are alleged to have caused or contributed to the cause of the property damage sustained during Hurricane Katrina. The plaintiffs' claims against the chemical companies and the oil companies are essentially tort claims that arise independent of any contractual issues and independent of any insurance issues. The chemical companies and the oil companies are alleged to have caused or contributed to the cause of the property damage the plaintiffs sustained during Hurricane Katrina. These legal theories and the underlying acts alleged to have been wrongful are so distinct as to negate, as a practical matter, any common issues of law and fact among the two groups of defendants (the insurers and mortgage lenders on the one hand and the oil companies and chemical companies on the other).

Thus, in my opinion, the joinder of all the proposed defendant classes in a single action exceeds the limits of Rule 20, F.R. Civ. P.

Given the preponderance of individual questions of damage, coverage, policy provisions, mortgage obligations, and the other relevant particulars involved in the case of each individual property owner who sustained damage as a result of Hurricane Katrina, I simply do not believe that the extremely broad classes of parties the plaintiffs are proposing are practical in the context of this civil suit. In my opinion, under the standards embodied in Rule 23, F.R. Civ. P., the questions of law and fact common to the members of the plaintiff class do not predominate over the questions affecting individual members of the plaintiff class. Nor do I believe that the questions of law and fact common to the insurers and mortgage holders predominate over the questions of law and fact affecting the individual insurers and the individual mortgage holders. And I do not believe that a class action of this nature is a superior method of resolving the issues that will arise, with respect to the insurance defendants and with respect to the mortgage holder defendants, in this litigation. Accordingly, I will require that the plaintiffs pursue individual actions limited to their own insurers and to their own mortgage lenders. Of course, by taking this action I do not imply any opinion concerning the merits of these actions.

Although leave to amend a complaint is to be freely given when justice so requires, there is no purpose to be served in allowing an amendment which is futile. In my opinion, the proposed second amended complaint, which seeks to further broaden this already expansive action would be an exercise in futility. This action, as it presently stands, is unmanageable; it is also inconsistent with the limitations of Rule 20, F.R. Civ. P.; and it cannot meet the requirements of Rule 23, F.R. Civ. P. Allowing the amendment the plaintiffs propose would only serve to make the litigation even less manageable and even more inconsistent with Rules 20 and 23, F.R. Civ. P.

Accordingly, I will deny the plaintiffs' motion for leave to file the second amended complaint they have proposed. Instead, in the exercise of my discretion under Rule 20 (b), F.R. Civ. P., I will require the plaintiffs to file separate actions against their insurers and mortgage lenders. To this end, I will dismiss this action as to the insurers and mortgage lenders without prejudice. Each of the plaintiffs (a husband and wife shall be considered to be a single plaintiff) shall be permitted to proceed against his insurer and his mortgage lender in an individual action. Each plaintiff shall identify the insurers and mortgage lenders against whom they have individual claims and against whom they may wish to proceed, and each plaintiff shall file a separate complaint. Each plaintiff will be permitted to sue only the insurance companies and the mortgage lenders with whom they have contractual relationships. Any plaintiffs who have the same insurer and the same mortgage lender may file separate complaints or they may proceed in a single action against these common defendants, should they choose to do so. Any plaintiffs who do not share a common insurer and mortgage lender must proceed in a separate action. All new complaints that must be filed in order to comply with this ruling will be considered to have been filed on the date this action was originally filed for all purposes, and each civil cover sheet for any subsequently filed complaint shall identify this action as a related civil proceeding.

As a result of my ruling, the parties remaining as defendants in this action will be the oil company defendants and the chemical company defendants. I will grant plaintiffs leave to file an amended complaint to clarify their claims against these defendants and to add any additional parties that the plaintiffs intend to bring in to this litigation. The plaintiffs shall, for the sake of clarity in this record, designate their amended complaint in this action a "third amended complaint."

Without in any way expressing an opinion on the merits of the plaintiffs' claims against these defendants, I will observe that there exists a sharp difference of opinion in the scientific community concerning the causes of global warming, and I foresee daunting evidentiary problems for anyone who undertakes to prove, by a preponderance of the evidence, the degree to which global warming is caused by the emission of greenhouse gasses; the degree to which the actions of any individual oil company, any individual chemical company, or the collective action of these corporations contribute, through the emission of greenhouse gasses, to global warming; and the extent to which the emission of greenhouse gasses by these defendants, through the phenomenon of global warming, intensified or otherwise affected the weather system that produced Hurricane Katrina. This is a task that the plaintiffs are free to undertake if that is their intention, and I am confident that due consideration will be given to the requirements of Rule 11, F.R. Civ. P. Under Rule 20, F.R. Civ. P., these claims cannot be litigated in a single action that also includes the plaintiffs' contractual claims against their insurers and their mortgage lenders. * * * I cannot, at this juncture, determine whether the plaintiffs' action against the oil companies and chemical companies named as defendants should proceed as a class action under Rule 23, F.R. Civ. P., and that issue will be determined in accordance with the requirements of that rule at the appropriate time.

NOTES AND QUESTIONS

(1) After the *Buente* opinions, Judge Senter made essentially the same decision in a policyholders' action against another large insurer. *See, e.g., Tuepker v. State Farm Fire & Cas. Co.*, 2006 U.S. Dist. LEXIS 45883 (S.D. Miss. May 24, 2006). The *Buente* decisions, particularly the April 11 opinion more than the March 24 opinion, were seen by insurers as a significant victory. *See, e.g.,* Daniel Hays, *Insurers Win Big Round in Flood Case*, NAT'L UNDERWRITER (Prop. & Cas. ed.), April 24, 2006 at 8. However, other commentators find that the policyholders gained significant ground as well. *See, e.g.,* Peter Geier, *Judges play Katrina suits down the middle*, NAT'L

L.J., July 3, 2006 at 6 ("Judge Senter gave homeowners the chance to prove that wind destroyed the premises before the flood got there, which was a big win for homeowners. But he also maintained the integrity of the insurers' flood exclusion.") (quoting insurer attorney Randy Maniloff).

(2) Which perspective seems closer to correct? Does the March 24 *Buente* opinion give something to both policyholders and insurers? How about the April 11 opinion? What must policyholders prove to collect under the two *Buente* opinions excerpted above? Is one legitimate policyholder criticism of the opinions that the Court seems not to put much weight on the rule of interpretation that requires exclusions to be strictly construed against the insurer and that the insurer be the one to prove the applicability of an exclusion (rather than requiring the policyholder to prove the inapplicability of the exclusion)?

(3) Can one reasonably quarrel with the Court's analysis of the text of what Judge Senter labels the "inundation exclusion"? Can a policyholder construct a less textual argument that the literal language of the exclusion defeats the policyholder's objectively reasonable expectations of coverage? If a home is smashed by a wave, does the average layperson think of this as damage due to a "flood"? Even if this is not the case, does the exclusion's mention of "waves" and "tidal water" successfully defeat reasonable expectation or ambiguity arguments? Would the policy be clearer if it stated "there is no coverage for storm surge damage"? Are there clearer ways to state the limits of coverage?

(4) Is the *Comer* opinion's resistance to class action treatment of the Katrina-related coverage disputes justified? The Court finds that each property hit by the Hurricane was "uniquely situated" and that the "particulars of coverage will vary from policy to policy"—so much so that the Court finds it would be "futile" to even permit the policyholder plaintiffs to frame the case as a putative class action. Although we all remember from Property class (or at least the Lexis *Questions & Answers* from Property class) that "each Blackacre is unique," doesn't this sentiment seem a little too 16th Century in light of the modern realities of property ownership and the potential efficiencies in adjudicating common questions. Modern housing tends to be based on a few standard floor plans and construction techniques. Damage from wind or flood may vary at the margin but can be separately classified. Personal lines property insurance such as homeowners' insurance and commercial business property coverage is highly standardized.

(5) In addition, Fed. R. Civ. P. 23 permits class actions as to common issues and permits the use of subclasses (e.g., all State Farm policyholders). Could this be used to obtain some efficiencies from class treatment for the parts of the claims that are more homogenous without steamrolling the individual aspects of claims? Would common trials work for topics such as the causal inquiry required to decide the disputes, the boundaries of covered windstorm and uncovered flood, the meaning of standard policy terms, and the means of measuring loss? Why or why not?

(6) In the absence of class treatment, can many of the same benefits be realized by having the court first decide representative cases. After a sufficient body of precedent has been formed, should this not sufficiently encourage settlement? But what if an insurer or insurers want to simply apply pressure to individual claimants by refusing to settle on fair terms? If the homeowner's claim is sufficiently small or if the economics of litigation are unattractive, does this give the insurer too much leverage in the absence of class action treatment? Conversely, does class treatment give policyholders (or class counsel) too much leverage?

(7) Judge Senter has also issued his share of procedural decisions in the case, including at least three remanding removed cases back to state court, usually because the plaintiff has properly sued a resident defendant, such as a Mississippi insurance agent, in addition to suing an non-resident insurance company. *See, e.g., Pierce v. Reynolds,* 2006 U.S. Dist. LEXIS 47539 (May 15, 2006); *Cleveland v. Nationwide Mut. Fire Ins. Co.,* 2006 U.S. Dist. LEXIS 28763 (S.D. Miss. May 1, 2006); *Carr v. Dennison,* 2006 U.S. Dist. LEXIS 28765 (S.D. Miss. May 1, 2006). *See also Leonard v. Nationwide Ins. Co.,* 2006 U.S. Dist. LEXIS 43198 (June 13, 2006) (denying plaintiff request for discovery concerning underwriting of insurer's Hurricane Coverage and Deductible Provision Endorsement after finding that Endorsement was not part of policy in dispute).

(8) After this visit to the epicenter of Katrina controversy, you should be able to answer this question: is Judge Senter a formalist or a functionalist? Why or why not? Would formalists and functionalist reach different results in these cases? Why or why not?

§ 10.05   SUBROGATION

[G]   The Loan Receipt Method

Page 673: [Add at the end of § 10.05[G]:]

[H]   Title Insurance

Title Insurance involves real property but it does not insure the real property or other physical property against loss. Rather, title insurance protects the purchaser of real estate if the title obtained by the buyer is impaired in some way. "Defects in titles may stem from sources such as forgery of public record, forgery of titles, invalid or undiscovered wills, defective probate procedures, and faulty real estate transfers." *See* JAMES S. TRIESCHMANN, ROBERT E. HOYT & DAVID W. SOMMER, RISK MANAGEMENT AND INSURANCE 187-88 (12th ed. 2004). The title insurer agrees to indemnity the property owner against loss suffered "by reason of unmarketability of the title: or from "loss or damage by reason of liens, encumbrances, defects, objections, estates, and interests" except those listed in a schedule of defects found during a title search of the property. The goal is for the title search to be done well and reveal all defects, with buyer and seller than negotiating impact of those defective on the terms of the sales transaction. Title insurance provides compensation for defects that are missed by the title search but does not insure the property against physical injury or the owner against commercial loss.

Title insurance also normally includes a duty to defend the owner in legal proceedings concerning title to the property. The premium is paid once and the policy remains in force from the time of issuance forward. However, if the property is sold or otherwise transferred, the title insurer's commit- ment ends and the new owner must purchase a new policy of title insurance.

"Title insurance is thus narrower than general property or liability insurance and backward-looking in that it assumes the risk of a deficient examination of title. By contrast, general property insurance and liability insurance is forward-looking in that it assumes the risk that adverse events will take place in the future." *See Stempel on Insurance Contracts* § 22.14[D] at 22-117.

Title insurance thus does not insure against potential future calamities but instead provides defense of title against adverse claims and compensa- tion if the title of property was more clouded than revealed by the title search. Because of its more limited scope and significant premiums in rela- tion to risk assumed, title insurance has been regarded by some as overpriced relative to the value of the product. *See also* Liam Pleven, *Deciphering Title Insurance: Regulators Take Closer Look Amid Concerns About Pricing; Garage on the Property Line*, WALL ST. J., Dec. 31, 2005 at B1, col. 1. Even if the criticisms are well-founded, it is still hard to imagine the modern American home market without title insurance. In addition, title insurance may serve a related useful role by encouraging better record- keeping regarding chain of title and by making real property markets more transparent and efficient. In that respect, title insurance may make for better real estate transactions and documentation just as the inspection component of boiler and machinery insurance has made for safer industrial equipment. Useful treatises on title insurance include D. BARLOW BURKE, LAW OF TITLE INSURANCE (3d ed. 2001).

A risk management cousin of sorts to title insurance is private mortgage insurance, which insures against the risk of defaults on mortgages. Pre- mium payment is commonly included as part of a buyer's regular mortgage payments. *See generally* Quintin Johnstone, *Private Mortgage Insurance*, 39 WAKE FOREST L. REV. 783 (2004).

Chapter 11

LIABILITY INSURANCE ISSUES

§ 11.05 DEFINING AND COUNTING THE LIABILITY INSURANCE "OCCURRENCE"

Page 700: [Add the following to § 11.05, Note (1):]

See also Owners Ins. Co. v. Salmonsen, 366 S.C. 336, 622 S.E.2d 525 (So. Car. 2005) (finding distribution of defective stucco to be one occurrence rather than multiple occurrences based on number of sales); *Ramirez v. Allstate Ins. Co.*, 811 N.Y.S. 2d 19 (N.Y. App. Div. 2006) (two infants ingestion of lead paint chips in apartment is one occurrence); *Bomba v. State Farm Fire & Cas. Co.*, 379 N.J. Super. 589, 879 A.2d 1252 (N.J. Super. Ct. 2005) (shooting of two police officers a single occurrence).

Bomba and Koikos (and the respective law of New Jersey and Florida) are obviously in tension if not completely inconsistent. The Koikos each-victim-is-an-occurrence approach is better assessment for cases involving shootings or similar acts of serial destruction by a single tortfeasor, particularly under the facts of the two cases. In both Bomba and Koikos, the assailants did not spray a single burst of fire but separately fixated on separate targets and shot separately, albeit within a very short time frame. And, as the Koikos Court emphasized, an occurrence requires injury; until a bullet hits someone (or at least comes close enough to inflict mental anguish), there is no injury. For product distribution cases, the Salmonsen approach or a finding of more occurrences linked to significant multiple junctures of sale or distribution may be more apt depending on the facts of the respective cases.

§ 11.08 IS LIABILITY INSURANCE COVERAGE LIMITED TO ONLY "TORT" CLAIMS?

Page 730: [Add to § 11.08 following the Notes and Questions after the Vandenberg case:]

(3) At least one other state supreme court has implicitly adopted the *Vandenberg* analysis in concluding that liability insurance (in particular automobile liability insurance) provides coverage even if a claim for bodily injury or property damage is styled as a contract claim rather than a tort claim. *See Lee v. USAA Casualty Insurance Co.*, 86 P.3d 562, 564-565 (Mont. 2004) (policy (contains no exclusion for liability arising out of a contract, which is an exclusion often included in these types of liability insurance policies.(). The case arose when a couple brought a car together and the

male promised to add the female to his auto policy if she would drop her auto policy (presumably to save money for the couple). Sure enough, the guy failed to follow through and, sure enough, the girl was in an accident in which the driver at fault had inadequate insurance. She then sought underinsured (UIM) motorist benefits under the guy's policy (see Chapter 13) only to find that she had not been added to his policy and that his insurer was declining coverage. The uncovered guy confessed liability and judgment in the amount of $284,005. She then sued his insurer for payment and prevailed because of the broad insuring agreement in his auto policy, which provided it would pay when the policyholder (becomes legally responsible because of an accident." The insurer screamed (figuratively) that it had sold an auto accident policy and not a breach-of-contract-by-irresponsible-guys policy. The Court rejected this argument, noting that: "Nowhere in the above list [of approximately 10 specific policy exclusions] does the USAA policy exclude liability coverage from the situation presented here" i.e., where a person is injured as a result of an automobile accident and another person becomes liable by breach of contract. Therefore . . . USAA had a duty to defend and justifiably denied coverage based on the policy language." *See* 86 P.3d at 565.

(4) Although *Lee v. USAA* did not cite *Vandenberg v. Superior Court*, it takes a similar view in finding that the legal styling of a complaint is not particularly important. What is important is the facts alleged by the complaint and the language of the insuring agreement. If the facts allege something falling within the coverage agreement, the claim can be successful despite the adage that liability insurance exists to cover tort claims rather than contract claims. The real truth is that insurance covers claims within the scope of the policy irrespective of the styling of the claim. Also, before shedding too many tears for USAA, which undoubtedly was a bit perplexed at being hit with this claim, consider the realities of the situation. Had the guy followed through and requested to add the girl to his auto policy in connection with a car they purchased together, the insurer almost certainly would have agreed and expressly assumed the risk presented. At the same time, however, USAA can complain that it was blindsided and had not opportunity to adjust premiums or otherwise examine the new risk. But USAA did draft the broad insuring agreement with no breach-of-contract exclusion. Under the rules of ordinary contract construction, the *Lee v. USAA* result, like the *Vandenberg* result, makes sense.

§ 11.10 INSURER'S LIABILITY FOR PREGRESSIVE INJURIES—WHEN DOES THE INJURY OCCUR?

Page 736: [Add at the end of § 11. 10:]

(6) When multiple policies in consecutive policy years are triggered, the "noncumulation of liability" clause commonly found in general liability policies may act to limit the amount of policy proceeds available. *See, e.g.,*

Liberty Mut. Ins. Co. v. Treesdale, Inc., 418 F.3d 330 (3d Cir. 2005) (applying Pennsylvania law) (limiting benefits under policy to limits of a single policy although asbestos-related claims spanned several policy years); *Hiraldo v. Allstate Ins. Co.*, 5 N.Y.3d 508, 840 N.E.2d 563 (N.Y. 2005) (limiting insurer's responsibility for lead poisoning claim under landlord's liability policy to one annual aggregate policy limit of $300,000 even though the injuries spanned three years). *But see Spaulding Composite Co., Inc. v. Aetna Cas. & Sur. Co.*, 176 N.J. 25, 819 A.2d 410 (N.J. 2003) (refusing to give effect to noncumulation clause as respects multi-year asbestos and instead determining liability insurer's coverage responsibility according to pre-ration formula generally applied in all cases involving coverage under consecutive liability policies). *See* § 11.12 regarding coordination of coverage and allocation of responsibilities among insurers.

A typical noncumulation clause such as the one at issue in *Hiraldo v. Allstate*, provides that "[r]egardless of the number of . . . policies involved" the insurer's maximum responsibility "resulting from one loss will not exceed the limit of liability" stated on the policy's declarations sheet. The noncumulation provisions typically also include a "batching" clause that provides that all injury resulting from one accident or "continuous or repeated exposure to the same general conditions" shall be considered to be a single loss. In *Hiraldo*, only one policy out of three issued by Allstate to a landlord was obligated to provide coverage for an underlying claim for bodily injury caused by residential exposure to lead paint. Each policy was subject to a $300,000 limit of liability and the underlying plaintiffs obtained judgments totaling approximately $700,000. Said the Court:

> If each of the successive policies had been written by a different insurance company, presumably each insurer would be liable up to the limits of its policy. Why should plaintiffs recover less money because the same insurer wrote them all? Some courts have held that successive policy limits may be cumulatively applied to a single loss, where the policies do not clearly provide otherwise. But here, the policies do clearly provide otherwise. The non-cumulation clause says that "regardless of the number of . . . policies involved, [Allstate's] total liability under Business Liability Protection coverage for damages resulting from one loss will not exceed the limit of liability . . . shown on the declarations page." That limit is $300,000, and thus Allstate is liable for no more.

840 N.E.2d at 564 (citations omitted). If the policy limits vary during consecutive years on which a single triggered liability insurer is on the risk, the policy year with the highest policy limits would presumably be the one invoked by a court.

§ 11.12 COORDINATION OF COVERAGE AND ALLOCATION OF INSURANCE PROCEEDS

Page 774: [Add to § 11.12 following the Notes and Questions after Goodyear Tire & Rubber Co. v. Aetna Cas. & Sur. Co.]

(3) *See also Federated Rural Elec. Ins. Exch. v. National Farmers Union Prop. & Cas. Co.*, 805 N.E.2d 456 (Ind. App. 2004) (where two policies triggered, coverage for the matter must be pro-rated between triggered concurrent insurers; policyholder can only recover proportional amount from each insurer).

§ 11.13 COMMON EXCLUSIONS

[A] Exclusions for the Ordinary Economic Risks of Commercial Activity

Page 781: [Add to § 11.13[A] at the conclusion of Weedo v. Stone-E-Brick:]

AMERICAN FAMILY MUTUAL INSURANCE COMPANY v. AMERICAN GIRL, INC.,

268 Wis. 2d 16, 673 N.W.2d 65 (Wis. 2004)

DIANE S. SYKES, J. This insurance coverage dispute presents an array of legal issues pertaining to the proper interpretation of coverage and exclusion language in several post-1986 commercial general liability ("CGL") and excess insurance policies. * * * The dispute initially focuses on the meaning of "property damage" and "occurrence" in the standard CGL insuring agreement's grant of coverage. The parties also dispute the applicability of several exclusions: for "expected or intended" losses; "contractually-assumed liability"; and certain "business risks" (a/k/a "your work" or "your product" exclusions). There is a question about the applicability of the "professional services liability" exclusion in certain excess policies. Finally, the parties dispute the effect of the economic loss doctrine on the availability of insurance coverage, as well as the application of the common law "known loss" doctrine to certain of the policies.

The factual context is a construction project gone awry: a soil engineering subcontractor gave faulty site-preparation advice to a general contractor in connection with the construction of a warehouse. As a result, there was excessive settlement of the soil after the building was completed, causing the building's foundation to sink. This caused the rest of the structure to buckle and crack. Ultimately, the building was declared unsafe and had to be torn down. * * * The general contractor, potentially liable to the building owner under certain contractual warranties, notified its insurance carriers of the loss. Contractually-required arbitration between the owner and the contractor was initiated and stayed pending resolution of coverage questions involving several of the contractor's insurers. The circuit court, on summary judgment, found coverage under some but not all of the policies. The court of appeals reversed, concluding that the "contractual liability" exclusion in each of the policies excluded coverage. We reverse.

The threshold question is whether the claim at issue here is for "property damage" caused by an "occurrence" within the meaning of the CGL policies' general grant of coverage. We hold that it is. The CGL policies define "property damage" as "physical injury to tangible property." The sinking, buckling, and cracking of the warehouse were plainly "physical injury to tangible property." An "occurrence" is defined as "an accident, including continuous or repeated exposure to substantially the same general harmful condition." The damage to the warehouse was caused by substantial soil settlement underneath the completed building, which occurred because of the faulty site-preparation advice of the soil engineering subcontractor. It was accidental, not intentional or anticipated, and it involved the "continuous or repeated exposure" to the "same general harmful condition." Accordingly, there was "property damage" caused by an "occurrence" within the meaning of the CGL policies.

We also conclude that the economic loss doctrine does not preclude coverage. The economic loss doctrine generally operates to confine contracting parties to contract rather than tort remedies for recovery of purely economic losses associated with the contract relationship. The doctrine does not determine insurance coverage, which turns on the policy language. That the property damage at issue here is actionable in contract but not in tort does not make it "non-accidental" or otherwise remove it from the CGL's definition of "occurrence." * * * We further hold that because the property damage at issue here was neither expected nor intended, the "expected or intended" exclusion does not apply.

The "contractually-assumed liability" exclusion (upon which the court of appeals rested its no-coverage conclusion) eliminates coverage for damages the insured is obligated to pay "by reason of the assumption of liability in a contract or agreement." We conclude that this language does not exclude coverage for all breach of contract liability. Rather, it excludes coverage for liability that arises because the insured has contractually assumed the liability of another, as in an indemnification or hold harmless agreement. There is no indemnification or hold harmless agreement at issue here, so this exclusion does not apply.

We also conclude that while the "business risk" or "your work" exclusions ordinarily would operate to exclude coverage under the circumstances of this case, the "subcontractor" exception applies here. The subcontractor exception to the business risk exclusion restores coverage if "the work out of which the damage arises" was performed by a subcontractor.

In addition, we conclude that the "professional services liability" exclusion in the excess policies applies under the circumstances of this case. And finally, coverage under the policies issued after the property damage loss was substantially known to the parties is barred by the "known loss" doctrine.

I. FACTS AND PROCEDURAL HISTORY

In 1994 The Pleasant Company ("Pleasant") entered into a contract with The Renschler Company for the design and construction of a large distribution center warehouse, dubbed the "94DC," on Pleasant's Middleton, Wisconsin, campus. Under the terms of the contract, Renschler warranted to Pleasant that the design and structural components of the 94DC would be free from defects, and that Renschler would be liable for any consequential damages caused by any such defects. (Pleasant changed its name to American Girl, Inc., several days before the issuance of this opinion; we will refer to the company as it was known throughout these proceedings.)

Renschler hired Clifton E.R. Lawson (Lawson), a soils engineer, to conduct an analysis of soil conditions at the site. Lawson concluded that the soil conditions were poor and recommended "rolling surcharging" to prepare the site for construction. Surcharging is a process by which soils are compressed to achieve the density required to support the weight of a building or other structure. The process usually involves placing large quantities of earth above the soil and allowing the earth to bear down on the soils. Typically this requires bringing in enough earth to cover the entire site, which can be very costly, and so for large projects like the 94DC, small areas of the site are compressed individually, and the earth is rolled from one area to the next.

The surcharging was done according to Lawson's professional advice, and the building was substantially completed in August 1994. Pleasant took occupancy, and soon thereafter the 94DC began to sink. By the spring of 1995 the settlement at one end of the structure had reached eight inches.

Renschler became aware of the problem in March 1995, and Lawson was subsequently advised. In the fall of 1995 Renschler re-hung approximately 30 exterior panels and windows that were leaking as a result of the settlement. The building continued to sink throughout 1996. By early 1997, the settlement approached one foot, the building was buckling, steel supports were deformed, the floor was cracking, and sewer lines had shifted. In January or February 1997, the parties met to discuss the settlement damage and the options for remediation. [The Court found that this meeting "triggered application of the know loss doctrine," making later injury uninsurable] In August 1997 Renschler notified its liability insurance carrier, American Family Mutual Insurance Company. * * * American Family conducted an investigation of the claim and at first concluded that coverage existed for the claim. In January 1998 the insurer reserved $750,000 for the claim, and in May 1998 paid Renschler $27,501 for services performed relating to remediation of the damage that had occurred up to that point. In early 1999 remediation alternatives were estimated to cost between $4.1 and $5.9 million. * * * Renschler hired engineers to conduct evaluations of the floor from March through September 1999. The engineers advised Renschler that the structural steel was so over-stressed that the building was no longer safe for occupancy. In late 1999 or early 2000 the building was dismantled. By that time, the settlement was approximately 18 inches. Renschler's geotechnical expert concluded that Lawson was negligent in the performance of his engineering/geotechnical work. It is undisputed that Lawson's faulty soil engineering advice was a substantial factor in causing the settlement of the 94DC.

The contract between Pleasant and Renschler provided for arbitration of disputes. Pleasant filed a demand for arbitration in December 1999 asserting breach of contract and negligence theories of recovery. Pleasant alleged that Lawson's negligence caused excessive settlement, resulting in damage to the building, and that Renschler thereby breached its contract with Pleasant. * * * In March 2000 American Family filed this action in Dane County Circuit Court seeking a declaratory judgment regarding coverage under the CGL and excess policies it had issued to Renschler from March 1993 to March 1997. Renschler joined four additional insurers: Ohio Casualty Insurance Company and West American Insurance Company, which had issued CGL and excess liability policies for April 1, 1997, through April 1, 1999, respectively, and General Casualty Insurance Company and Regent Insurance Company, which had issued CGL and umbrella liability policies thereafter. Arbitration was stayed pending resolution of the coverage issues.

[The trial court] concluded that American Family's CGL policies for the years 1994-95, 1995-96, and 1996-97 provided coverage, but its 1993-94 policy did not, as it pre-dated the loss. The circuit court held that Pleasant's claim against Renschler was covered under the language of the insuring agreement in the 1994-97 policies, and that none of the policy exclusions applied. The court also concluded that neither the economic loss doctrine nor the known loss doctrines precluded coverage under these policies. The circuit court also concluded that the "professional services liability" exclusions in American Family's excess policies excluded coverage under those policies. With respect to the four other insurers, the circuit court held that the known loss doctrine precluded coverage, because the extent of the settlement problem was known before any of those policies came into effect. * * * The court of appeals [holding] that the exclusion for property damage "for which the insured is obligated to pay damages by reason of the assumption of liability in a contract or agreement" precluded coverage, because Renschler's liability to Pleasant derived entirely from its obligations under the construction contract. The court of appeals also held that there was no coverage under American Family's excess policies, as well as the policies of the other insurers, on the basis of identical "contractual liability" exclusions in those policies. The court did not address the other coverage issues. We accepted review.

* * *

Exclusions are narrowly or strictly construed against the insurer if their effect is uncertain. We analyze each exclusion separately; the inapplicability of one exclusion will not reinstate coverage where another exclusion has precluded it. Exclusions sometimes have exceptions; if a particular exclusion applies, we then look to see whether any exception to that exclusion reinstates coverage. An exception pertains only to the exclusion clause within which it appears; the applicability of an exception will not create coverage if the insuring agreement precludes it or if a separate exclusion applies.

III. DISCUSSION

A. The CGL policies

The precursor of today's standard commercial liability insurance contract was promulgated in 1940 and has since undergone five principal revisions, the most recent of which came into use in 1986. Today, most CGL insurance in the United States is written on standardized forms developed by the Insurances Services Office, Inc. (ISO). . . . Jeffrey W. Stempel, Law of Insurance Contract Disputes §§ 14.01, 14.02 (2d ed. 1999). * * * Until 1966, standard CGL policies provided coverage for liabilities arising out of injury or damage "caused by an accident." 16 Eric Mills Holmes, Holmes' Appelman on Insurance § 117.3, 240 (2d ed. 2000). In response to uncertainty over whether the term "accident" included harm caused by gradual processes, the insurance industry removed the "accident" language from the insuring agreement and replaced it with the broader term "occurrence," defined as an accident, but also including gradual accidental harm; this coverage language is used to this day. * * * Standard CGL policies, including those at issue in this case, now cover "sums that the insured becomes legally obligated to pay as damages because of 'bodily injury' or 'property damage' . . . caused by an 'occurrence' that takes place in the 'coverage territory.' "

The CGL insuring agreement is a broad statement of coverage, and insurers limit their exposure to risk through a series of specific exclusions. There are exclusions for intended or expected losses; for contractually-assumed liabilities; for obligations under worker's compensation and related laws; for injury and damage arising out of aircraft and automobiles; and for several so-called "business risks." * * * The "business risk" exclusions, also known as "your work," "your product," and "your property" exclusions, have generated substantial litigation. 2 Stempel, supra, § 14.13, 14-127. "Insurers draft liability policies with an eye toward preventing policyholders from . . . converting their liability insurance into protection from nonfortuitous losses such as claims based on poor business operations. The 'own work' and 'owned property' exclusions are two important and frequently litigated policy provisions designed to accomplish this purpose." The 1986 version of the CGL contains a modified "business risk" exclusion that provides an exception for the work of subcontractors, id., and will be discussed in greater detail below.

The CGL policies at issue here contain 15 separate exclusions lettered "a" through "n" of subsection I.A.2. This case requires an examination of several of these: exclusion (a), for expected or intended losses; exclusion (b), for contractually-assumed liabilities; and exclusions (j) and (l), the business risk exclusions for property damage to the insured's work. As we have noted, however, our first task is to determine whether the claimed loss is covered by the language of the insuring agreement's initial grant of coverage.

B. The CGL's insuring agreement

* * *

i. "Property damage" and the economic loss doctrine

The policy defines "property damage" as "physical injury to tangible property, including all resulting loss of use of that property." The sinking, buckling, and cracking of the 94DC as a result of the soil settlement qualifies as "physical injury to tangible property." * * * American Family characterizes Pleasant's claim against Renschler as one for economic loss rather than property damage, and argues that the economic loss doctrine bars coverage. The economic loss doctrine generally precludes recovery in tort for economic losses resulting from the failure of a product to live up to contractual expectations. The economic loss doctrine is "based on an understanding that contract law and the law of warranty, in particular, is better suited than tort law for dealing with purely economic loss in the commercial arena." * * * The economic loss doctrine operates to restrict contracting parties to contract rather than tort remedies for recovery of economic losses associated with the contract relationship. The economic loss doctrine is a remedies principle. It determines how a loss can be recovered-in tort or in contract/warranty law. It does not determine whether an insurance policy covers a claim, which depends instead upon the policy language.

The economic loss doctrine may indeed preclude tort recovery here (the underlying claim is in arbitration and not before us); regardless, everyone agrees that the loss remains actionable in contract, pursuant to specific warranties in the construction agreement between Pleasant and Renschler. To the extent that American Family is arguing categorically that a loss giving rise to a breach of contract or warranty claim can *never* constitute "property damage" within the meaning of the CGL's coverage grant, we disagree. "The language of the CGL policy and the purpose of the CGL insuring agreement will provide coverage for claims sounding in part in breach-of-contract/breach-of-warranty under some circumstances." 2 Stempel, supra, § 14A.02[d],14A-10. This is such a circumstance. Pleasant's claim against Renschler for the damage to the 94DC is a claim for "property damage" within the meaning of the CGL's coverage grant.

ii. "Occurrence"

Liability for "property damage" is covered by the CGL policy if it resulted from an "occurrence." "Occurrence" is defined as "an accident, including continuous or repeated exposure to substantially the same general harmful conditions." The term "accident" is not defined in the policy. The dictionary definition of "accident" is: "an event or condition occurring by chance or arising from unknown or remote causes." Webster's Third New International Dictionary of the English Language 11 (2002). Black's Law Dictionary defines "accident" as follows: "The word 'accident,' in accident policies, means an event which takes place without one's foresight or expectation. A result, though unexpected, is not an accident; the means or cause must be accidental."

No one seriously contends that the property damage to the 94DC was anything but accidental (it was clearly not intentional), nor does anyone argue that it was anticipated by the parties. The damage to the 94DC occurred as a result of the continuous, substantial, and harmful settlement of the soil underneath the building. Lawson's inadequate site-preparation advice was a cause of this exposure to harm. Neither the cause nor the harm was intended, anticipated, or expected. We conclude that the circumstances of this claim fall within the policy's definition of "occurrence." [In footnote 5, the majority noted that "Justice Roggensack's dissent asserts that the soil settlement and resultant property damage were expected by the parties because the construction contract contained a warranty against defects. While the warranty in question was specifically inserted in the construction contract under the subheading "Additional Warranties," it is nevertheless stated in broad and general terms. The provision of a general warranty against defects does not support a conclusion that the contract parties expected a particular loss to occur."]

American Family argues that because Pleasant's claim is for breach of contract/breach of warranty it cannot be an "occurrence," because the CGL is not intended to cover contract claims arising out of the insured's defective work or product. We agree that CGL policies generally do not cover contract claims arising out of the insured's defective work or product, but this is by operation of the CGL's business risk exclusions, not because a loss actionable only in contract can never be the result of an "occurrence" within the meaning of the CGL's initial grant of coverage. This distinction is sometimes overlooked, and has resulted in some regrettably overbroad generalizations about CGL policies in our case law. * * * Despite this broad generalization, however, there is nothing in the basic coverage language of the current CGL policy to support any definitive tort/contract line of demarcation for purposes of determining whether a loss is covered by the CGL's initial grant of coverage. "Occurrence" is not defined by reference to the legal category of the claim. The term "tort" does not appear in the CGL policy.

[Prior precedent] interpreting pre-1986 CGL policies, never discussed the insuring agreement's initial grant of coverage; rather, the cases were decided on the basis of the business risk exclusions. * * * Hence we need not address the validity of one of the carrier's initially-offered grounds of non-coverage, namely, that the policy did not extend coverage for the claims made even absent the exclusions." Weedo [v. Stone-E-Brick] does not hold that losses actionable as breaches of contract cannot be CGL "occurrences," * * * If, as American Family contends, losses actionable in contract are never CGL "occurrences" for purposes of the initial coverage grant, then the business risk exclusions are entirely unnecessary. The business risk exclusions eliminate coverage for liability for property damage to the insured's own work or product—liability that is typically actionable between the parties pursuant to the terms of their contract, not in tort. If the insuring agreement never confers coverage for this type of liability as an original definitional matter, then there is no need to specifically exclude it. Why would the insurance industry exclude damage to the insured's own work or product if the damage could never be considered to have arisen from a covered "occurrence" in the first place?

The court of appeals has previously recognized that the faulty workmanship of a subcontractor can give rise to property damage caused by an "occurrence" within the meaning of a CGL policy. In Kalchthaler v. Keller Construction Co., 224 Wis. 2d 387, 395, 591 N.W.2d 169 (Ct. App. 1999), a general contractor subcontracted out all the work on a construction project; the completed building subsequently leaked, causing over $500,000 in water damage. The court of appeals noted that the CGL defined "occurrence" as "an accident," and further noted that "an accident is an 'event or change occurring without intention or volition through carelessness, unawareness, ignorance, or a combination of causes and producing an unfortunate result.' " The court of appeals concluded that the leakage was an accident and therefore an occurrence for purposes of the CGL's coverage grant. * * * The same is true here. * * * This brings us to the policy exclusions. American Family invokes several.

C. The "expected or intended" exclusion

Exclusion (a) eliminates coverage for " 'property damage' expected or intended from the standpoint of the insured.' " American Family argues that given the poor soil conditions at the site, and Renschler's recognition that special measures were required to prepare the soil to carry the weight of the 94DC, Renschler expected that some settlement would occur, and therefore this exclusion applies. We disagree.

American Family does not argue that "property damage" was expected or intended by the insured (which is what the exclusion requires), only that some degree of settlement must have been expected under the circumstances. This is insufficient to trigger the exclusion. * * *

D. The "contractually-assumed liability" exclusion

The court of appeals held that exclusion (b), for contractually-assumed liabilities, applied to preclude coverage under all the policies at issue in this case. Exclusion (b) states:

This insurance does not apply to: . . . .

b. "Bodily injury" or "property damage" for which the insured is obligated to pay damages by reason of the assumption of liability in a contract or agreement. This exclusion does not apply to liability for damages:

(1) Assumed in a contract or agreement that is an "insured contract," provided the "bodily injury" or "property damage" occurs subsequent to the execution of the contract or agreement; or

(2) That the insured would have in the absence of the contract or agreement.

* * *

"The key to understanding this exclusion . . . is the concept of liability assumed." 2 Rowland H. Long, The Law of Liability Insurance § 10.05[2], 10-56, 10-57 (2002). As one important commentator has noted,

> Although, arguably, a person or entity assumes liability (that is, a duty of performance, the breach of which will give rise to liability) whenever one enters into a binding contract, in the CGL policy and other liability policies an "assumed" liability is generally understood and interpreted by the courts to mean the liability of a third party, which liability one "assumes" in the sense that one agrees to indemnify or hold the other person harmless.

21 Holmes, supra, § 132.3, 36-37.

The term "assumption" must be interpreted to add something to the phrase "assumption of liability in a contract or agreement." Reading the phrase to apply to all liabilities sounding in contract renders the term "assumption" superfluous. We conclude that the contractually-assumed liability exclusion applies where the insured has contractually assumed the liability of a third party, as in an indemnification or hold harmless agreement; it does not operate to exclude coverage for any and all liabilities to which the insured is exposed under the terms of the contracts it makes generally.

This reading is consistent with the general purposes of liability insurance because it enables insurers to enforce the fortuity concept by excluding from coverage any policyholder agreements to become liable after the insurance is in force and the liability is a certainty. See 2 Stempel, supra, § 14.14, 14-141. Limiting the exclusion to indemnification and hold-harmless agreements furthers the goal of protecting the insurer from exposure to risks whose scope and nature it cannot control or even reasonably foresee. The relevant distinction "is between incurring liability as a result of a breach of contract and specifically contracting to assume liability for another's negligence."

Courts in other jurisdictions have held that the contractually-assumed liability exclusion "refers to a specific contractual assumption of liability by the insured as exemplified by an indemnity agreement." * * * This interpretation of exclusion (b) is consistent with the evolution of the CGL policy over time. Prior to the 1986 revision, the exclusion for contractually-assumed liabilities was achieved through language in the insuring agreement that granted coverage for "contractual liabilities." Coverage was extended to certain types of contractual obligations but not others. With the 1986 revision, however, this language was moved into the exclusions section, and the basic coverage for certain contractual obligations was retained by inserting an exception to the exclusion for "insured contracts." * * * This case does not involve a claim for "contractually-assumed liability," properly understood. The breach of contract/warranty liability at issue here is Renschler's direct liability to its contract partner, Pleasant, pursuant to warranties in the construction contract. Renschler is not claiming coverage for a claim made against it pursuant to a third-party indemnification or hold harmless agreement.

E. The "business risk" exclusions

The business risk exclusions (j) through (n) preclude coverage generally for property damage to the work of the insured. Several of these are implicated here. The first, exclusion (j), contains the following language:

This insurance does not apply to:

j. "Property damage" to: . . . .

(6) That particular part of any property that must be restored, repaired or replaced because "your work" was incorrectly performed on it. . . . .

Paragraph (6) of this exclusion does not apply to "property damage" included in the "products-completed operations hazard.

The policy defines "your work" as:

a. Work or operations performed by you or on your behalf; . . . .

"Your work" includes:

a. Warranties or representations made at any time with respect to the fitness, quality, durability, performance or use of "your work;"

Renschler's work on the 94DC, as well as Lawson's engineering work under subcontract to Renschler, both fall within the definition of "your work." Exclusion (j) comes into play because Pleasant's claim against Renschler involves the repair and replacement of the 94DC.

However, if the property damage that occurred falls within the "products-completed operations hazard," exclusion (j) does not apply. The "products-completed operations hazard" includes:

All "bodily injury" and "property damage" occurring away from premises you own or rent and arising out of "your product" or "your work" except:

(1) Products that are still in your physical possession; or

(2) Work that has not yet been completed or abandoned.

The damage to the 94DC occurred away from premises that Renschler owns or rents, and it arose out of Renschler's "own work" because, as we have indicated, Renschler's work on the 94DC falls within the policy definition of "your work." Work on the 94DC was substantially completed in August 1994, and Pleasant occupied the premises at that time. The settlement was noticed in March 1995. Damage to the property therefore occurred after the work had been completed, so exception (2) does not apply. Thus the property damage at issue in this case falls within the "products-completed operations hazard" and exclusion (j) does not apply.

This brings into play exclusion (l), for "property damage to your work" inside the "products-completed operations hazard":

> This insurance does not apply to:
>
> l. "Property damage" to "your work" arising out of it or any part of it and included in the "products-completed operations hazard."
>
> This exclusion does not apply if the damaged work or the work out of which the damage arises was performed on your behalf by a subcontractor.

By its terms, exclusion (l) would operate to exclude coverage under the circumstances of this case but for the exception that specifically restores coverage when the property damage arises out of work performed by a subcontractor. It is undisputed that Lawson's negligent soils engineering work was a cause of the soil settlement and resultant property damage to the 94DC.

This subcontractor exception dates to the 1986 revision of the standard CGL policy form. Prior to 1986 the CGL business risk exclusions operated collectively to preclude coverage for damage to construction projects caused by subcontractors. Many contractors were unhappy with this state of affairs, since more and more projects were being completed with the help of subcontractors. In response to this changing reality, insurers began to offer coverage for damage caused by subcontractors through an endorsement to the CGL known as the Broad Form Property Damage Endorsement, or BFPD. Introduced in 1976, the BFPD deleted several portions from the business risk exclusions and replaced them with more specific exclusions that effectively broadened coverage. Among other changes, the BFPD extended coverage to property damage caused by the work of subcontractors. In 1986 the insurance industry incorporated this aspect of the BFPD directly into the CGL itself by inserting the subcontractor exception to the "your work" exclusion. Cases in Wisconsin and in other jurisdictions have consistently recognized that the 1986 CGL revisions restored otherwise excluded coverage for damage caused to construction projects by subcontractor negligence. In Kalchthaler, the court of appeals concluded that "the only reasonable reading of [the 1986 exception] is that it restores coverage for damage to completed work caused by the work of a subcontractor."

The court of appeals' straightforward reading of the subcontractor exception to the business risk exclusion in Kalchthaler was buttressed by a similar holding in a case from Minnesota, O'Shaughnessy v. Smuckler Corp., 543 N.W.2d 99 (Minn. Ct. App. 1996), in which the Minnesota Court of Appeals found coverage for improper subcontractor performance that caused damage to a residential home project. * * * Like the O'Shaughnessy court, the court in Kalchthaler recognized that the effect of the 1986 revision of the CGL could not be defeated by reliance upon broad judicial holdings interpreting pre-1986 policies that did not contain the subcontractor exception. "For whatever reason, the industry chose to add the new exception to the business risk exclusion in 1986. We may not ignore that language when interpreting case law decided before and after the addition. To do so would render the new language superfluous."

Courts in other jurisdictions have reached the same conclusion when interpreting the post-1986 subcontractor exception or policy endorsements containing identical language. American Family cites conflicting authorities which appear to hold that damage to an insured's work caused by a subcontractor is not covered because of the "your work" exclusion, but these authorities are no longer controlling because they construed policies that did not include the subcontractor exception. Noting the apparent conflict between O'Shaughnessy, Kalchthaler, and similar cases on the one hand, and contrary cases on the other, one commentator has pointed out that "those cases [finding no coverage] involved the older policy language while the current policy specifically provides that the 'own work' exclusion does not apply 'if the damaged work or the work out of which the damage arises was performed on your behalf by a subcontractor.'" 2 Stempel, supra, § 14.13[a], 14-132.

This interpretation of the subcontractor exception to the business risk exclusion does not "create coverage" where none existed before, as American Family contends. There is coverage under the insuring agreement's initial coverage grant. Coverage would be excluded by the business risk exclusionary language, except that the subcontractor exception to the business risk exclusion applies, which operates to restore the otherwise excluded coverage. * * * Accordingly, Renschler's CGL base policies with American Family cover Pleasant's claim. We also agree with the circuit court's application of the "continuous trigger . . . . The continuous trigger theory interprets the term "occurrence" in CGL policies to include continual, recurring damage as well as damage that occurs at one moment in time. * * * The property damage to the 94DC occurred continuously over a period extending from the later part of the 1994-95 policy term, throughout the 1995-96 policy term, and well into the 1996-97 policy term. Settlement had reached eight inches by the spring of 1995, when the first policy was still in force, and continued throughout 1996 and into 1997, by which time it was approaching one foot. Accordingly, under the continuous trigger holdings of Society Insurance and Wisconsin Electric, the policies for the years 1994-95, 1995-96, and 1996-97 cover this loss.

F. American Family's excess policies

Renschler also had excess liability policies with American Family for the years 1993-94, 1994-95, 1995-96, and 1996-97. The circuit court held that there was no coverage under the 1993-94 policy because there had been no occurrence before the end of the 1993-94 policy term, and no coverage under the remaining excess policies because the professional services liability exclusions in those policies excluded coverage. * * * The court of appeals affirmed, but did so because of the contractually-assumed liability exclusion in the policies. We have rejected the court of appeals' interpretation of the contractually-assumed liability exclusion. We agree, however, with the circuit court's conclusion that the professional services liability exclusion in the excess policies excludes coverage. * * * Renschler's Commercial Blanket Excess Liability Policy contains the following endorsement:

> Professional liability exclusion.

> Insurance under this policy does not apply to any liability arising out of the rendering of or failure to render professional services in the conduct of **your** business or profession. (Emphasis in original.)

It is undisputed that Lawson's inadequate soil engineering advice was a substantial factor in causing the excessive soil settlement and resulting property damage to the 94DC. Renschler is responsible to Pleasant for the flaws in Lawson's professional services pursuant to the broad warranty in the construction contract. Accordingly, the liability here arises out of the rendering of professional services, and by its terms, this exclusion applies.

G. The four other insurers

Renschler also had insurance policies from four other insurers: Ohio Casualty Insurance Company and West American Insurance Company, which issued CGL and excess liability policies respectively for April 1, 1997, through April 1, 1999, and General Casualty Insurance Company and Regent Insurance Company, which issued CGL and umbrella liability policies, respectively, thereafter. The circuit court held that the known loss or loss-in-progress doctrine precluded coverage under all of these policies. We agree. * * * The known loss doctrine holds that insurers are not obligated to cover losses which are already occurring when the coverage is written or which has already occurred. Here, the fact that settlement was occurring on the 94DC was known as early as March of 1995, and the extent of the damage was substantially known by the time of the meeting in January or February, 1997. The policies of these remaining insurers postdate this period. Accordingly, the known loss doctrine precludes coverage under these policies. The decision of the court of appeals is reversed and the cause remanded for proceedings consistent with this opinion.

N. PATRICK CROOKS, J. *(dissenting).* I disagree with the majority's conclusion that there is coverage under the CGL policies issued by American Family. Although I agree with Justice Roggensack's dissent, I write separately to address an issue the majority concedes is relevant, yet touches on only briefly. In this case, there are contract claims for breach of warranty resulting in economic loss. Breach of contract/breach of warranty resulting in economic loss is not a covered "occurrence" under the plain language of the CGL policies' general grant of coverage. American Family and the other CGL insurers have no duty to defend or indemnify Renschler against Pleasant's damage claims, since the CGL policies at issue do not cover the contract claims, and the economic loss doctrine prevents any tort claim as well. Thus, I conclude there can be no coverage in this case, as the requirements for both liability and recovery of damages are not satisfied.

* * *

PATIENCE D. ROGGENSACK, J. (dissenting). Before considering exceptions to coverage in the American Family insurance policy, we must first conclude that there has been an "occurrence" because the policy does not provide coverage under any circumstances unless the " 'property damage' is caused by an 'occurrence.' " Renschler Company asserts that the act that caused damage to the Pleasant Company's building was Clifton Lawson's allegedly inaccurate advice concerning compaction of the subsoil prior to the building's construction, which permitted the building to sink. However, it was known that if subsoil compaction was not properly done, the completed building would sink and the damage to the building that has occurred would very likely occur. Therefore, the cause of the damage was simply the continuation of prior existing unstable subsoil conditions. Accordingly, I conclude the property damage at issue here was not caused by an accident, which is how "occurrence" is defined in the policy. Without an "occurrence," there is no potential coverage under Renschler's CGL policy. Because the majority concludes otherwise, I respectfully dissent.

The majority bottoms its analysis of the "occurrence" issue in the following major premise: "No one seriously contends that the property damage to the [building] was anything but accidental (it was clearly not intentional), nor does anyone argue that it was anticipated by the parties." That assertion is contrary to the central argument American Family is making: Pleasant and Renschler, the parties to the construction contract, recognized the risk that the subsoil might not be sufficient to support the building. As American Family points out, Pleasant, the purchaser of the completed building, was so aware of the possibility of the building settling that it secured a warranty from Renschler in which Renschler agreed to shoulder the risk of financial loss if settling occurred as a result of the continuation of the unstable subsoil conditions.

The majority's equation of "accidental" with "unintentional" begs the question presented here: whether the sinking of the building was an unforeseen event or one that resulted from an unknown cause. "Accident" is the operative word in the policy definition of "occurrence." An "accident" has been variously defined as: "an event that takes place without one's foresight or expectation—an event that proceeds from an unknown cause, or is an unusual effect of a known cause, and therefore not expected. "10 Couch on Insurance § 139:14 (3d ed. 2000); or "an event or condition occurring by chance or arising from unknown or remote causes . . . ." Webster's Third New International Dictionary of the English Language, Unabridged, 11 (3d ed. 1961); or "The word 'accident,' in accident policies, means an event which takes place without one's foresight or expectation. A result, though unexpected, is not an accident; the means or cause must be accidental. (Emphasis added)." Black's Law Dictionary, 15 (7th ed. 1999). Here, the settling was not an unexpected outcome of construction. It was a known possibility. Furthermore, the settling did not take place due to an unknown cause. It was well recognized that the soil conditions were unfavorable to construction and if they continued there would be problems.

In sum, all the definitions of "accident" require, at a minimum, an unexpected event or an unexpected cause. Here, it does not matter whether we focus on the sinking building or the continuation of unstable subsoil conditions, neither was unexpected. The unstable subsoil conditions were known and their correction required to prevent the building from sinking. In fact, the risk that the building would sink after construction was assumed by Renschler in its contract with Pleasant, showing a continuation of the unstable subsoil conditions was a potential and known risk of constructing the building on the site Pleasant chose. * * * Furthermore, we have equated "accident" with negligence. However, negligence is a tort, and as we have earlier explained, Pleasant cannot sue Renschler for a tort. Therefore, if we use the definition in Doyle, there will be no coverage under the policy because Renschler will never be "legally obligated to pay" Pleasant based on negligence.

Additionally, this analysis fits squarely within the purpose of a CGL policy. It is written to cover the risks of injury to third parties and damage to the property of third parties caused by the insured's completed work. It is not written to cover the business risk of failing to provide goods or services in a workmanlike manner to the second party to the contract. * * * And finally, the happening of an accident is entirely unpredictable; by its very definition, it is not something one can plan to occur. Therefore, a contractor would have difficulty budgeting to meet that risk; hence the need for insurance. However, here, the risk that the unstable subsoil conditions would continue was a known risk. If Renschler did not want to shoulder that risk, it could have required a performance bond or a warranty from Lawson similar to the one Pleasant obtained from it.

The majority also asserts that if contract claims are never "occurrences" then there is no need to have the business risk exclusion. That argument ignores the fact that the policy at issue is a standard CGL policy. It is issued to many contractors to cover myriad circumstances that may be very dissimilar from the facts that form the basis for Pleasant's claim. Therefore, in a claim based on different facts, there may be an occurrence and yet the business risk exclusion may preclude coverage. For example, if a contractor builds a building and a wall spontaneously collapses on a passer-by because of poor workmanship in constructing the wall, there would be an occurrence in regard to the unforeseen falling of the wall, and the damage to the injured person would be covered. However, the repair of the defective wall would be excluded from coverage under the business risk exclusion.

AUTO-OWNERS INSURANCE COMPANY v. HOME PRIDE COMPANIES, INC.

268 Neb. 528, 684 N.W.2d 571 (Neb. 2004)

Gerrard, J.

Auto-Owners Insurance Company (Auto-Owners) instituted this declaratory judgment action to determine its obligations to its insured, Home Pride Companies, Inc. (Home Pride). The district court determined that the policy issued by Auto-Owners to Home Pride did not cover Home Pride's claim and granted summary judgment in favor of Auto-Owners. The main issue on appeal is whether a standard commercial general liability (CGL) insurance policy covers an insured contractor for the faulty workmanship of a subcontractor that it hired.

Because this action is based upon an underlying action filed in April 2002, we digress to trace the history of the original action. Appletree Apartments, Inc. (Appletree), is a wholly owned subsidiary of J.A. Peterson Enterprises, Inc. (Peterson). Appletree and Peterson entered into a contract with JT Builders, Inc., to install new shingles on a number of Appletree's apartment buildings. Thereafter, JT Builders subcontracted with Craig Industries, Inc., to do the work. After becoming dissatisfied with Craig Industries' work, JT Builders terminated its contract with Craig Industries and subcontracted the work to Home Pride. Home Pride then entered into a subcontract with Ron Hansen, doing business as Ron Hansen Construction, to install the shingles.

Sometime in 1996, Ron Hansen Construction completed the project. Soon thereafter, Appletree began to notice problems with the roof. Appletree notified Home Pride of the problems, and after receiving what it believed to be an unsatisfactory response, Appletree and Peterson filed suit against Home Pride, JT Builders, and Craig Industries. In their petition, Appletree and Peterson claimed that the aforementioned parties failed to install the shingles in a workmanlike manner and that such faulty workmanship caused substantial and material damage to the roof structures and buildings. Appletree and Peterson also alleged that the shingles were defective and included in the action the manufacturer of the shingles, Certain Teed Corporation, and G.S. Roofing Products Co., a company that merged with Certain Teed Corporation after Appletree purchased the shingles.

After the suit was filed, Home Pride made a claim to its insurer, Auto-Owners, for coverage under its CGL policy. Pursuant to a reservation of rights, Auto-Owners assumed the defense of Home Pride. Thereafter, Auto-Owners instituted this declaratory judgment action against Home Pride, Appletree, Peterson, JT Builders, Craig Industries, Certain Teed Corporation, G.S. Roofing Products Co., and Ron Hansen, doing business as Ron Hansen Construction. Essentially, Auto-Owners claimed that the insurance policy did not provide coverage because the faulty workmanship of a subcontractor is not an "occurrence" under a CGL policy.

Both Auto-Owners and Home Pride moved for summary judgment. The district court determined that any alleged property damage was not caused by an "occurrence" and granted summary judgment in favor of Auto-Owners. Home Pride filed a timely notice of appeal. * * * Home Pride assigns that the district court erred in determining that its CGL policy did not provide coverage.

Broadly speaking, this appeal requires us to determine whether damage caused by faulty workmanship is covered under a standard CGL insurance policy. Although this issue has been frequently examined by a number of courts, it is a matter of first impression in Nebraska. * * * The meaning of an insurance policy is a question of law, in connection with which an appellate court has an obligation to reach its own conclusions independently of the determination made by the lower court. In construing insurance policy provisions, a court must determine from the clear language of the policy whether the insurer in fact insured against the risk involved. In an appellate review of an insurance policy, the court construes the policy as any other contract to give effect to the parties' intentions at the time the writing was made. Where the terms of a contract are clear, they are to be accorded their plain and ordinary meaning. * * * As relevant here, Home Pride's policy states:

SECTION I-COVERAGES

COVERAGE A. BODILY INJURY AND PROPERTY DAMAGE LIABILITY

1. Insuring Agreement.

a. We will pay those sums that the insured becomes legally obligated to pay as damages because of "bodily injury" or "property damage" to which this insurance applies. . . .

. . . .

b. This insurance applies to "bodily injury" and "property damage" only if:

(1) The "bodily injury" or "property damage" is caused by an "occurrence" that takes place in the "coverage territory" . . . .

2. Exclusions.

This insurance does not apply to: . . . .

1. "Property damage" to "your work" arising out of it or any part of it and including in the "products-completed operations hazard".

This exclusion does not apply if the damaged work or the work out of which the damage arises was performed on your behalf by a subcontractor.

As an initial matter, we note that Home Pride appears to argue that coverage exists because the policy contains a subcontractor exception to the "your work," or "1," exclusion found in section 2. We disagree. The provision Home Pride relies on is merely an exception to an exclusion and, therefore, incapable of providing coverage. Stated otherwise, the exception contained within exclusion "1" is irrelevant until two conditions precedent are met: (1) There is an initial grant of coverage and (2) exclusion "1" operates to preclude coverage. If, and only if, these two conditions are met may the subcontractor exception to the exclusion be applicable.

In order to determine if coverage exists, we must first determine if there was "property damage" caused by an "occurrence." On both accounts, Auto-Owners contends that there is not. As to the former, the policy states that "property damage" is "physical injury to tangible property, including all resulting loss of use of that property" as well as "loss of use of tangible property that is not physically injured." In their amended petition, Appletree and Peterson alleged that shingles were breaking apart and falling off the roofs at Appletree's apartments, resulting in substantial and material damage to the roof structures and buildings. Such allegations state a cause for physical injury to tangible property and, therefore, "property damage" under the policy.

At the core of Auto-Owners' appellate argument is its contention that faulty workmanship does not constitute an "occurrence" under the policy. The policy defines "occurrence" as "an accident, including continuous or repeated exposure to substantially the same general harmful conditions." While the term "accident" is not defined in the policy, we have previously stated that "an accident within the meaning of liability insurance contracts includes any event which takes place without the foresight or expectation of the person acted upon or affected thereby."

Whether faulty workmanship fits within the aforementioned definition of accident is a difficult question, and courts have answered it in a variety of ways. For example, a relatively small number of courts have determined that the damage that occurs as a result of faulty or negligent workmanship constitutes an accident, so long as the insured did not intend for the damage to occur. * * * However, the majority of courts have determined that faulty workmanship is not an accident and, therefore, not an occurrence. * * * Although it is clear that faulty workmanship, standing alone, is not covered under a standard CGL policy, it is important to realize that there are two different justifications for this rule. On the one hand, the rule has been justified on public policy grounds, primarily on the long-founded notion that the cost to repair and replace the damages caused by faulty workmanship is a business risk not covered under a CGL policy. Today, the business risk rule is part of standard CGL policies in the form of "your work" exceptions to coverage. Therefore, the business risk rule does not serve as an initial bar to coverage, but, rather, as a potential exclusion, via the "your work" exclusions, if an initial grant of coverage is found.

On the other hand, rather than relying on the business risk rule, a majority of courts have determined that faulty workmanship, standing alone, is not covered under a CGL policy because, as a matter of policy interpretation, "the fortuity implied by reference to accident or exposure is not what is commonly meant by a failure of workmanship." Because the majority rule is based on an actual interpretation of policy language, as opposed to a mere exposition of policy, and comports with our prior definitions of the term "accident," we believe that it represents the better rule. Consequently, we conclude that faulty workmanship, standing alone, is not covered under a standard CGL policy because it is not a fortuitous event.

Important here, although faulty workmanship, *standing alone*, is not an occurrence under a CGL policy, an accident caused by faulty workmanship is a covered occurrence. Stated otherwise, although a standard CGL policy does not provide coverage for faulty workmanship that damages only the resulting work product, if faulty workmanship causes bodily injury or property damage to something other than the insured's work product, an unintended and unexpected event has occurred, and coverage exists. For example, in *L-J, Inc. v. Bituminous Fire and Marine*, a subcontractor was hired to clear, grub, grade, and construct the subbase for a road construction project. The subcontractor failed to remove a number of tree stumps in the roadbed and moisture seeped into the road base, deteriorating the road. After stating the general rule that "faulty workmanship, standing alone, does not constitute an 'accident' and cannot therefore be an 'occurrence,'" the court noted faulty workmanship that causes an accident is covered under a standard CGL policy.

> Had the pavement not failed and [the developer] brought an action to recover the cost of removing the tree stumps from the roadbed, the defective work, standing alone, would not have been "property damage" or an "occurrence" under the policy. The damages, however, extend beyond the cost of removing the tree stumps because the failure to properly compact the roadbed led to property damage, namely, the failure of the road surfaces. These remote damages were an "accident" not expected or intended by the insured.

Similarly, in *High Country Assocs. v. N.H. Ins. Co.*, a homeowners' association sued the builders of a number of condominiums for negligently constructing the condominiums' exterior walls. Initially, the court noted the rule that claims for faulty workmanship, standing alone, do not constitute an "occurrence" within the meaning of a CGL policy. The court then went on to point out that the homeowners' association's petition not only requested compensation to repair and replace the poorly constructed exterior walls, but also requested compensation for the water damage that allegedly occurred as a result of the builders' faulty workmanship, including decay of the sheathing, harm to the structural studding, loss of structural integrity, and damage to the vertical siding. *Id.* Determining that these consequential damages constituted accidental damage to property other than the insured's own work product, the court held that the homeowners' association had made out a claim for property damage caused by an occurrence and that therefore, the insurer was obligated to provide coverage for the insured builder.

In the instant case, Appletree and Peterson alleged that JT Builders, through its subcontractors Craig Industries and Home Pride (hereinafter contractors), negligently installed shingles on a number of apartments, which caused the shingles to fall off. Additionally, the amended petition alleged that as a consequence of the faulty work, the roof structures and buildings have experienced substantial damage. This latter allegation represents an unintended and unexpected consequence of the contractors' faulty workmanship and goes beyond damages to the contractors' own work product. Therefore, the amended petition properly alleged an occurrence within the meaning of the insurance policy.

Because Appletree and Peterson's amended petition alleges property damage caused by an occurrence, the policy provides an initial grant of coverage. Therefore, we now turn to the policy exclusions. Under established law, the burden to prove that an exclusionary clause applies rests upon the insurer. On appeal, Auto-Owners contends that coverage is excluded by exclusions "n(2)" and "n(3)." These exclusions state:

SECTION I-COVERAGES

COVERAGE A. BODILY INJURY AND PROPERTY DAMAGE LIABILITY . . . .

2. *Exclusions.*

> This insurance does not apply to: . . . .
>
> **n.** Damages claimed for any loss, cost or expense incurred by you or others for the loss of use, withdrawal, recall, inspection, repair, replacement, adjustment, removal or disposal of: . . . .
>
> **(2)** "Your work"; or
>
> **(3)** "Impaired property";
>
> if such . . . work or property is withdrawn or recalled from the market or from use by any person or organization because of a known or suspected defect, deficiency, inadequacy or dangerous condition in it.

Generally speaking, the "your work" exclusions, of which "n(2)" is one, operate to prevent liability policies from insuring against an insured's own faulty workmanship, which is a normal risk associated with operating a business. Essentially, the rationale behind the "your work" exclusions is that they discourage careless work by making contractors pay for losses caused by their own defective work, while preventing liability insurance from becoming a performance bond.

In the instant case, exclusion "n(2)" does not serve to exclude Appletree and Peterson's damage claim because their claim extends beyond the cost to simply repair and replace the contractors' work, i.e., to reshingle the roofs. As previously noted, Appletree and Peterson alleged that the contractors' faulty workmanship resulted in substantial damage to the roof structures and buildings. Therefore, their claimed damages to the roof structure and buildings fall outside of the exclusion. * * * Similarly, in regard to exclusion "n(3)," the policy states that property is not "impaired" unless it is capable of being restored by the "repair, replacement, adjustment or removal of . . . 'your work'; or . . . your fulfilling the terms of the contract or agreement." Therefore, because damage to the roof structures and buildings cannot be repaired or restored by simply reshingling the apartment roofs, they are not "impaired property" within the meaning of exclusion "n(3)." Consequently, exclusion "n(3)" is inapplicable.

For the foregoing reasons, we conclude that Auto-Owners has a duty to defend Home Pride, and to the extent that Home Pride may be found liable for the resulting damage to the roof structures and the buildings, Auto-Owners is obligated to provide coverage. The district court erred in granting summary judgment in favor of Auto-Owners and in not granting summary judgment in favor of Home Pride. The judgment entered in favor of Auto-Owners and against Home Pride is reversed, and the district court is directed to enter judgment in favor of Home Pride consistent with this opinion. * * * Reversed and remanded with directions.

NOTES AND QUESTIONS

(1) [continue with text]

Page 784: [Add to the Notes and Questions concluding on page 784:]

(2) Which is more persuasive in *American Family v. American Girl*: the majority or the dissent?

(3) Which case is easier to decide: *American Girl* or *Home Pride*? Why?

(4) An additional insurance coverage issue that frequently crops up in construction defect or other liability claims related to commercial operations involves the status of "additional insureds" under a potentially applicable policy. Recall that the primary or "named" insured generally purchases the policy and that some individuals or entities are "insureds" under the policy by operation of the policy language. Commercial liability policies also frequently designate entities other than the main policyholder as "additional insureds" by name. For example, a general contractor may insist as part of its arrangements with subcontractors that the general contractor be named as an additional insured on all subcontractor policies. This gives the general contractor more protection generally and specifically helps the general contractor if it should be sued because of mistakes made by a subcontractor.

(5) Controversies can arise as to the scope of liability coverage offered to an additional insured. For example, a common controversy is whether the insurance provides coverage only where the additional insured is accused of "active" negligence or is sued merely for vicarious liability. You can see how this would matter in many construction defect claims in which a general contractor did not actually do the allegedly defective work but the plaintiff seeks to hold the contractor responsible for mistakes made by

subcontractors. Although there is division among the courts, the majority approach has traditionally been to cover additional insured for both active negligence and vicarious exposure.

(6) Relatively recent versions of additional insured endorsements or policy language tend to restrict coverage to additional insureds. However, broader endorsements remain in common use as well. *See generally* Randy J. Maniloff, *Coverage for Additional Insured-Venders: Recent Markdowns By ISO and New York's High Court*, 19-36 MEALEY'S LITIG. REPORT: INSURANCE 1 (July 26, 2005); Randy J. Maniloff, *Additional Insured Coverage and Legislative Changes On The Horizon—Taking ISO's 07 04 Additional Insured Revisions A Step Further*, 19-22 MEALEY'S LITIG. REP. INS. 11 (2005) (also found at FC&S CASUALTY & SURETY VOLUME (April 2005) at M.24-1); F, C & S CASUALTY & SURETY VOLUME, *Additional Insured Endorsements: ISO's Revisions* (May 2004) at M.23-1; Laurence A. Steckman & Bruce M. Strikowsky, *Recurring Problems in Additional Insured Litigation*, 18-23 MEALEY'S LITIG. REP. INS. 14 (April 20, 2004). On construction defect coverage litigation generally, *see* Randy J. Maniloff, *Construction Defect Coverage in Flux: No Hope For Bob The Builder: Three Recent Supreme Court Decisions and Three Different Approaches*, 18-3 MEALEY'S LITIG. REPT: INS. (Sept. 21, 2004).

[C]   The "Absolute" Pollution Exclusion

Page 793: [Add to § 11.13[C] following the conclusion of the Kent Farms case:]

THE QUADRANT CORPORATION v. AMERICAN STATES INSURANCE COMPANY

154 Wn.2d 165, 110 P.3d 733 (Wash. 2005)

EN BANC Bridge, J.—A tenant in an apartment building was overcome by fumes and became ill after a restoration company applied sealant to a nearby deck. The tenant sued the restoration company and the owners of the apartment building. Both the restoration company and the building owners settled and the owners now claim that their business liability insurance should cover the loss.

The business liability policies at issue here both contain absolute pollution exclusion clauses, which the insurers now argue apply to exclude coverage for the tenant's claim. The building owners contend that after this court's decision in *Kent Farms, Inc. v. Zurich Insurance Co.* 998 P.2d 292 (2000), the pollution exclusion cannot be applied to exclude occurrences that are not "traditional environmental harms." The owners also assert that if it is applied as the insurers suggest, the pollution exclusion would render the policy illusory with regard to the restoration company.

We hold that the plain language of the absolute pollution exclusion clause encompasses the injuries at issue here and therefore the tenant's claim is excluded from coverage. We find that the *Kent Farms* case is distinguishable on its facts and instead we adopt the reasoning of *Cook v. Evanson*, 920 P.2d 1223 (1996), a case similar to this one in that it involved injuries that resulted from toxic fumes. Furthermore, we conclude that the pollution exclusion clause does not render the policies illusory with respect to the building owners because the insurance policy will still cover a variety of claims, including slip and fall accidents, despite the pollution exclusion. We note that the restoration company is not a party to this case and, thus, the question of whether the insurance contract is illusory with respect to the restoration company is not properly before us. The insureds' request for attorney fees is denied. * * *

The facts of this case are not in dispute. Roy Street Associates owns an apartment building located at 200 Roy Street in Seattle. In 1996, the building owners hired Pacific Restoration to make repairs and improvements on the building. In the course of completing the repair work, Pacific Restoration applied waterproofing sealants to the surface of a deck. The parties agree that Pacific Restoration used PC-220 and Polyglaze AL, manufactured by Polycoat Products. Both contain various chemicals, including a toxic substance called toluene diisocyanate (TDI), whose fumes can irritate the respiratory tract and, in high concentrations, can cause central nervous system depression. * * * Delores Kaczor was a tenant in the apartment adjacent to the deck. Pacific failed to warn Kaczor that it would be applying the sealant and then failed to properly ventilate the area. Fumes entered her apartment as the deck dried, making her ill enough to require hospitalization. Specifically, Kaczor's estate claimed that exposure to the fumes caused "exacerbation of her preexisting chronic obstructive pulmonary disease" and led to her "debilitating and declining health." Kaczor filed a lawsuit against Pacific Restoration and the building owners claiming personal injury and property damage. Kaczor died in 1998 and her lawsuit was dismissed without prejudice. In 1999, her estate filed a second lawsuit based on Kaczor's injuries. That suit was settled for $30,000 and dismissed in July 2000.

In early 1996, Pacific Restoration held a general liability policy from American States Insurance Company. The policy provided liability coverage to Pacific Restoration and to the apartment owners as additional insureds. The American States policy was subject to the following exclusion: This insurance does not apply to: . . . .

f. Pollution

(1) "Bodily injury" or "property damage" arising out of the actual, alleged or threatened discharge, dispersal, seepage, migration, release or escape of pollutants:

(a) At or from any premises, site or location which is or was at any time owned or occupied by, or rented or loaned to, any insured; . . .

(d) At or from any premises, site or location on which any insured or any contractors or subcontractors working directly or indirectly on any insured's behalf are performing operations:

(i) if the pollutants are brought on or to the premises, site or location in connection with such operations by such insured, contractor or subcontractor; . . . .

Pollutants means any solid, liquid, gaseous or thermal irritant or contaminant, including smoke, vapor, soot, fumes, acids, alkalis, chemicals and waste. Waste includes materials to be recycled, reconditioned or reclaimed.

Similarly, Roy Street Associates held a general liability insurance policy from State Farm Fire and Casualty Company, which included Quadrant and Holly Corporation as additional insureds. The policy was subject to a nearly identical exclusion. Based on the pollution exclusions, the insurers denied coverage for the Kaczor claim.

The insureds filed this action, claiming that the insurers wrongfully denied their request for defense and indemnity with respect to the Kaczor claim. Both the insurers and the insureds filed motions for summary judgment based on agreed facts, arguing whether Kaczor's claim would be covered by the policy as a matter of law. The insurers claimed that the plain language of the pollution exclusion renders it applicable in these circumstances and, therefore, they were justified in denying coverage. In contrast, the insureds claimed that after this court's decision in *Kent Farms*, the absolute pollution exclusion must be interpreted to apply only to traditional environmental harms, not personal injuries arising from ordinary negligence. Because this claim arguably did not involve traditional environmental pollution, the insureds asserted that the exclusion cannot apply under these circumstances.

The trial court granted summary judgment in favor of the insurers and denied the insureds' motion. The insureds appealed and the Court of Appeals affirmed, holding that *Kent Farms* was factually distinguishable and this case was instead comparable to *Cook*, a similar case in which toxic fumes had caused the injury. The Court of Appeals also held that the exclusion was not so broad that it rendered the insurance contracts illusory. The insureds filed a petition for review, which this court granted.

* * *

The rise of absolute pollution exclusions sparked new controversy over whether the exclusion applied to incidents that did not involve so-called classic environmental pollution. *Id.* Many courts have interpreted absolute pollution exclusions specifically in the context of claims for bodily injuries arising out of the release of toxic fumes. Some have concluded that the absolute pollution exclusion does not apply where personal injury has resulted from the negligent release of fumes during the ordinary course of the insured's business. Others have concluded that because the historical purpose of the prior qualified pollution exclusion was to shield insurers from sweeping liability for environmental cleanups, the absolute pollution exclusion clause could be reasonably interpreted to apply only to traditional environmental harms. Finally, some courts have concluded that a "common-sense approach" is necessary and the pollution exclusion should not be read to apply to "injuries resulting from everyday activities gone slightly, but not surprisingly, awry." * * * However, a majority of courts has concluded that absolute pollution exclusions unambiguously exclude coverage for damages caused by the release of toxic fumes.

Absolute Pollution Exclusions in Washington: The Washington Court of Appeals first interpreted an absolute pollution exclusion in 1996. In *Cook*, the insured contractor applied a concrete sealant to a building. The material safety data sheet described the sealant as a " '[r]espiratory irritant,' " and the product information contained warnings regarding adequate ventilation. The contractor failed to seal off an air intake vent, fumes were sucked into the building, and some of the building's occupants suffered respiratory damage. The insurer argued that the pollution exclusion clause in the contractor's insurance policy, one that is substantially the same as the exclusion in this case, precluded coverage.

The *Cook* appellants argued that the pollution exclusion should be interpreted to cover only traditional environmental harms, but not injuries arising from normal business operations. They contended that the drafting history of the pollution exclusion clause supported limiting the clause's application to traditional environmental pollution cases. But the *Cook* court concluded that when the language of an insurance policy is clear and unambiguous, a court must enforce the contract as written. The court noted that "[a] party can present drafting history to assist in determining a reasonable construction *after* the court finds a clause ambiguous. We cannot use the drafting history to *find* the clause ambiguous, however." * * * The plain language of the *Cook* policy made no distinction based on "classic environmental pollution," the exclusion specifically included injuries at the insured's work site, and a reasonable person would recognize the sealant as a pollutant. *Id.* at 154. Therefore, the policy language was unambiguous and, absent ambiguity, the court could not limit the exclusion. This court denied review.

* * *

Then, in 2000, this court accepted review of an absolute pollution exclusion case. *Kent Farms* [in which] The court explained that the *Kent Farms cause of action was "rooted in negligence, not in environmental harm caused by pollution," because the plaintiff alleged "negligence in the maintenance and design of a fuel storage facility that resulted in immediate bodily injury when a high-pressure jet of liquid struck him." In other words, it was the defect in the shutoff valve, not the toxic character of the fuel, that was central to the injury. Thus, the court framed the issue as whether the mere fact that a pollutant "appears in the causal chain" can trigger the application of the exclusion clause. * * * While this court noted that the Court of Appeals had labeled the pollution exclusion ambiguous, it did not explicitly determine whether the clause was in fact ambiguous. Instead, the Kent Farms* court explained that to resolve the issue, it had to "determine the purpose and scope of the exclusion." Relying on Queen City Farms, 126 Wn.2d 50, 882 P.2d 703, a case in which this court interpreted a qualified pollution exclusion, the Kent Farms court concluded that it was required to "view the exclusion in light of the whole policy to determine whether, in that context, the exclusion applies." Kent Farms, 140 Wn.2d at 400. The court began by "examining what the exclusion and similar exclusions are intended to accomplish."

The Kent Farms court explained that the qualified pollution exclusion clause, was initially adopted so that insurers could avoid the " 'yawning extent of potential liability arising from the gradual or repeated discharge of hazardous substances into the environment.' " Later, various forms of the absolute pollution exclusion clause were incorporated into insurance policies in the wake of expanded environmental liability under federal law; thus, the absolute pollution exclusion clauses "were clearly intended to exculpate insurance companies from liability for massive environmental cleanups required by CERCLA and similar legislation." Therefore, the exclusion specifically addressed "those situations in which injury was caused by environmental damage."

The Kent Farms court reasoned that the injured deliveryman was not "polluted" by diesel fuel and more importantly, the fuel was not "acting as a 'pollutant' when it struck him." To hold otherwise would "broaden the application of the exclusion far beyond its intended purpose." The average purchaser of a comprehensive liability policy reasonably expects broad coverage for liability arising from business operations and exclusions should be strictly construed against the insurer. Kent Farms would have reasonably believed that injuries arising from faulty equipment would be beyond the scope of the exclusion and would be covered.

* * *

Application of the Absolute Pollution Exclusion in this Case: With this background in mind, we now turn to the case at hand. In this case, the Court of Appeals held that the underlying injury and cause of action were primarily the result of the toxic character of the pollutant and therefore the pollution exclusion would apply. The Court of Appeals concluded Cook and Washington's other "fumes" cases remain good law because the facts of those cases are distinguishable from the facts of Kent Farms. Unlike the diesel fuel in Kent Farms, Cook involved a substance whose toxicity could cause injury even when used as intended. Thus, the Cook reasoning and not the Kent Farms rule would control when fumes caused injury and where the pollutant was being used as it was intended. See id. Because the tenant in this case was injured by fumes emanating from water proofing material that was being used as intended, the air in her apartment was "polluted." Thus, the pollution exclusion applied and the court affirmed the summary judgment dismissal of the insureds' suit. We agree.

* * *

In this case, the policy language clearly states that the liability coverage does not apply to *bodily injury* or *property damage arising out of the dispersal, seepage, migration, release, or escape of a gaseous irritant, including vapors, fumes and chemicals, at any premises owned by the insured or any premises onto which a contractor or subcontractor hired by the insured has brought a pollutant.* The language clearly applies to bodily injury and property damage; it is not limited to actions for cleanup costs. * * * *When considering the facts of this case, it is difficult to see how a reasonable person could interpret the policy language such that it would not encompass the claim at issue here. The Kaczor estate claims that she suffered bodily injury and property damage when the deck sealant fumes drifted or migrated into her apartment. The sealant was applied at property owned by the insureds. In addition, Pacific Restoration was hired to apply the sealant; they brought the sealant onto the premises for the purpose of applying it to the deck owned by the insureds. The parties agree that the sealants at issue here, PC-220 and Polyglaze AL, contained TDI, a toxic substance which can irritate the respiratory tract and, in high concentrations, can cause central nervous system depression. CP at 176. The material safety data sheet for these products indicates that their ingredients are toxic and recommends precautions such as adequate ventilation, respiratory protection, protective clothing, and eye protection. CP at 197. Furthermore, the Federal Clean Air Act lists TDI as a hazardous air pollutant. The contents of the sealant unambiguously fall within the policy definition of pollutant.*

The insureds argue that this court's decision in *Kent Farms requires* us to conclude that the absolute pollution exclusion can be applied only to exclude liability for "traditional environmental pollution." The *Kent Farms* court examined the history of the absolute pollution exclusion, but to do so, the court must have concluded that the exclusion was ambiguous with regard to the facts of that case. An absolute pollution exclusion clause can be ambiguous with regard to the facts of one case but not another. The *Kent Farms* facts are not present here. Where, as here, the exclusion unambiguously applies to the facts of the case at hand, the plain language must be applied without reference to extrinsic evidence regarding the intent of the parties. * * * The insureds also contend that the *Kent Farms* holding was so sweeping that it overruled *Cook* and *Harbor Insurance*. Thus, they argue that Washington's "fumes" cases are inapplicable and the absolute pollution exclusion must now be applied only to cases of traditional environmental pollution. However, it is important to note that while *Cook* was discussed in the *Kent Farms* Court of Appeals decision, this court did not mention *Cook* . . . . *Kent Farms* opinion. [*Cook*] case was [not] explicitly rejected. * * * Furthermore, the *Kent Farms* court did not implicitly reject the reasoning of those cases. While the *Kent Farms* case included language regarding the purpose behind the pollution exclusion, the court was careful to explain that the exclusion applies to " 'occurrences' involving the pollutant *as a pollutant*." In other words, the *Kent Farms* court distinguished between cases in which the substance at issue was polluting at the time of the injury and cases in which the offending substance's toxic character was not central to the injury.

* * *

Therefore, we conclude that the *Kent Farms* discussion of traditional environmental harms is limited by the facts of that case. Here, we adopt the reasoning of the *Cook* court; TDI meets the policy's definition of a pollutant and Kaczor's injuries fall squarely within the plain language of the pollution exclusion clause. Where the exclusion specifically includes releases or discharges occurring on the owner's property or as the result of materials brought onto the property at the behest of the insured, and a reasonable person would recognize the offending substance as a pollutant, the policy is subject to only one reasonable interpretation and the exclusion must not be limited.

In sum, because *Cook* follows the clear and longstanding rules for insurance contract interpretation adopted by this court, we apply the *Cook* reasoning in this case. We note that *Kent Farms* is distinguishable on its facts. Given Washington's clear rules for insurance contract interpretation, we reject the reasoning of other states that have declined to apply the pollution exclusion in fumes cases. The pollution exclusion at issue here unambiguously precludes coverage for the Kaczor claim and we decline to find ambiguity where none exists. Therefore, we affirm the Court of Appeals holding that the absolute pollution exclusion applies to these facts, distinguishing *Kent Farms* and adopting the reasoning in *Cook*.

Illusory Contract

The insureds contend that if the pollution exclusion is interpreted broadly, the exclusion will swallow all covered occurrences, making the policy illusory. * * * We conclude that because the pollution exclusion does not preclude coverage for many accidents that could occur on the building owners' property, the exclusion does not render the insurance contracts illusory. For example, slip and fall injuries would clearly fall outside of the pollution exclusion. Therefore the covered "occurrences" and excluded incidents are not mutually exclusive, and the exclusion does not render the insurance contracts illusory.

* * *

Conclusion

Washington law clearly requires this court to look first to the plain language of an insurance policy exclusion. If the exclusionary language is unambiguous, then the court cannot create an ambiguity where none exists. If the language is plain there is no need to consider extrinsic evidence of the parties' intent. The language of the absolute pollution exclusion is unambiguous when applied to the facts of this case. The deck sealant at issue here is clearly a pollutant as defined in the policy and Kaczor's injury falls squarely within the exclusionary language. Thus, there is no need to turn to evidence regarding the history and purpose of the standard pollution exclusion. Finally, because there are cases to which the absolute pollution exclusion would not apply, the insurance contract at issue here is not illusory.

CHAMBERS, J. (dissenting)—The majority embarks upon the noble quest of clarifying the law. Unfortunately, the majority confuses the "occurrence," or coverage triggering event, with the consequent damages. Specifically, the majority confuses a non polluting *event* covered by the policy with the resulting *damages*, which were caused by pollutants. Because we look at the occurrence to determine coverage, not the resulting damage, I respectfully dissent.

Our jurisprudence has been consistent in analyzing pollution exclusions. "The relevant inquiry is whether there has been a polluting event." In my view, the pollution exclusion operates only on polluting events. But if the "occurrence" triggering coverage was not a polluting event, then there is coverage. As we said, " '[i]f the initial event, the "efficient proximate cause," is a covered peril, then there is coverage under the policy regardless whether subsequent events within the chain, which may be causes-in-fact of the loss, are excluded by the policy.' " This initial event, the efficient proximate cause, should not be confused with the resulting damage. * * * This is not new. This court has long adopted the "efficient proximate cause" rule for determining whether an event is covered or not.

> "Where *a peril specifically insured against sets other causes in motion* which, in an unbroken sequence and connection between the act and final loss, produce the result for which recovery is sought, *the insured peril is regarded as the 'proximate cause' of the entire loss.*
>
> "It is the efficient or predominant cause which sets into motion the chain of events producing the loss which is regarded as the proximate cause, not necessarily the last act in a chain of events."

Consider an auto accident in which a driver was saturated in fuel, and suffered specific injuries from the irritating nature of the chemical compound and its noxious fumes. There would be coverage for this "occurrence" and the resulting damages. In this example, the occurrence is the alleged negligent act which caused the motor vehicle collision. The mere fact that a pollutant was involved in the causal chain of events does not trigger the pollution exclusion. There is coverage so long as "a covered peril sets in motion a causal chain" even when "the last link of which is an uncovered peril." The covered peril here was the alleged negligence of the contractor and apartment owner in performing routine work necessary to maintain the apartment building.

* * *

[T]he policies at issue are commercial comprehensive general liability policies. For our purposes, the apartment owners are insured under both policies. Because these are broad and comprehensive policies we must not only interpret them as would an average person purchasing insurance but we must also strictly construe any exclusions against the insurers. * * * Here, coverage is broad. The Americans States' policy says, "We will pay those sums that the insured becomes legally obligated to pay as damages because of 'bodily injury' or 'property damage' to which this insurance applies." As any exclusion must be read within the context of the coverage provided, we must first examine the definitions of "occurrence" within the policies. Both policies have the identical definition of occurrence: " 'Occurrence' means an accident, including continuous or repeated exposure to substantially the same general harmful conditions." Thus, the insured is led to understand that his insurance coverage extends to the continuous or repeated exposure to harmful conditions.

Next we must examine the pollutions exclusion. * * * Pollutant is broadly defined as any "irritant . . . or contaminant" in solid, liquid, gaseous or thermal form. CP at 209 (American States); *accord* 308 State Farm). Here, a contractor was hired by the insured to apply waterproofing to the exterior wood surface of the apartment complex. The specific allegation of negligence against the apartment owner was the failure to prevent exposure to toxic fumes and the failure to warn its tenant. Inherent in applying any water proofing material including stains and paints is the exposure of toxic fumes. But the specific contentions against the apartment owner was the failure to assure proper ventilation or to warn of the fumes.

The question before this court is whether the average purchaser of a comprehensive liability policy understand that the act or applying waterproofing to the exterior wall of an apartment building would be an act of "discharge, dispersal, seepage, migration, (or) release" of a pollutant. * * * This court has never held that mere injury by a pollutant triggers a pollution exclusion. This court has always examined the pollution exclusion by determining whether the "occurrence" was a polluting event. A polluting event is the discharge, dispersal, seepage, migration, release or escape of pollutants. This court, when addressing this question within the plain, ordinary, and popular meaning in accord with the understanding of the average purchaser of insurance has adopted the traditional meaning of pollution. This court has also always viewed pollution exclusions from their traditional purpose of avoiding massive exposure for environmental damage. This history is an integral part of a proper understanding of the clauses. * * * An excellent summation is found in *Kent Farms*:

> The qualified pollution exclusion clause, a precursor to the clause
> at issue here, came into existence so insurers could avoid the
> "yawning extent of potential liability arising from the gradual or
> repeated discharge of hazardous substances into the environment."
> Later, various forms of absolute pollution exclusion clauses, includ-
> ing the clause here, were incorporated into insurance policies in the
> wake of expanded environmental liability under the Comprehensive
> Environmental Response, Compensation, and Liability Act of 1980,

42 U.S.C. §§ 9601-9675 (1995) (CERCLA). These clauses were clearly intended to exculpate insurance companies from liability for massive environmental cleanups required by CERCLA and similar legislation. The insurance companies' objective in creating both clauses was to avoid liability for environmental pollution. To read the absolute exclusion clause more broadly ignores the general coverage provisions.

Kent Farms, (quoting *Waste Mgmt. of Carolinas, Inc. v. Peerless Ins. Co.* (N.C. 1986)) & citing *Queen City Farms, Inc. v. Cent. Nat'l Ins. Co. of Omaha* (Wash. App.1992) (surveying the history of the clause)); *see also generally* Jeffrey W. Stempel, *Reason and Pollution: Correctly Construing the "Absolute" Exclusion in Context and in Accord with its Purpose and Party Expectations*, 34 Tort & Ins. L.J. 1, 5 (1998).

The majority recognizes that it is dramatically departing from prior interpretation of pollution exclusions, but seems to justify departing from precedents by distinguishing the policy provisions before us as "absolute pollutions exclusions" to be distinguished from "qualified" exclusions, and by pointing to substantially irrelevant factual differences. The majority acknowledges that pollution exclusions originated from insurers' efforts to avoid sweeping liability for long-term release of hazardous waste. The majority then concludes that the exclusions before us are absolute, not qualified, and for that reason our former jurisprudence holding that pollution exclusions are interpreted in light of their purpose of avoiding massive exposure of environmental damage should no longer apply. But in *Kent Farms*, the exclusion at issue was also an absolute pollution exclusion.

* * *

The majority distinguishes *Kent Farms* on the grounds that *Kent Farms* did not explicitly recite that it found the clause ambiguous. Therefore, it concludes, *Kent Farms* discussion of the history of the clause was, apparently, not binding on future courts. But read as a whole, it is clear the court believed that the clause was ambiguous, at least as applied to the facts of *Kent Farms*, as it referred approvingly to the Court of Appeals holding that the clause was ambiguous and proceeded to review the drafting history of the clause.

Against that backdrop, it is clear that applying the clause to exclude this type of harm is appropriate only if the "occurrence" that triggers coverage is a polluting event. In my view, the average consumer of a general liability policy would not understand that applying wood preservative to the exterior of an apartment building was a polluting event. As this court has already noted, expanding the exclusion to cover any type of occurrence that involves pollution would be an "opportunistic afterthought," outside the intent of the drafters. I conclude this does violence to the meaning of the exclusion and our recent unanimous *Kent Farms* opinion. Accordingly, I respectfully dissent.

NAV-ITS, INC. v. SELECTIVE INSURANCE CO.

183 N.J. 110, 869 A.2d 929 (N.J. 2005)

Justice WALLACE delivered the opinion of the Court.

This case concerns the applicability of a pollution exclusion provision in a commercial general liability insurance policy. The question presented is whether the exclusion for injuries caused by the "discharge, dispersal, release or escape of pollutants" bars coverage for personal injury allegedly caused by the exposure to toxic fumes that emanated from a floor coating/sealant operation performed by the insured. An exception to the pollution exclusion allows coverage where the injury takes place inside a building "within a single 48-hour period and the exposure occurs within the same 48-hour period." We conclude that the pollution exclusion provision applies to traditional environmental pollution claims and is not a bar to coverage in this case.

The material facts are relatively simple. Plaintiff NAV-ITS, Inc. (Nav-Its), is a construction contractor specializing in tenant "fit-out" work, including the building of partitions, the laying of concrete, the installation of doors, and the application of finishes, such as paint, sealants, and coatings.

On April 22, 1998, Nav-Its entered into a contract to perform fit-out work at the Parkway Shopping Center (Center) in Allentown, Pennsylvania. Nav-Its obtained Comprehensive General Liability (CGL) insurance coverage for its activities at the Center from defendant Selective Insurance Company of America (Selective). Nav-Its hired T.A. Fanikos Painting (Fanikos) as a subcontractor on the project to perform painting, coating and floor sealing work. Fanikos performed that work from July 27 to August 5, 1998. During that time, Dr. Roy Scalia, a physician with office space in the Center, was allegedly exposed to fumes that were released while Fanikos performed the coating/sealant work. As a result of that exposure, Dr. Scalia suffered from nausea, vomiting, light-headedness, loss of equilibrium, and headaches. He sought medical treatment in September 1998.

In December 2000, Dr. Scalia filed a complaint against Nav-Its and several others for personal injuries arising out of his exposure to fumes at his office from July 27 through July 31, 1998, and from August 3 through August 5, 1998. Nav-Its forwarded the complaint to Selective, seeking defense and indemnification. Relying on the pollution exclusion in its policy, Selective refused to provide coverage to Nav-Its. Dr. Scalia's case against Nav-Its was subsequently resolved through binding arbitration.

Nav-Its then commenced the present action against Selective, seeking a declaratory judgment that Selective was obligated to defend and indemnify it in connection with the underlying personal injury action. Nav-Its also sought reimbursement for the costs incurred in defending the suit filed by Dr. Scalia. * * * Early in the litigation, Selective moved for summary judgment, and Nav-Its filed a cross-motion for partial summary judgment. The trial court denied Selective's motion and granted partial summary judgment in favor of Nav-Its, finding that Selective had an obligation to defend and indemnify Nav-Its in accordance with its insurance policy. The trial court concluded that Nav-Its had a reasonable expectation that liability arising out of normal painting operations would be covered under the policy. Selective moved for reconsideration, but once again the trial court denied relief. In a written decision, the trial court expanded its reasoning and concluded that the pollution exclusion clause in the policy applied only to traditional environmental pollution claims. * * * The trial court also found that the exception to the exclusion applied because Dr. Scalia suffered individual exposures every day he entered his office, namely that each exposure began and ended in a less than forty-eight hour period.

On appeal, in an unpublished opinion, the Appellate Division reversed, finding that pollution exclusion clauses are not necessarily limited to the clean up of traditional environmental damage. Nevertheless, the panel found that a jury must decide whether each period of time that Dr. Scalia was at work represented a separate exposure of less than forty-eight hours, or one continuous period of exposure. * * * We granted Nav-Its' petition for certification and Selective's cross-petition.

* * *

The policy defined pollutants as "any solid, liquid, gaseous, or thermal irritant or contaminant, including smoke, vapor, soot, fumes, acids, alkalis, chemicals and waste." Under the policy, "[w]aste includes materials to be recycled, reconditioned or reclaimed." It also defined "Pollution Hazard" to mean "an actual exposure or threat of exposure to the corrosive, toxic or other harmful properties of any 'pollutants' arising out of the discharge, dispersal, seepage, migration, release or escape of such 'pollutants.' "The policy also contained a limited exception to the pollution exclusion. That exception provided that the pollution exclusion does not apply to:

B. Injury or damage arising from the actual discharge or release of any "pollutants" that takes place entirely inside a building or structure if:

1. the injury or damage is the result of an exposure which takes place entirely within a building or structure; and

2. the injury or damage results from an actual discharge or release beginning and ending within a single forty-eight (48) hour period; and

3. the exposure occurs within the same forty-eight (48) hour period referred to in 2. above; and

4. within thirty (30) days of the actual discharge or release:

a. the company or its agent is notified of the injury or damage in writing; or

b. in the case of 'bodily injury,' the 'bodily injury' is treated by a physician, or death results, and within ten (10) additional days, written notice of such injury or death is received by the company or its agents.

Strict compliance with the time periods stated above is required for coverage to be provided.

* * *

The central question presented in this case is whether we should limit the applicability of the pollution exclusion clause to traditional environmental pollution claims. We begin our analysis by noting the often-stated principles for interpretation of insurance policy language. * * * Generally, "[w]hen interpreting an insurance policy, courts should give the policy's words 'their plain, ordinary meaning.' If the policy language is clear, the policy should be interpreted as written. *Ibid.* If the policy is ambiguous, the policy will be construed in favor of the insured. Because of the complex terminology used in the policy and because the policy is in most cases prepared by the insurance company experts, we recognize that an insurance policy is a "contract [] of adhesion between parties who are not equally situated." As a result, "courts must assume a particularly vigilant role in ensuring their conformity to public policy and principles of fairness." "Consistent with that principle, courts also [] endeavor [] to interpret insurance contracts to accord with the objectively reasonable expectations of the insured." * * * "[t]he insured's 'reasonable expectations in the transaction may not justly be frustrated and courts have properly molded their governing interpretative principles with that uppermost in mind.' Moreover, we have recognized the importance of construing contracts of insurance to reflect the reasonable expectations of the insured in the face of ambiguous language and phrasing, and in exceptional circumstances, when the literal meaning of the policy is plain." * * * We have applied the reasonable expectations doctrine to all forms of insurance contracts. * * * Important to our analysis is the principle that exclusions in the insurance policy should be narrowly construed. Nevertheless, if the exclusion is " 'specific, plain, clear, prominent, and not contrary to public policy,' "it will be enforced as written.

* * *

The insurance industry presented testimony to the insurance regulators as to the intended purposes of the absolute pollution exclusion. One commentator reviewed the transcripts of the hearings before the New Jersey insurance regulators and stated:

In 1985, for example, the New Jersey State Insurance Department held hearings to determine whether to approve what became the 1986 exclusion. In those hearings, the New Jersey insurance commissioners heard testimony from various members of the insurance industry regarding the [absolute pollution exclusion]. The regulators were concerned that the then-proposed exclusion sought to sweep too many potential non-environmental liabilities within its reach.

The insurance industry sought to allay those fears and, thus, secure the needed approval of this exclusion. Michael A. Averill, a manager of the Insurance Services Office, Inc. ("ISO"), an insurance industry trade organization, Commercial Casualty Division, stated that the insurance industry did not intend to use the revised pollution exclusion as a bar to coverage: '[The purpose of the change in policy language] is to introduce a complete on-site emission and partial off-site exclusion for some operations. *For some operations. It is not an absolute exclusion.*' []

Another speaker, Robert J. Sullivan, Vice President of Government Affairs for Crum & Forster in Morristown, New Jersey, testified that the exclusion would not preclude coverage for liability for a policyholder's products and completed operations. [Lorelie S. Masters, *Absolutely Not Total: State Courts Recognize the Historical Limits of the "Absolute" and "Total" Pollution Exclusions, Envtl. Claims J.* Vol. 15, No. 4, 453-54 (Autumn 2003) (emphasis [***29] in the original); see also *Kimber Petrol. Corp. v. Travelers Indem. Co.*, 298 N.J. Super. 286, 298, 689 A.2d 747, 753-54 (App.Div.1997) (noting evidence presented by insurance industry to Department of Insurance supporting absolute pollution exclusion clause).]

Additionally, commentators have explained that the absolute pollution exclusion was developed to address the expansion of liability for remediating hazardous waste imposed under the Comprehensive Environmental Response, Compensation & Liability Act (CERCLA, 42 *U.S.C.* § 9601 et. seq.) in 1980. *Masters, supra, Envtl. Claims. J. at 457; Jeffrey W. Stempel, Reason and Pollution: Correctly Construing the "Absolute" Exclusion In Context and in Accord with Its Purpose and Party Expectations, 34 Tort & Ins. L.J. 1, 29-32 (1998) ("[T]he available evidence most strongly suggests that the absolute pollution exclusion was designed to serve the twin purposes of eliminating coverage for gradual environmental degradation and government-mandated cleanup such as Superfund response cost reimbursement.")*

We have reviewed the development of the pollution exclusion to assist our interpretation of the pollution exclusion in the Selective policy. Based on that review, we are confident that the history of the pollution-exclusion clause in its various forms demonstrates that its purpose was to have a broad exclusion for traditional environmentally related damages. Notably, we have not been presented with any compelling evidence that the pollution exclusion clause in the present case, when approved by the Department of Insurance, was intended to be read as broadly as Selective urges. *See Stempel, supra, 34 Tort & Ins. L.J. at 33.* ("If the absolute exclusion was intended to reach as broadly as now contended, one would expect to see conclusive ISO memoranda and similar documents"). To be sure, read literally, the exclusion would require its application to all instances of injury or damage to persons or property caused by "any pollutants arising out of the discharge, dispersal, seepage, migration, release or escape of . . . any solid, liquid, gaseous, or thermal irritant or contaminant, including

smoke, vapor, soot, fumes, acids, alkalis, chemicals and waste." If we were
to accept Selective's interpretation of its pollution exclusion, we would
exclude essentially all pollution hazards except those falling within the
limited "exception" for exposure within a structure resulting from a release
of pollutants "within a single forty-eight hour period." We reject Selective's
interpretation as overly broad, unfair, and contrary to the objectively
reasonable expectations of the New Jersey and other state regulatory
authorities that were presented with an opportunity to disapprove the
clause.

The decisions of the highest courts in California, Illinois, Massachusetts,
Ohio, New York and Washington are consistent with our decision to limit
the pollution exclusion to those hazards traditionally associated with
environmentally related claims.

* * *

We find no need to address the ramifications of the 48-hour exception
and whether it should be read to expand the pollution exclusion clause. We
interpret that exception to limit the reach of the pollution clause, i.e. if the
environmental pollution occurs within a building within a single forty-eight
hour period, and the other conditions are met, then the insured may receive
coverage for that environmental pollution claim. Simply put, if the pollution
exclusion is not applicable, neither is the exception to the pollution
exclusion.

As a final observation, the insurance industry has revised its policies in
the past to provide for the exclusion of certain coverages. We will review
each change on the record presented. We emphasize that industry-wide
determinations to restrict coverage of risks, particularly those that affect
the public interest, such as the risk of damage from pollution, environmental or otherwise, must be fully and unambiguously disclosed to regulators
and the public.

NOTES AND QUESTIONS

(1) What's going on regarding the opinions of the Washington Supreme
Court in *Kent Farms* and *Quadrant Corp.*? Can the cases be reconciled on
their different facts or is something else at work such as changes in the
Court's membership or the Court's views of contract and insurance law?
Which case do you expect to become the dominant law of Washington?

(2) Which case's analysis is most persuasive: *Deni; Kent Farms; Quadrant; Nav-Its*? Which perspective do you expect to win out over time? Or
will the states simply remain divided over the scope and applicability of
the absolute pollution exclusion. Remember, the exclusion has been around
in substantially this form for more than 20 years.

(3) *See also Employers Mut. Cas. Co. v. Industrial Rubber Products, Inc.*,
2006 U.S. Dist. LEXIS 9242 (D. Minn. Feb. 23, 2006) (coverage barred for

claim related to steel grit blasting done in the ordinary course of policyholder's business); *City of Chesapeake v. States Self-Insurers Risk Retention Group, Inc.*, 271 Va. 574, 628 S.E.2d 539 (Va. 2006) (claim related to presents of trihalomethanes or THMs in city drinking water excluded, a result that would appear to be justified by both a formal textual approach and a functional approach stressing insuring intent and purpose; however, if the third party claim is that the city improperly purified its water rather than that the city itself discharged THMs into the water supply (the reported opinion is unclear on this point), the City would have a strong argument that the third party claim is one of negligent water treatment and not one of water pollution); *Madison Const. Co. v. Harleysville Mut. Ins. Co.*, 735 A.2d 100 (Pa. 1999) (pollution exclusion bars injury suffered by third party at job site from fumes released by cement curing agent). *But see Lititz Mut. Ins. Co. v. Steeley*, 785 A.2d 975 (Pa. 2001) (despite 1999 decision in *Madison Construction* holding pollution exclusion nonetheless did not bar coverage for lead-based paint. Even after concluding that lead-based paint was a pollutant, the court found another rationale to avoid the applicability of the pollution exclusion: "One would not ordinarily describe the continual, imperceptible, and inevitable deterioration of paint that has been applied to the interior surface of a residence as a discharge ("a flowing or issuing out"), a release ("the act or an instance of liberating or freeing"), or an escape ("an act or instance of escaping")." *Lititz Mutual* at 981. Given that some New Jersey policyholders no doubt conduct business in neighboring Pennsylvania and vice-versa, the stage is likely set for policyholders and insurers in some pollution-related claims with these dual-state contacts to have different ideas about which state's law applies.

(4) [continue with main text on page 793]

§ 11.14   THE PROBLEM OF GOVERNMENT-MANDATED EXPENDITURES

Page 794: [Add to § 11.14 before the Questions:]

Not only do courts applying the same law differ on this issue, at least one state supreme court has reversed itself within a relatively short time. *See Johnson Controls, Inc. v. Employers Insurance of Wausau*, 264 Wis. 2d 60, 665 N.W.2d 257 (Wis. 2003) (holding that CERCLA response costs are covered under standard CGL policy, reversing *City of Edgerton v. General Casualty Co. of Wisconsin*, 184 Wis. 2d 750, 517 N.W.2d 463 (1994), *cert. denied*, 514 U.S. 1017 (1995) on the basis of additional information regarding the background and drafting history of CGL provision providing coverage regarding actions "for damage").

Compare Certain Underwriters at Lloyd's v. Superior Court (Powerine Oil Companies), 24 Cal. 4th 945, 16 P.3d 94, 103 Cal. Rptr. 2d 672 (Cal. 2001) (*Powerine I*) (standard CGL insuring agreement to cover liability for "damages" does not apply to pollution clean costs from administrative order compliance) *with Powerine Oil Co., Inc. v. Superior Court*, 118 P.3d 589,

33 Cal. Tptr. 3d 562 (Cal. 2005) (*Powerine II*) (excess/umbrella policy language reflected insurer commitment to pay policyholder's reasonable costs in complying with state administrative agency's pollution, cleanup, and abatement orders). The *Powerine I* holding regarding the standard CGL policy and indemnity coverage is consistent with the California Supreme Court's opinion (excerpted in Chapter 9 at p. 708) in *Foster-Gardner, Inc. v. National Union Fire Ins. Co.*, 18 Cal. 4th 857, 959 P.2d 265, 77 Cal. Rptr. 2d 107 (Cal. 1998) ((CGL duty to defend language for "suite seeking damages" limited to civil suits prosecuted in court and does not apply to administrative proceedings). However, *Powerine II* is as yet only a partial or tentative victory for the policyholder as the court stated:

> Although other policy provisions or exclusion clauses yet to be litigated could ultimately defeat coverage as this litigation progresses, the express wording of the central insuring agreement in these nine excess/umbrella policies [at issue in the case] goes well beyond mere coverage for court-ordered money "damages," and is broad enough to include coverage for the liability of environmental cleanup and response costs ordered by an administrative agency. Under a literal reading of these policies, we conclude such would be the objectively reasonable expectation of the insured.

See *Powerine II*, 188 P.3d at 593.

QUESTIONS

(1) The California Supreme Court, like most courts, obviously puts great stock in the text the insurance policy at issue. But as noted in Chapter 2, the policy, like any writing, is not actually "the contract" of the parties. The contract is the agreement of the parties. The memorialization of that agreement in an insurance policy, mortgage, purchase agreement form, etc., is "merely" a contract document that is supposed to accurately record the agreement (but may not, making judicial review of the contract more difficult).

(2) The law displays great deference to written contract documents, so much so that laypersons, lawyers, and courts frequently err by assuming that the written paper is "the contract" and controls adjudicative outcomes even when there is strong evidence to suggest that the agreement of the parties did not include what is written on the paper. In many cases, of course, at least one of the parties had no particular understanding of a written term in the contract document. Consider your frequent entry into standardized contracts such as software licensing, and credit card applications. In these situations, courts usually are particularly deferential to the text of contract documents because there is nothing to the contrary in the parties' "negotiations" (which may have been confined only to price, quantity, and delivery in the case of most standardized policies) or the context of the transaction. Reasonable standardized terms are also usually consistent with the purpose of the contract. Although you may not have thought about it before you applied for the Visa card, you should not be surprised

that Visa charges interest if you fail to pay the balance at the end of the month and that the interest rate is higher than that charged by commercial banks for secured loans such as a home mortgage. Similarly, it is not unfairly surprising to find out that if you default on mortgage payments, the bank has the right to foreclose and sell the secured asset.

(3) But what about insurance text? Should courts focus so intently on written text rather than the transaction? Does the degree of standardization or manuscripting of a policy matter? For example, as noted in § 11.02, when a commercial policyholder procures a liability insurance program, it typically has a significant deductible or retention, a primary insurance policy of $1 million or more, and several layers of excess or umbrella insurance coverage. Normally, excess policies are expected to "follow-form" to the underlying insurance while umbrella policies follow form concerning coverages below and also provide additional coverage of some type.

(4) One can debate whether *Powerine I* and *Foster-Gardner* were correctly decided (see the *Hazen Paper v. USF&G* case adjacent to *Foster-Gardner* in Chapter 9, p. 701) but under a typical commercial liability program, one would reasonably expect excess insurance to follow form to primary insurance. Consequently, *Powerine II's* presumptive grant of coverage on the basis of the literal language of an excess policy form may be a little jarring to pure excess insurers, who expect to be held to the same contours of coverage as the underlying CGL insurer. For umbrella insurers, the Powerine II Court's focus on policy text makes more sense in that both policyholder and umbrella carrier expect that the umbrella coverage will be broader than the underlying liability policy. But what if the umbrella language were more restrictive concerning defense of and coverage for administrative enforcement proceedings? For example, if Powerine Oil were a Massachusetts company subject to the Hazen Paper, decision, could Powerine Oil's excess or umbrella insurer provide less coverage than the underlying CGL on the basis of that more restrictive language in the policies memorializing the insuring arrangement? If there were no other evidence of policy meaning, should the Massachusetts Court in this hypothetical case rely more on the language of the excess/umbrella policies or upon the industry norm of coverage following form?*

(5) Is the sharp focus on policy text by the California Supreme Court in *Powerine II* good or bad insurance coverage jurisprudence? Review the California Supreme Court cases in this book. The "scorecard" for insurers and policyholders appears to be about even. Recall that in *Vandenberg v. Superior Court* (§ 11.08 at p. 724), the Court's focus on policy language (insuring agreement covering claims for "property damage" without regard to the characterization of the legal action seeking compensation) defeated the insurer argument that "everyone knows" that liability insurance is only for tort claims. We think this is clearly the right result. Could the California Court have reached it through a less textual analysis? Regardless of who wins and who loses, what is the appropriate degree of judicial deference to the policy language? In order to construe coverage in a manner at odds with the natural reading of policy text, should courts require some

particular evidence of specific party intent to the contrary or is evidence of traditional understanding, custom, practice, or industry norm sufficient? What about the purpose of the insurance program and the surrounding circumstances? Where policy or contract document text is unclear, of course, consideration of extrinsic evidence, party intent, purpose, and public policy then become bases for decision even for courts that prefer textualism if the clarity of the language at issue permits.

(6) [continue with text at bottom of page 794]

§ 11.16 COVERAGE "B" OF THE COMMERCIAL GENERAL LIBAILITY POLICY: "PERSONAL INJURY" AND "ADVERTISING INJURY"

Page 797: [Add the following to § 11.16:]

The following case provides an illustration of the scope of Coverage B and also provides a refresher course concerning the duties and liability exposure of insurance brokers because, as the song says, "things fall apart" and "you can count on bad, bad weather." Or maybe you will agree with the broker that the case is "like a sunburn." Enough with the bad references to the policyholder's popular songs, let's read the case.

THIRD EYE BLIND, INC. v. NEAR NORTH ENTERTAINMENT INSURANCE SERVICES, LLC

127 Cal. App. 4th 1311; 26 Cal. Rptr. 3d 452 (Cal. Ct. App. 2005)

McGuiness, P. J., with Pollak, and Parrilli, JJ., concurring.

When an insured sues its insurer for coverage and also brings negligence claims against its business manager and insurance broker for failing to advise about a policy exemption and failing to obtain additional coverage, are the negligence claims barred as a matter of law if the court rules in the insured's favor on the coverage claim? In this case, after the trial court concluded on a motion for summary adjudication that an insurer breached its duty to defend appellants, respondents filed motions for judgment on the pleadings arguing this ruling negated appellants' negligence claims against them as a matter of law. The trial court agreed and granted the motions without leave to amend, and appellants dispute this ruling on appeal. We conclude the judgment must be reversed because the prior order did not negate an element of the causes of action alleged against respondents. We also conclude attorney fees appellants incurred in pursuing coverage are a recoverable item of damages in their claims against respondents.

Appellants are members and associated corporate entities of the musical performance group Third Eye Blind. During the relevant time period, appellants' business manager, respondent Provident Financial Management (Provident), was responsible for, among other things, assessing the band's insurance needs, facilitating insurance planning and obtaining appropriate insurance policies. Appellants also retained an insurance broker, respondent Near North Entertainment Insurance Services, LLC (Near North), a company they selected based on its claimed expertise in the field of entertainment insurance and risk management.

Respondents obtained a commercial general liability (CGL) insurance policy for appellants from North American Specialty Insurance Company (NAS) covering the period of January 31, 1999, to January 31, 2000. Provident paid premiums on the policy and was responsible for obtaining renewals. Despite their responsibilities and expertise, however, neither Provident nor Near North advised appellants that the NAS policy excluded coverage for some liability under a Field of Entertainment Limitation Endorsement (FELE). The FELE in appellants' policy excludes coverage for personal injury or advertising injury arising out of the "Field of Entertainment Business." Specifically, coverage is excluded for claims of: (1) invasion, infringement or interference of the right to privacy or publicity; (2) copyright or trademark infringement; (3) defamation, except for claims arising out of a public appearance unrelated to the band's professional entertainment work; (4) plagiarism, piracy or unfair competition regarding unauthorized use of others' ideas or works; and (5) breach of contract regarding the band's professional entertainment work.

In January 2000, Third Eye Blind, Inc., fired one of its band members, Kevin Cadogan. Cadogan immediately threatened to sue the band, claiming any further performances it gave under the name Third Eye Blind would violate Cadogan's rights under the Lanham Act. (15 U.S.C. § 1125(a).) Cadogan ultimately filed suit against appellants, and others, in June 2000. In addition to several other claims against individual band members, the complaint in *Cadogan v. Third Eye Blind et al.* alleged appellants had misappropriated Cadogan's right of publicity by making unauthorized use of his name, likeness and goodwill and had violated the Lanham Act by creating public confusion regarding Cadogan's affiliation with the band and his role in creating or sponsoring the band's music. Cadogan also claimed appellants' continued use of the name Third Eye Blind constituted trademark infringement under the Lanham Act.

Shortly after it was filed, appellants tendered the *Cadogan* complaint to NAS for defense and indemnity. NAS denied the claim a month later, asserting the FELE in appellants' policy excluded coverage for the *Cadogan complaint's Lanham Act claims and claims alleging a violation of Cadogan's right of publicity. Although appellants sought reconsideration based on case law holding the FELE's language ambiguous, NAS continued to refuse coverage. Appellants therefore proceeded to defend the Cadogan suit on their own and ultimately settled the case. Appellants estimate the amount of settlement proceeds paid, combined with attorney fees and costs they incurred, exceeds $3 million.*

On March 15, 2002, appellants filed the instant action against NAS and respondents Provident and Near North. The complaint alleged NAS had breached its policy obligations by unreasonably refusing to defend and indemnify appellants in the *Cadogan* case. In addition to breach of contract and declaratory relief claims against NAS, the complaint alleged causes of action against respondents for negligence, breach of implied contract and declaratory relief. Appellants alleged that, despite their claimed expertise in the field of entertainment industry insurance and despite the duties they owed appellants, respondents failed to advise or notify them that the NAS policy contained an FELE, such that an additional errors and omissions insurance policy would be necessary to guarantee full coverage. Appellants further alleged they would have obtained an errors and omissions policy if they had been so advised. The complaint sought general damages from respondents, including "all covered defense costs" appellants had incurred.

In the summer of 2002, appellants and NAS filed cross-motions for summary judgment and summary adjudication regarding NAS's duty to defend the *Cadogan* suit. After two hearings, the court (Hon. A. James Robertson, II) concluded Cadogan's claims against appellants were potentially covered under the CGL policy and NAS therefore had a duty to defend appellants in the *Cadogan* lawsuit. In granting appellants' motion for summary adjudication against NAS, the court also ruled the FELE was ambiguous as applied to the allegations and claims set forth in the *Cadogan* complaint. This court summarily denied NAS's petition for writ of mandate on November 7, 2002, and the trial court denied a motion for reconsideration of the order on December 20, 2002. During this time, counsel for NAS advised appellants' attorney that NAS believed the trial court's rulings were erroneous and NAS planned to appeal any final judgment. Appellants and NAS participated in two mediation sessions in January 2003 and ultimately reached a settlement.

On February 28, 2003, Provident filed a motion for judgment on the pleadings, arguing the complaint did not state a cause of action against it in light of the court's recent summary judgment and summary adjudication orders. Characterizing these orders as a judicial determination that NAS owed appellants a duty to defend the *Cadogan* lawsuit, Provident asserted it could not be held liable on the complaint's claims for breach of implied contract, negligence and declaratory relief because "these claims were alleged as alternative causes of action, and predicated on a finding that the NAS policy did not cover [appellants'] underlying claim." A week later, Near North filed a motion for judgment on the pleadings reciting the same arguments. Both motions requested judicial notice of the court's orders granting appellants' motion for summary adjudication and denying NAS's motion for summary judgment. After a hearing, the trial court * * * granted the requests for judicial notice and granted the motions for judgment on the pleadings without leave to amend. The order explained appellants' causes of action against Provident and Near North no longer stated claims for relief because they were "predicated" on a claim that the NAS policy was insufficient to provide coverage in the *Cadogan* lawsuit, yet the court had found in prior orders that the policy *was* sufficient. Accordingly, the trial court also denied appellants' claim for attorney fees.

* * *

I. *Complaint Alleged Claims Against Respondents Independent of Coverage*

Appellants argue the trial court erred in granting judgment on the pleadings because they alleged independent causes of action against respondents and the court's prior ruling regarding NAS's duty to defend did not resolve or negate any element of these claims. Respondents, of course, disagree. They contend appellants' claims against them are "precluded" by the NAS ruling because these claims were "predicated" on a finding that the CGL policy did not provide coverage for the *Cadogan* lawsuit. We conclude there are several problems with this argument and the judgment in favor of respondents must be reversed.

First, respondents distort the nature of the claims against them when they rely on language taken out of context from the complaint to argue these claims were predicated on an absence of coverage under the CGL policy. In support of their argument, respondents quote the following paragraph from the introductory section of the complaint (emphasizing the opening clause): "Alternatively, if this Court determines that NAS has no obligation to provide defense or indemnity for the *Cadogan* suit, Plaintiffs seek compensatory damages against Provident and/or Near North Entertainment arising out of their failure to obtain adequate and reasonable insurance coverage, and in particular, an errors and omissions policy." However, read in context, the complaint alleges claims against respondents that are not premised on any conclusions as to the sufficiency of the CGL policy. Indeed, although respondents summarize its allegations this way, the complaint does not simply assert that respondents were negligent because they procured an insufficient policy. Rather, it alleges that, despite their superior insurance knowledge and expertise, respondents failed to notify appellants that the policy contained an FELE—under which coverage for certain events might be excluded—and failed to advise them that an errors and omissions policy would be necessary to cover this potential shortfall. These claims do not depend on an assumption that the CGL policy was deficient. The point is that respondents failed to alert appellants that the FELE would give NAS a viable basis for refusing coverage under some circumstances and, consequently, failed to recommend that appellants purchase errors and omissions insurance to ensure complete, uncontestable coverage.

Based on their oversimplified articulation of the claims against them, respondents proceed to argue that the NAS ruling conclusively established they fulfilled any duty of care they owed to appellants. In similar fashion, they contend the prior ruling established NAS was fully responsible for appellants' losses. Because respondents did not do something to cause NAS to deny coverage, they argue their conduct cannot be considered a proximate cause of any injury to appellants. But again, these arguments merely knock down straw men while ignoring the actual legal theories alleged in the complaint. Appellants alleged respondents breached their duty to notify appellants of the existence of the FELE and to advise them of the need to obtain errors and omissions insurance to protect them from a potential gap in coverage. Whether respondents failed to give competent advice to appellants is an independent question and does not depend on whether NAS was justified in denying coverage under the CGL policy.

Likewise, while it is true the complaint does not allege respondents actively caused NAS to deny coverage, respondents fail to recognize that this is not the only way in which their breach of duty could cause appellants' losses. Appellants allege that if respondents had advised them about the FELE they would have obtained an errors and omissions policy to cover any potentially excluded claims, such as Cadogan's. Because they did not have such a policy to provide clear coverage of the *Cadogan* suit, appellants were forced to assume their own defense, incurring attorney fees, costs and indemnity. The complaint also alleges NAS is responsible for these losses, but the two theories are not mutually exclusive, as respondents argue. Rather, the law recognizes that there may be multiple causes of a plaintiff's injury. " 'It is not essential to a recovery of damages that a defendant's wrongful act be the sole and only cause of the injury; it is sufficient if it be a proximate cause which in the natural course of events produced, either by itself or in conjunction with other causes, the damage.' " [Citation.]

Division Two of this court recently rejected a similar causation argument. In *Lombardo v. Huysentruyt* (Cal. App. 2001), an attorney drafted an amendment to name the appellants beneficiaries of a trust. After a probate court found this amendment ineffective, the appellants settled with the probate estate and then sued the attorney for malpractice. However, the trial court concluded no reasonable judge would have found the trust amendment ineffective, and thus the probate court's order was a superseding cause of the appellants' alleged damages. On appeal from an entry of nonsuit, the appellate court rejected this reasoning based on hornbook law that " '[a]n independent intervening act is a superseding cause relieving the actor of liability for his negligence only if the intervening act is highly unusual or extraordinary and hence not reasonably foreseeable. [Citation.] Because the appellants offered evidence to show that a reasonable attorney would have taken steps before execution of the trust amendment to avoid the rejection appellants ultimately suffered in probate court, the probate court's order—even if erroneous—was, for nonsuit purposes, a foreseeable result of the attorney's negligence. Likewise, here, appellants have alleged that, as a result of respondents' negligent failure to advise them about the FELE and the need for errors and omissions insurance, they suffered the foreseeable harm of having to defend a lawsuit without adequate insurance coverage. Although NAS may have been wrong to deny coverage of the *Cadogan* suit, the complaint alleges this was a foreseeable harm that could have been avoided if respondents had competently advised appellants.

Similar allegations of proximate cause have been found sufficient to withstand a challenge to the pleadings. In *Kurtz, Richards, Wilson & Co. v. Insurance Communicators Marketing Corp.* (Cal. App. 1993) (*Kurtz*), the plaintiff (KRW) hired an insurance broker to obtain group insurance for its employees. When KRW later made large claims on its policy due to the serious illness of an employee, the insurer denied coverage, citing an inaccurate certificate KRW had submitted through its broker. The insurer sued KRW to rescind the policy, and KRW filed a cross-complaint against the insurer, for breach of contract and other claims, and against the insurance broker and its president for negligence and fraud. Much like the procedural history in the case before us, the broker defendants successfully demurred to the cross-complaint after the trial court granted KRW's motion for summary judgment against the insurer. On appeal, the broker defendants maintained it was not reasonably foreseeable that any false information they may have given the insurer would cause the insurer to cancel the policy and bring suit against KRW. As support, they cited KRW's own allegations in the cross-complaint that the insurer "used the inaccurate information in the application to 'create a pretense' for cancelling the policy." However, the appellate court concluded the demurrer should have been overruled because the complaint alleged it was "entirely foreseeable" the insurer would seek to rescind the policy on this basis, even if the attempted rescission was not ultimately successful. In an observation that seems equally apt in the present case, the *Kurtz* court noted: "KRW's challenge to the legality of its insurer's actions does not insulate respondents from liability."

Although the precise question under review was different, much of the Supreme Court's analysis in *Jordache Enterprises, Inc. v. Brobeck, Phleger & Harrison* (Cal. App. 4th 1998) (*Jordache*) also supports our conclusion. In *Jordache*, the Brobeck firm defended a client in a lawsuit but did not investigate whether there was potential insurance coverage for the suit. As a result of the attorneys' alleged negligence, Jordache provided its own defense for several years. In addition, because Jordache delayed tendering its defense to the insurer, the insurer could—and ultimately did—raise a "late notice" defense to coverage. After Jordache settled a coverage lawsuit against the insurer, it sued Brobeck for legal malpractice. The issue before the Supreme Court in *Jordache* was when the client suffered "actual injury" for purposes of triggering the statute of limitations on claims against Brobeck. In an analogous argument to the one respondents raise here, Jordache asserted its malpractice claims against Brobeck did not ripen until resolution of the coverage action. Jordache argued, and the Court of Appeal agreed, that the causal connection between Brobeck's negligent advice and Jordache's damages was not established until the trial court issued findings regarding coverage and the late notice defense and Jordache settled with the insurer. The Supreme Court disagreed, however, based on the nature of the claims Jordache asserted and the alleged damages.

Similar to the claims appellants assert against respondents here, Jordache claimed its attorneys' neglect allowed the insurer to raise an objectively viable defense to coverage. The insurer's assertion of this defense caused Jordache to incur costs to litigate its coverage claims and also reduced those claims' settlement value. In addition, as a result of the attorneys' alleged neglect, Jordache incurred costs in providing its own defense in the third party action for several years. Likewise here, appellants claim respondents' negligence caused them to incur costs in defending a third party action and in litigating coverage with NAS. Although the trial court here believed a summary judgment ruling on coverage conclusively negated appellants' claims against respondents, the Supreme Court concluded the same detrimental effects Jordache had alleged regarding its attorneys' negligence "were *not* contingent on the outcome of the coverage action." The court reasoned: "Ultimately . . . Jordache's insurance coverage litigation could not determine the existence or effect of Brobeck's alleged negligence. As Brobeck notes, the alleged failure to advise Jordache on insurance matters was not at issue in the coverage lawsuits. Thus, the resolution of that litigation would not determine whether Brobeck breached its duty to Jordache. For the same reason, the coverage litigation could not determine the consequences resulting from Brobeck's alleged breach of duty. The coverage litigation's resolution was relevant to Brobeck's alleged negligence only insofar as it potentially affected the amount of damages Jordache might recover from Brobeck."

The same is true here. Nevertheless, respondents argue the finding that NAS had a duty to defend appellants in the *Cadogan* suit conclusively negates any liability they might have had for procuring the NAS policy with an FELE attached. While that may be so regarding this particular theory of liability, the finding did not preclude respondents' potential liability for failing to help appellants secure more direct, and certain, coverage through an errors and omissions policy. Indeed, the Supreme Court rejected a similar argument—i.e., that a favorable finding on the "late notice" issue in Jordache's coverage litigation would mean any negligence by Brobeck caused no injury—by observing Brobeck could still be liable for failing to obtain a more timely and certain insurer-funded defense for the client. Thus, "Although the outcome of the [***21] coverage litigation may have reduced Jordache's damages, that action could neither necessarily exonerate Brobeck, nor extinguish Jordache's action against Brobeck for failure to render timely advice on insurance issues.

Respondents seek to distinguish *Jordache* by suggesting the attorneys' negligence actually caused Jordache's coverage litigation, in that the court found Brobeck's neglect gave the insurer an objectively viable defense. Respondents note the complaint does not allege that anything they did, or failed to do, decreased appellants' rights under the NAS policy. However, once again respondents oversimplify appellants' claims. Just as in *Jordache*, appellants here allege the respondents' negligence caused them to have to spend large sums in suing their insurer for coverage. Had they been properly advised about the FELE in the NAS policy, appellants allege they would have obtained errors and omissions insurance. There is no dispute an errors and omissions policy would have provided clear coverage for the

Cadogan suit, thus appellants would have had no need to sue NAS and no need to defend themselves in *Cadogan*. Since the very purpose of respondents' hiring was to ensure appellants had adequate insurance coverage, such coverage litigation was a foreseeable result of their alleged negligence in fulfilling this purpose.

In short, the complaint properly alleges multiple causes of appellants' losses. * * * Finally, even assuming the causes of action against respondents could be viewed as alternative pleadings to primary claims alleged against NAS, such that their viability was dependent upon the outcome of the claims against NAS, there are additional reasons why the judgment on the pleadings was not well taken. It is well established that "a party may plead in the alternative and may make inconsistent allegations." However, the trial court dismissed appellants' "alternative" claims based on nothing more than its prior order finding NAS had a duty to defend. In this respect, the judgment on the pleadings was tantamount to a ruling that appellants were collaterally estopped from arguing they did not enjoy full coverage under the NAS policy for the *Cadogan* suit. Although respondents carefully avoid mentioning the doctrine, their assertions that appellants' claims against them are "precluded" or "barred" by the NAS order raise concerns typically addressed in the context of res judicata or collateral estoppel. But, just as the trial court's NAS ruling was not binding on all parties under the law of the case doctrine—a point Near North concedes on appeal -it also could not have a preclusive effect on claims appellants alleged against respondents for their independent breaches of duty. First, the order granting summary adjudication was not necessarily a final ruling. "While an insured may obtain an early summary adjudication of a defense obligation, the insurer is entitled to seek a contrary ruling at *any time* it acquires the requisite evidence to conclusively eliminate any potential for coverage." * * * Second, the ruling may not have been entitled to collateral estoppel effect because the parties settled before trial. "A settlement which avoids trial generally does not constitute actually litigating any issues and thus prevents application of collateral estoppel. [Citations.][noting "a consent judgment is not usually given preclusive effect in subsequent litigation on a different cause of action, unless the parties manifest an intent in the consent judgment to give it such preclusive effect"].)

II. *Attorney Fees in Pursuing Coverage May Be Recovered as Damages*

In granting respondents' motion for judgment on the pleadings, the trial court also denied appellants' claim for attorney fees in pursuing coverage from NAS. This ruling was erroneous because appellants are entitled to seek such fees as an item of damages caused by respondents' alleged negligence. * * * "Under California law, it is a well-established principle that attorney fees incurred through instituting or defending an action as a direct result of the tort of another are recoverable damages. Attorney fees in this context are to be distinguished from "attorney's fees *qua* attorney's fees," such as those the plaintiff incurs in suing the tortfeasor defendant. Rather, when a defendant's tortious conduct requires the plaintiff to sue a third party, or defend a suit brought by a third party, attorney fees the plaintiff incurs in this third party action "are recoverable as damages resulting from a tort in the same way that medical fees would be part of the damages in a personal injury action." The "tort of another" doctrine has been applied to permit recovery of attorneys fees resulting from an insurer's tortious conduct, and we see no reason why it should not also apply to fees incurred as a result of an insurance broker's alleged negligence.

As a result of respondents' allegedly negligent failure to advise appellants about the FELE and the need for errors and omissions insurance, appellants were required to sue NAS for coverage. Appellants allege that if they had been competently advised they would have obtained an errors and omissions policy, which would have provided more definite coverage for the *Cadogan* action. Because they had no errors and omissions policy to rely on, appellants were required to litigate coverage with NAS as a direct result of respondents' alleged negligence; thus, the attorney fees and costs incurred in the coverage litigation may be recovered as damages if appellants prevail in their claims against respondents.

For reasons already discussed, the fact that NAS's denial of coverage *also* caused appellants to incur fees and costs in the coverage litigation does not absolve respondents of their own responsibility for damages proximately caused by their negligence. The trier of fact is presumably capable of apportioning responsibility for these losses among NAS and the respondents. Nor is there a problem because the attorney fees were incurred in the same lawsuit in which appellants now seek their recovery. The Supreme Court long ago observed: "In the usual case, the attorney's fees will have been incurred in connection with a prior action; but there is no reason why recovery of such fees should be denied simply because the two causes (the one against the third person and the one against the party whose breach of duty made it necessary for the plaintiff to sue the third person) are tried in the same court at the same time." More recently, the high court stated: "The fact that . . . the fees claimed as damages are incurred in the very lawsuit in which their recovery is sought, does not in itself violate [Code of Civil Procedure] section 1021's general requirement that parties bear their own costs of legal representation, though it may make the identification of allowable fees more sophisticated." Allowable attorney fees and costs here must be limited to only those attributable to appellants' pursuit of coverage against NAS, and may not include amounts expended litigating their claims against respondents. With appropriate instructions, we presume the trier of fact is capable of making such an allocation.

The judgment is reversed. Respondents shall bear costs of the appeal.

NOTES AND QUESTIONS

(1) What exactly is the standard for brokers set forth by *Third Eye Blind* Court? What did the broker do wrong? What should it have done better (or done at all)?

(2) Brokers have a responsibility to understand the needs of a policyhold-er-client sufficiently well so that they attempt to procure coverage appropri-ate to the client's needs. What do the "advertising injury" and "personal injury" coverages provide to a policyholder? Does every business require such coverage? When might it make sense to except exclusions or sublimits on such coverage or even forego it altogether? (Of course, since Coverage B is part of ISO's standardized CGL, it will be hard-to-impossible to per-suade an insurer to sell coverage limited to Part A in return for a reduced premium).

(3) Beyond conventional norms (e.g., an advertising agency should have advertising injury coverage), brokers also take specific direction from clients and seek to procure coverage specifically requested by the client. Usually, the client's request comes after consultation with the broker, who has a duty to use reasonable care and offer reasonable advice regarding insurance needs and potentially available products. But what if the client wants only a skeletal product that the broker thinks is inadequate? Should the broker refuse and perhaps even resign? Conversely, what if the client wants more insurance than it reasonably needs? Should the broker merely follow orders or refuse to aid and abet overinsurance? Does it make a difference if the broker is compensated in whole or in part by commissions paid by insurers who accept a client solicitation by the broker? What should the broker be telling the client about its commission arrangements (even in the absence of Eliot Spitzer)?

(4) Brokers attempt to obtain insurer subscription to the commercial policyholder's proposed insurance program? What if an insufficient number of insurers (or perhaps no insurers) are willing to participate at reasonable premium prices? What should the broker do then?

(5) Brokers are also responsible for pulling together the documentation of an insurance program and keeping records for the client. As discussed above, the broker may propose a program designed for the individual client's needs and even provides a broker-drafted form to use as the template for the program, with participating insurers using or following the broker's form. But the actual policy forms will then be issued by the insurer under its own name. Commonly, insurers will want to use their own format and language for at least some aspects of the insurance. For example, the insurer may want to use slightly different language for some exclusions because its reinsurers insist on the particularly language. Or the insurer may have its own language regarding the form of notice or proof of claim. These differences from the followed policy should not be material unless specifically negotiated and agreed to by the parties because the standard operating procedure for placing commercial risks is that insurers participating in a program agree to follow the program, which can be based on a broker-provided form, a standardized ISO or ACCORD form, or a selected primary insurance policy that serves as the building block of the program. When policies begin to flow (or trickle) into the broker, which may take weeks or months after the initial agreement, what should a broker

do if the insurer's policy forms are at variance with the followed policy? How quickly must the broker act? What if the insurer refuses to revise problematic language that arguably effects a material change in the insuring agreement or is otherwise inconsistent with the program?

(6) Because advertising involves media, technological changes can produce new varieties of claims. For example, the invention of the fax machine enabled mass advertising by "junk faxes" akin to junk mail, which in turn spawned litigation by recipients of the unwanted faxes against the senders of junk faxes. Most courts have found that such claims are covered under the advertising injury provisions of the CGL policy absent a specific junk fax exclusion. *See, e.g., Park University Enter., Inc. v. American Cas. Co.*, 442 F.3d 1239 (10th Cir. 2006) (applying Kansas law) (transmission of fax is publication of advertisement and its receipt can constitute invasion of recipient's privacy; CGL insurer must defend junk fax claim against policyholder); *Hooters of Augusta, Inc. v. American Global Ins. Co.*, 2005 U.S. App. LEXIS 26765 (11th Cir. Dec. 6, 2005) (applying Georgia law) (same; generalize "publishing liability exclusion" does not negate coverage because insuring agreement trumps exclusion where rules of construction require strict interpretation against insurer bearing burden of persuasion as to exclusion's applicability); *Valley Forge Ins. Co. v. Swiderski Elec., Inc.*, 834 N.E.2d 562 (Ill. Ct. App. 2005), *appeal granted*, 844 N.E.2d 972 (Ill. 2006) (same; volitional sending of faxes does not in itself make policy's "expected or intended injury" exclusion applicable; insurer bears burden to demonstrate that policyholder sent fax with subjective intent of inflicting injury).

§ 11.17　ADDITIONAL TYPES OF LIABILITY COVERAGE

This Chapter has focused on general liability insurance because it is by far the most common and commonly litigated type of liability insurance. In a basic casebook of finite length (although the book may seem interminable to you at this point in the semester), it would be hard to justify any different approach. But be aware that there are other types of liability insurance that are also pervasive, important, and the source of many coverage disputes.

[A]　Errors and Omissions Insurance

Errors and Omissions Insurance ("E&O") insurance is, as the name implies, insurance that covers professionals or quasi-professionals for mistakes of professional judgment (or lack of judgment) that injure their clients/customers. For example, the broker in the *Third Eye Blind/Hooters of Augusta* case in § 11.16 probably has E & O insurance. Like CGL insurance, E & O coverage generally includes a duty to defend claims and attempt to defeat or settle them without trial. The broker in *Third Eye Blind/Hooters of Augusta* may even have been defended by its E & O carrier.

Unlike CGL insurance, E & O coverage is more commonly written on a claims-made basis (see § 11.15) and the costs expended on defense are more commonly subtracted from the policy limits available to settle claims or pay judgments against the policyholder. This is "defense within limits" or "burning limits" coverage as contrasted with the "defense outside of limits" coverage typically available in general liability policies. Many of the other types of more specialized liability policies, particularly professional liability policies, are likely to share the claims-made and burning limits policies found in E & O policies.

What rationales might support such differences? Does the presence of burning limits create additional opportunities for insurer bad faith or misjudgment? How? *See generally* Gregory S. Munro, *Defense Within Limits: The Conflicts of "Wasting" or "Cannibalizing" Insurance Policies Hooters of Augusta*, 62 MONT. L. REV. 131 (2001).

[B]   Professional Liability

Professional liability or malpractice insurance is sold to doctors, lawyers, and other professionals. Like D & O insurance, it is commonly sold on a claims-made basis and may or may not have burning limits regarding defense costs. The primary coverage battlegrounds in reported cases involves intentional infliction of harm to a patient or client or the question of whether a professional's misconduct was part of the mis-rendering of professional services or was instead simply tortuous conduct that took place outside the professional role and was merely committed by a tortfeasor who happened to be a lawyer or doctor. An example of the former category is assault and battery or fraud by the professional. An example of the latter is the professional defaming a client or having an affair that leads to charges of alienation of affections by the wronged spouse.

[C]   Directors and Officers Liability Insurance

Directors and Officers Liability ("D & O") Insurance is again a product that does what its name suggests: defense and insure directors and officers of corporations or similar business entities. For reasons related to corporate law, securities law, and business torts, directors and officers are often named as defendants in suits stemming from alleged corporate wrongdoing. The phenomenon stems from the nature of the business entity, which is its own legal "person" but which is actually run by its constituents: officers, directors, middle managers, lawyers, accountants, and other workers. When a rank-and-file worker makes a mistake, this most likely leads to a general liability claim as when the company driver is in an accident or a factor produces adulterated food or beverages. But where corporate misfeasance is found, this usually involves upper management and directors. Contemporary news accounts of the great corporate collapses of the early 21st Century suggest that much of the directors' contribution or fault may stem from being inattentive or too compliant with management while officers such as the late Kenneth Lay, Jeffrey Skilling and Andrew Fastow are more likely to be the active perpetrators of corporate wrongdoing.

A significant number of claims against businesses involve something far milder than the raptors of Enron. For example, a company may be sued over an allegedly misleading proxy statement or press release, particularly if the company proves not to have been as close to FDA approval of a wonder drug, obtaining of oil leases in Mineralistan, etc. Plaintiff and Defense lawyers and their respective allies continue to argue over the merits and worth of such suits. Plaintiffs argue that corporate misstatement works fraud on the market and injures investors while defendants characterize many of these suits as raids by voracious lawyers seeking compensation that will go in large part to the lawyers simply because a company has not performed as well as indicated. Regarding the politics of business liability and the frequency of corporate wrongdoing, both sides can claim victory. Plaintiffs have the Sarbanes-Oxley Act of 2002 while defendants have the Private Securities Litigation Reform Act of 1995, the Securities Law Uniform Standards Act of 1998, and (at least to a degree) the Class Action Reform Act of 2005. *See generally* Jeffrey W. Stempel, *Class Actions and Limited Vision, Opportunities for Improvement Through a More Functional Approach to Class Treatment of Issues*, 83 WASH. U. L.Q. 1127, 1139-1154 (2006) (reviewing legislation and public policy debate over utility of class actions against businesses).

Whatever the merits of the respective positions in this ongoing debate, the fact remains that there remains much litigation directed at both allegedly errant companies and their directors and officers. Consequently, there is a brisk market for D & O insurance (which got even better after Sarbanes-Oxley). Premiums per amount of coverage are comparatively high and policyholders may have substantial retentions but few companies of any size go without it. Modern D & O policies typically provide coverage in one section for the individual directors and officers while in another section providing coverage for the corporate entity itself, although many policies in force still follow the traditional approach of insuring the individual directors and officers only. The distinction is important because a typical securities class action or business wrongdoing claim will have multiple counts, some against only individuals, some against the entity, some against all, and some against others such as outside accountants, lawyers, or bankers. Because most litigation settles, there can be significant battles over how much of a settlement is subject to applicable D & O Insurance. *See Hooters of Augusta Stempel on Insurance ContractsHooters of Augusta* § 19.06.

In addition to battles over allocation and apportionment regarding settlement, there are of course straight out coverage battles. For example, D & O insurance, like general liability insurance, typically excludes coverage for intentionally inflicted injury or criminal wrongdoing, which presents definitional problems akin to general liability battles over the intentional act exclusion. In addition, a single claim may present elements of both negligence and worse. D & O policies can have either a duty to defend or a duty to reimburse the policyholder for defense costs. In the latter situation, there can be issues regarding the reasonableness of defense costs and the timing of reimbursement. Like E & O coverage, D & O coverage is normally written on a claims-made basis and a "defense within limits" basis. *See generally Stempel on Insurance Contracts*, § 19.01.

[D] Environmental Claims Liability Insurance

As discussed in §§ 11.13 and 11.14, the issue of general liability coverage for pollution and environmental cleanup claims has been a major battleground during the past 25 years even though the standard CGL policy has since 1986 contained an "absolute" pollution exclusion. Litigation continues both because some claims involve older policies without the exclusion (remember, groundwater contamination can take place for decades before it is noticed) and because some cases present divisive issues of whether the exclusion properly applies (e.g., carbon monoxide poisoning from a leaky furnace; toxic fumes from construction work, chemical burns from handling equipment).

For the most part, however, the absolute pollution exclusion has been effective in doing what the insurance industry intended to do: bar general liability coverage for waste disposal, contamination, and cleanup claims. As a result, a policyholder that has exposures in these areas cannot expect coverage from its CGL policy. To have coverage, the policyholder will need to either "buy" its way out of the exclusion by paying a higher premium in return for an endorsement excising the exclusion or will need to procure a separate policy covering environmental pollution and related claims. These types of policies are available as separate purchases, typically with relatively high premiums and low policy limits in relation to general liability policies. This is perhaps expected. A reasonable insurer approached by BelchCo, a smelting company, undoubtedly knows that the prospective policyholder is seeking this separate coverage because it knows it presents a larger than normal risk in this area. A local bookstore is unlikely to present such claims, no matter how bad the coffee produced by its attached cafe.

Like other liability products thought to involve higher than normal risks, environmental claims policies tend to be written on a claims basis and defense within limits. They may also have a high policyholder retention and specific exclusions. For example, InsureCo may be willing to insure most of BelchCo's operations but not the infamous Kill City facility that has old technology and is already under investigation by the EPA. In writing coverage, InsureCo would use a specific exclusion to "laser-out" coverage for any liabilities arising out of the operations of the Kill City plant.

[E] Employer's Liability, Workers Compensation, and Employment Practices Insurance

General liability insurance is structured to protect the policyholder from claims by third parties. Employees of an insured company may or may not be third parties, depending on the claim and one's point of view. Certainly, insurers do not view the CGL policy as providing coverage for employment-related claims and it contains exclusions designed to avoid coverage for employee claims. The notion is that employee claims should be under a different insurance product. Historically, Employers' Liability ("EL") or Workers' Compensation ("WC") policies have been those products, although there are occasionally worker claims held to fall within CGL coverage. Over time, insurers have revised the CGL to make this less likely. *See Stempel on Insurance Contracts* § 21.02. Consequently, the EL and WC coverages of a company are important to protecting it from employee claims. In addition, because claims of race and gender discrimination are not usually covered under these policies, a relatively recent product, employment practices liaiblity ("EPL") has come into the market with some force.

[1] Workers' Compensation

Workers' compensation insurance generally tracks the workers' compensation statutes in effect in the employer's state and sets forth the benefits the employer must pay. Employer liability for on-the-job injuries is strict and without regard to fault but the WC insurer has a right to investigate and defend claims. Certain defenses such as "serious and willful misconduct" are available. For example, if a factory worker is horsing around and injures himself trying to do a triple somersault into a cleaning vat, this probably is not covered (but remember, each case is different as are state laws and court decisions). Similarly, if the worker throws out his shoulder attempting to hit a co-worker, this is probably not covered. However, the same worker who burns his hand on a sodering iron is typically covered under WC insurance. Injury from clear violation of health and safety laws may also be excluded. *See generally* ARTHUR LARSON & LEX K. LARSON, LARSON'S WORKERS' COMPENSATION LAW (2002); PETER J. KALIS, THOMAS M. REITER & JAMES R. SEGERDAHL, POLICYHOLDER'S GUIDE TO THE LAW OF INSURANCE COVERAGE § 12.02 (1997).

A major source of much workers' compensation litigation is the question of whether the employee was acting within the scope of his or her employment when injured. If the answer is "yes," then the employee is covered by WC insurance, which also means under the statutes of nearly every state that recovery against the employer is limited to WC benefits, although other entities contributing to the injury might also be sued in tort. One explanation for the popularity of product liability actions against manufacturers is that injured workers may receive relatively modest WC benefits when injured at work while using a manufacturer's equipment. As a means of seeking additional compensation, the rational worker might be more inclined to also blame the product maker for the injury. Like much in litigation, this is a two-edged sword. A jury might have no trouble finding the worker seriously injured but find the product liability claim farfetched if the injury appears to result clearly from an unsafe workplace rather than a defectively designed or manufactured product. What most lay jurors do not know, of course, is that the employer cannot be sued in tort and that the employer's liability is cabined by the WC statute and benefits.

If the answer about on the job injury is "no," of course, then WC insurance is not applicable and the injured worker must pursue other avenues of relief. In some cases, an injury may not be job related for purposes of WC coverage but may result in a court action implicating CGL coverage or other insurance held by the employer or another entity arguably responsible for the worker's injury. In such cases, the respective insurers may have adverse interests and argue for different characterizations of whether the injury was sufficiently work-related to be subject to WC treatment. For example, if a worker is injured while attending a business "team building" exercise involving white water rafting during a conference/meeting at a hotel/resort, the WC insurer may argue that this is not a work-related injury while the CGL carrier will argue that it was. Depending on the answer, a different insurer may pay and the amount recoverable may vary. In addition, the nature of employer immunities frequently found in WC statutes can create some arguable gaps in coverage. *See, e.g., Bias v. Eastern Associated Coal Corp.*, 2006 W. Va. LEXIS 43 (W. Va. June 8, 2006.)

NOTES AND QUESTIONS

(1) Remember that workers' compensation was enacted in the late 19th and early 20th Centuries in order to provide workers with a remedy because the tort law of the time, which had strong employer defenses based on assumption of risk and the fellow servant rule, made recovery in tort very difficult for workers at a time when workplaces were far more dangerous than today. Has a century of business evolution made workers' compensation an unwitting enemy of the worker? Are revisions to the system in order?

(2) Alternatively, employers and insurers frequently argue that WC insurance has become excessively costly because its no-fault premise and broad coverage make it easy for malingering workers to claim injury, prevail on dubious claims, and extend their absences through over-extended recuperation and rehabilitation periods (with expensive physical therapy or other treatment). Without doubt, WC insurance premium are relatively high compared to other forms of liability insurance even though WC benefits are set by a schedule rather than ad hoc by courts or juries. Does this mean workplace injury is still too frequent in society? That workers are taking unfair advantage? That insurers are overpricing the product or failing to control and monitor claims? During the 2002 California gubernatorial campaign, then-candidate Arnold Schwartzenegger actually used WC insurance rates as a campaign issue, making reform to lower rates part of his platform. What is the current state of political debate, if any, regarding workers' compensation in your state?

[2] Employers' Liability Insurance

EL insurance is designed to protect the employer against liability from traditional physical injury torts that may be brought by an employee and wall outside of WC coverage. EL insurance is designed to fill gaps between the basic WC policy and CGL coverage. Consequently, it is not unusual to see these policies sold as a package or at least assembled as a package by the policyholder's broker in order to attempt to avoid gaps in coverage. *See Stempel on Insurance Contracts* § 21.03.

[3] Employment Practices Liability Insurance

EPL insurance is designed to provided defense against and indemnity for the non-traditional liability for worker claims alleging discrimination. Recall that prior to the 1964 Civil Rights Act, race, gender, and religious discrimination by private employers was perfectly legal. Although a few reactionaries seem to want to return to this state of the world, there is little dispute that liability for discrimination is here to stay, which means that a demand for insurance is probably here to stay as well. *See* James B. Dolan, Jr., *The Growing Significance of Employment Practices Liability Insurance*, THE BRIEF (Winter 2005) at 30. EPL insurance products became significantly available in the mid-1990s and initially could be had only for relatively low limits at high premiums. Since then, the product has become more affordable and protective. Regarding EPL coverage generally, see CLARANCE E. HAGGLUND, BRITTON D. WEIMER, T. MICHAEL SPEIDEL & ANDREW F. WHITMAN, EMPLOYMENT PRACTICES LIABILITY: GUIDE TO RISK EXPOSURES & COVERAGE (1998); ANDREW KAPLAN, RACHEL MCKINNEY, BETH A. SCHROEDER & LEONARD SURDYK, THE EPL BOOK: A PRACTICAL GUIDE TO EMPLOYMENT PRACTICES LIABILITY AND INSURANCE (1997); Barbara A. O'Donnell, *The First Wave of Decisions Interpreting Employment Practices Liability Policies*, THE BRIEF (Fall 2005) at 39.

In addition, EPL insurance, like Boiler & Machinery insurance (see *Stempel on Insurance Contracts* § 22.04), can have a preventive effect in reducing the number of claims against the employer by spotting potential problems before they turn into actual losses or claims. Before a B & M insurer will provide coverage, it has its expert engineers inspect the machinery to be insured. If the machinery is suffering from material defects, the insurer will not write B & M coverage. However, the prospective policyholder now knows that Boiler No. 3 needs to be repaired or replaced before it can get insurance. Fixing Boilder No. 3 now is ordinarily much less expensive than having it explode in the middle of manufacturing operations. Many policyholders purchase B & M coverage in order to obtain the inspection as much as for the coverage. Similarly, a wise EPL insurer will not write discrimination coverage until it is assured that the policyholder has in place adequate anti-discrimination protocols and procedures by which an employee may seek help if harassed on the job.

Like other policies, EPL insurance may be written with a specified exclusion for claims arising out of a certain facility or from the actions of a particular person. For example, the insurer's investigation may reveal that the Bugtussle office of AcmeCo is a little Peyton Place awash in inter-office affairs. Even if the liaisons started as consensual, these things have a way of leading to sexual harassment claims. Similarly, former regional manager Bill Bigot may have just been forced out of the company after his membership in the Aryan Nations came to light. Even if Bigot no longer works for Acme, he may have engaged in acts of discrimination that will lead to claims during the policy period. In such cases, a prudent EPL insurer would either demand a higher premium or by endorsement exclude claims related to Bigot or the Bugtussle office.

[F] Suretyship

Suretyship is an agreement in which one contracting party agrees to act in the event of a contingency. As a result, it is often considered to be the equivalent of insurance and at other times considered distinct from insurance. Although "either too much or too little can be made of the technical differences between surety ship and insurance," traditional orthodoxy of insurance has posited that the two differ primarily in that:

(a) the surety bond involves three parties (surety, principal, and obligee) while the insurance policy involves two parties (insurer and insured), although with liability insurance third party claimants are always waiting in the wings. This may be important for purposes of "its effect on misrepresentation, concealment, or other fraud." The fraud of a contractor, unlike the fraud of a co-insured, cannot extinguish the surety's liability. "Only when principal and obligee conspire to defraud the surety will fraud void the surety arrangement."

(b) the surety arrangement generally permits the surety to seek indemnity from a contractor whose negligence caused the default requiring the surety to pay. By contrast, the insurer usually has no claim for indemnity or other relief (e.g., subrogation) as a result of negligence on the party of the policyholder. "The ability to seek reimbursement for losses from its own insured is an important distinction between suretyship and insurance."

See MARK S. DORFMAN,, INTRODUCTION TO RISK MANAGEMENT AND INSURANCE 410-11 (7th ed. 2002) (boldface in original). *See also Surety Underwriters v. E & C Trucking, Inc.*, 10 P.3d 338 (Utah 2000) (contract under which surety agreed to issue $50,000 bond if obligor gave surety consideration was "insurance contract" under Utah law and required license for engaging in such business; absent license, contract was unenforceable.

Neither of these traditional distinctions, however important, bears on the question of whether sureties should be liable for bad faith conduct toward the policyholder, an issues that has divided courts. The distinctions, or lack thereof, between suretyship and insurance may become important to questions of regulation and liability. It has become particularly important in recent years because of differing precedent over the issue of whether a

bad faith claim can be made against a surety as it can be made against
a conventional insurer.

In general, the rules and norms of contract construction applicable to
insurance policies are also applicable to surety agreements. At the margin,
however, the surety agreement may be more strictly construed by some
courts in order to protect the interests of the surety. Historically, a surety
has been described as a "favorite of the law." However, that maxim arose
at a time when sureties were usually individual guarantors rather than
the large insurance companies that act as sureties today.

The modern insurer-surety accepts risk transfer and spreads contingent
risk much in the manner of a conventional insurer. As a result, judicial
treatment of insurance and suretyship appears to be converging, including
attendant bad faith exposure for sureties. Sureties and their counsel,
however, usually argue with considerable success that sureties are different
than insurers and should be immunized from bad faith and punitive
damages exposure. The principal or obligor of a surety payment or performance bond will argue to the contrary where it believes it has been treated
with bad faith by a surety. The recent judicial trend generally favors
permitting insurance-like bad faith claims against sureties but the jurisdictions remain divided.

As you read the case below, ask yourself which view of surety bad faith
liability is more persuasive. *See generally* Troy J. Harris, *Good Faith,
Suretyship, and the Ius Commune*, 53 MERCER L. REV. 581 (2002); Aron
J. Frakes, Note, *Surety Bad Faith: Tort Recovery for Breach of a Construction Performance Bond*, 2002 U. ILL. L. REV. 497 (2002). *See also Stempel
on Insurance Contracts* § 22.13.

TRANSAMERICA PREMIER INSURANCE COMPANY v. BRIGHTON SCHOOL DISTRICT 27J

940 P.2d 348 (Colo. 1997)

CHIEF JUSTICE VOLLACK delivered the Opinion of the Court.

We granted certiorari to review the court of appeals decision to determine
whether Colorado recognizes the existence of a common law tort claim
against a commercial surety who fails to reasonably proceed with the
payment of a claim under a performance bond. The court of appeals held
that the trial court did not err in submitting an obligee's bad faith claim
to the jury. We conclude that allowing this cause of action to proceed in
the commercial surety context is justified by the special nature of the suretyship agreement and by the reasoning set forth in our prior decisions
authorizing bad faith actions against insurers. For this reason, we affirm
the court of appeals.

I.

On May 13, 1991, Brighton School District 27J (the school district)
entered into a contract with Adco Mechanical Contractors, Inc. (Adco) to

perform the mechanical work on a construction project at Brighton High School. Pursuant to section 38-26-106(1), 16A C.R.S. (1982), Adco provided the school district with a performance bond on which Transamerica Premier Insurance Company (Transamerica) agreed to act as commercial surety to guarantee Adco's performance under its contract with the school district.

Adco began work on the project in June of 1991 and soon fell behind schedule. The construction manager and the school district repeatedly advised Adco of the need to proceed on schedule, but Adco fell further behind and continued to miss deadlines throughout the winter of 1991-92. Adco was also notified both orally and in writing that various problems with its work had been discovered, but it failed to address most of these problems. On April 30, 1992, solder, wood chips, and rocks were discovered in a unit ventilator which controlled the temperature in one of the classrooms. Further inspection revealed numerous instances of Adco's incomplete or defective work as well as repeated failures to comply with the architect's drawings and specifications. Following its investigation, the school district gave Adco written notice on May 19, 1992, that it had been removed from the project. That same day, the school district filed a claim with Transamerica on the performance bond. Adco filed suit on June 8, 1992, in Adams County District Court, alleging that the school district violated the terms of the construction contract.

The school district met with Transamerica representatives on June 10, 1992, to devise a remedial plan to correct the errors in Adco's work. At the meeting, the school district stressed the importance of completing the remedial project by the start of the 1992-93 school year. A Transamerica representative stated that the school district was proceeding properly and expressed Transamerica's desire to have the school district obtain between three and five bids for the remedial work. * * * On June 29, 1992, the school district filed an answer, counterclaim, and third-party complaint asserting breach of warranty, breach of contract, negligence, and fraud claims against Adco and asserting that Transamerica had breached the terms of the performance bond by not performing its commercial surety obligations.

* * *

In Colorado, every contract contains an implied duty of good faith and fair dealing. Actions based upon a breach of this duty were traditionally limited to contract damages because the duty of good faith and fair dealing concerned the faithful performance of a contract's terms. * * * "The motivation of the insured when entering into an insurance contract differs from that of parties entering into an ordinary commercial contract. By obtaining insurance, an insured seeks to obtain some measure of financial security and protection against calamity, rather than to secure commercial advantage. The refusal of the insurer to pay valid claims without justification, however, defeats the expectations of the insured and the purpose of the insurance contract. It is therefore necessary to impose a legal duty upon the insurer to deal with its insured in good faith." * * * In Travelers Insurance Co. v. Savio (Colo. 1985), we extended the "basic rationale" of Trimble to authorize actions in tort where an insurer was alleged to have handled a first-party workers' compensation claim in bad faith. We noted that, "since workers compensation serves [**8] the same purpose as insurance in general, the Trimble rationale demands that the provider of such compensation deal fairly and in good faith with an employee asserting a compensable injury." We also elaborated on the proper standard for evaluating such claims as follows:

In the first-party context an insurer acts in bad faith in delaying the processing of or denying a valid claim when the insurer's conduct is unreasonable and the insurer knows that the conduct is unreasonable or recklessly disregards the fact that the conduct is unreasonable. * * * Section 38-26-106(1), 16A C.R.S. (1982), provides that every contractor that is awarded a public works contract for more than $50,000 must submit a performance bond executed by a qualified commercial surety to the public entity in charge of the project. Under the terms of the performance bond, in the event the contractor (the principal) fails to fulfill its obligations to the public entity (the obligee) under the public works contract, the commercial surety must guarantee performance and/or satisfy debts resulting from unpaid labor and materials.

The issue in this case concerns whether we should extend our [insuer bad faith] holdings to include situations in which a commercial surety company fails to act in good faith when processing claims made by an obligee pursuant to the terms of a performance bond. We conclude that the rationale for providing insureds with a cause of action in tort for an insurer's bad faith in processing a claim applies with equal force in the commercial surety context. * * * We have previously explained that commercial sureties receiving consideration for the issuance of surety bonds serve a purpose similar to that of insurers: "Generally speaking, a contract of suretyship by a surety company is governed by the same rules as the contracts of other sureties, but some distinctions are made by the courts in construing such contracts. The doctrine that a surety is a favorite of the law, and that a claim against him is strictissimi juris, does not apply where the bond or undertaking is executed upon a consideration by a corporation organized to make such bonds or undertakings for profit. While such corporations may call themselves 'surety companies,' their business is in all essential particulars that of insurers."

The insurance statutes reflect a legislative intent to include sureties as part of the regulatory scheme governing insurance. Section 10-1-102(8), 4A C.R.S. (1994), defines the term "insurer" as "every person engaged as principal, indemnitor, surety, or contractor in the business of making contracts of insurance." Similarly, section 10-3-1102(2), 4A C.R.S. (1994), of the Deceptive Practices Statute, §§ 10-3-1101 to -1114, 4A C.R.S. (1994 & 1996 Supp.), defines the terms "insurance policy" and "insurance contract" to include suretyship agreements. The Deceptive Practices Statute expressly prohibits unfair claim settlement practices and lists a variety of penal measures available in the event a commercial surety engages in unfair settlement practices. See § 10-3-1104(h), 4A C.R.S. (1994); § 10-3-1108, 4A C.R.S. (1994). Furthermore, section 10-3-1113(1), 4A C.R.S. (1994), provides: "In any civil action for damages founded upon contract, or tort, or both against an insurance company, the trier of fact may be instructed that the insurer owes its insured the duty of good faith and fair dealing, which duty is breached if the insurer delays or denies payment without a reasonable basis for its delay or denial." These statutes indicate persuasive legislative support for treating a commercial surety contract as a form of insurance agreement and for treating a commercial surety which fails to settle its obligations in good faith in the same way that our tort law treats insurers who process a claim in bad faith.

More specifically, most other jurisdictions that have considered this issue have recognized a separate cause of action in tort for a commercial surety's bad faith in processing claims made under a surety bond. * * * We agree with the reasoning of those cases which authorize a bad faith cause of action in the commercial surety context and conclude that a similar result in the present case represents a logical extension of our [insurer bad faith precedents].

A special relationship exists between a commercial surety and an obligee that is nearly identical to that involving an insurer and an insured. When an obligee requests that a principal obtain a commercial surety bond to guarantee the principal's performance, the obligee is essentially insuring itself from the potentially catastrophic losses that would result in the event the principal defaults on its original obligation. When the principal actually defaults, the commercial surety must assume or correct any flaws in performance pursuant to the terms of the original contract, thereby eliminating the obligee's risk of loss in the venture.

Although the parties to a suretyship agreement are on equal footing in terms of bargaining power when they enter into the agreement, it is the commercial surety who controls the ultimate decision of whether to pay claims made by the obligee under the terms of the surety bond. For this reason, the commercial surety has a distinct advantage over the obligee in its ability to control performance under the secondary agreement. As with insurers, commercial sureties must proceed with the payment of claims made pursuant to a surety bond in good faith. Otherwise, the core purpose of the suretyship agreement, which is to insulate the obligee from the risk of a default, is defeated.

Recognizing a cause of action in tort for a commercial surety's breach of its duty to act in good faith compels commercial sureties to handle claims responsibly. When the commercial surety withholds payment of an obligee's claim in bad faith, contract damages do not compensate the obligee for the commercial surety's misconduct and have no deterrent effect to prevent such misconduct in the future. As the Arizona Supreme Court explained in Dodge, contract damages "offer no motivation whatsoever for the insurer not to breach. If the only damages an insurer will have to pay upon a judgment of breach are the amounts that it would have owed under the policy plus interest, it has every interest in retaining the money, earning the higher rates of interest on the outside market, and hoping eventually to force the insured into a settlement for less than the policy amount."

Transamerica argues that the unique features of suretyship distinguish it from insurance and that the suretyship agreement is, in essence, a financial service. We disagree. As explained above, the suretyship agreement provides the obligee with financial security by eliminating the risk of default in the original agreement between the principal and the obligee. While there may be differences in the form of the suretyship agreement and the obligations of the parties, its substance is essentially the same as insurance.

[In footnote 4, the Court noted that "We recognize that the commercial surety is put in an awkward position in handling simultaneous claims made by the principal and the obligee. The Supreme Court of Hawaii has explained the surety's dilemma as follows:

Clearly, the surety owes a duty of good faith and fair dealing to both the principal and the obligee on the bond. If the surety pays too quickly to the obligee, it may invite liability claims from the principal. Conversely, if it refuses to pay anything pending an arbitration or judicial proceeding to determine its liability on the bond, the surety may incur liability to the obligee for failing to act promptly on a valid claim. Although the commercial surety's obligations may be more complex than those of an insurer, this complexity does not authorize a commercial surety to disregard its obligation to act in good faith.]

[In footnote 5, the Court stated: "In Suver v. Personal Service Insurance Co., the Supreme Court of Ohio elaborated on the differences and similarities between insurers and sureties as follows: "It is true that a financial responsibility bond is not the same as an insurance policy and that a surety is not an insurer and may therefore act in its own interest. But the nature of the differences between the two is neither complete nor absolute. Rather, the financial responsibility bond and the insurance policy differ primarily in whom they protect and to whom the duty runs. . . .These differences are not so pronounced as to require the creation of a cause of action in one case and its denial in the other. Precisely the same policy arguments and rationale hold true in both settings. . . . Moreover, to insulate the issuer of a financial responsibility bond from liability for the deliberate refusal to pay its obligations arising from the bond is to encourage the routine denial of payment of claims for as long as possible. This court should not provide an incentive to act in bad faith."]

Accordingly, we hold that Colorado common law recognizes a cause of action in tort for a commercial surety's failure to act in good faith when processing claims made by an obligee pursuant to the terms of a performance bond. In evaluating these causes of action, we adopt the rule . . . .

that a commercial surety acts in bad faith when the surety's conduct is unreasonable and the surety knows that the conduct is unreasonable or recklessly disregards the fact that its conduct is unreasonable. By imposing this legal duty on the commercial surety, our holding ensures that the expectations of the obligee and the purposes of the suretyship agreement are given effect while recognizing the surety's right to refuse invalid claims.

JUSTICE KOURLIS dissenting:

The majority recognizes a common law cause of action in tort for a commercial surety's failure to act in good faith when processing claims made by an obligee pursuant to the terms of a performance bond. In support of that result, the majority concludes that "the rationale for providing insureds with a cause of action in tort for an insurer's bad faith in processing a claim applies with equal force in the commercial surety context." Because I believe that there are essential differences between the surety/obligee relationship and the insurer/insured relationship, I would decline to recognize a bad faith claim in this case. Therefore, I respectfully dissent.

* * *

We have predicated the existence of a special relationship upon various factors, including quasi-fiduciary obligations, protection against unforeseeable loss, and unequal bargaining power. In my view, none of those factors exist in the suretyship context. Specifically, Transamerica did not have a quasi-fiduciary obligation to the school district; Transamerica was not insuring the school district against an unforeseeable calamity, but rather against a completely foreseeable possibility; and the school district was not hampered by an unequal bargaining position, but could have contracted for whatever remedies it felt were necessary to protect against possible loss. Therefore, the elements of a special relationship are not present.

Additionally, I disagree with the extension of the remedy because it does not provide a clear stopping point. For example, although the majority limits its opinion to commercial sureties, the reasoning could extend to guarantors and bondsmen who also provide financial security by assuring payment in the event of a party's default on an agreement, thereby subjecting those guarantors or bondsmen to the possibility of a bad faith tort cause of action in addition to their contractual liabilities for failure to perform their obligations. * * * For those reasons, I would limit the school district to the remedies provided by the contract.

The majority asserts that "[a] special relationship exists between a commercial surety and an obligee that is nearly identical to that involving an insurer and an insured." However, in my view, several of the key elements which make the relationship between insurer and insured "special" are absent from the surety/obligee relationship.

First, unlike the relationship between an insurer and an insured, a relationship between a surety and obligee is not quasi-fiduciary. When an insurance company handles claims of third persons against its insured, the insurance company stands in a position similar to that of a fiduciary because the "insurer retains the absolute right to control the defense of actions brought against the insured, and the insured is therefore precluded from interfering with the investigation and negotiation for settlement." Where a person purchases an insurance policy, "[he barters] to the insurance company all of the rights possessed by him to discover the extent of the injury and to protect himself as best he can from the consequences of the injury. He has contracted with the insurer that it shall have the exclusive right to settle or compromise the claim, to conduct the defense, and that he will not interfere except at his own cost and expense."

Because the insurer retains these valuable rights, it is obligated to act reasonably in denying or delaying payment of a claim. By contrast, a surety is in no way responsible for third party claims against an obligee. The obligee does not cede any right to represent his interests to the surety by virtue of the suretyship agreement and retains the rights to pursue, defend, settle, or compromise claims with the principal, surety, or third parties. As the majority recognizes, the surety has obligations both to the obligee and to the principal. Those obligations are defined by the contract of suretyship, and are not of a fiduciary nature. Therefore, to the extent our holding in Trimble was based upon the existence of a quasi-fiduciary relationship arising from the insured's surrender of rights to the insurer, that holding does not support the majority's result.

When an obligee files an action against a surety for bad faith failure to pay a claim on a performance bond, the situation is more analogous to a first-party direct coverage case. The rationale for the creation of a tort for bad faith breach of insurance contract in a first-party direct coverage case is the concern that a contract claim for insurance proceeds may not effectively protect an injured party once a calamity has befallen him or her.

"Insurers, backed by sufficient financial resources, are encouraged to delay payment of claims to their insureds with an eye toward settling for a lesser amount than that due under the policy . . . . The inequity of this situation becomes particularly apparent in the area of disability insurance in which the insured, often pursued by creditors and devoid of bargaining power, may easily be persuaded to settle for an amount substantially lower than that provided for in the insurance contract."

The majority contends that this same concern arises in the suretyship context because "it is the commercial surety who controls the ultimate decision of whether to pay claims made by the obligee under the terms of the surety bond. For this reason, the commercial surety has a distinct advantage over the obligee in its ability to control performance under the secondary agreement."

The concern that a surety may take advantage of a bond obligee in the claims resolution process overlooks fundamental differences between liability insurance contracts and surety bonds. In contrast with a liability insurance contract, which involves only the insurer and insured, "suretyship involves a tripartite relationship between a surety, its principal, and the bond obligee, in which the obligation of the surety is intended to supplement an obligation of the principal owed to the bond obligee." The surety's obligation to the bond obligee is secondary to the obligation owed by the surety's principal to that obligee. Thus, in contrast with a party sustaining a loss covered under a liability insurance contract who can look only to an insurer for recovery, a bond obligee has a remedy against the principal. For this reason, an obligee is not necessarily left in the same vulnerable position that an insured may face in the wake of a calamity.

The foreseeability of the loss is another distinction between suretyship and insurance. Insurance by its very nature protects against unforeseen losses. In contrast, a surety bond secures to the obligee the cost necessary to complete a project. Before the suretyship agreement is entered into, the obligee is aware of the losses that may result if the principal breaches the contract. The obligee is also aware of any damages that may result from the surety's breach of the suretyship agreement. "Generally, the measure of damages for a breach of contract is the loss in value to the injured party of the other party's performance caused by its failure or deficiency, plus any other incidental or consequential loss caused by the breach, less any cost or other loss that the injured party has avoided by not having to perform. The damages that may result from the surety's breach are reasonably foreseeable, unlike the situation in which calamity strikes and leaves an insured party without the means to face the demands of his or her creditors.

The majority argues that by requiring the principal to obtain a surety bond, the obligee is "essentially insuring itself from the potentially catastrophic losses that would result in the event the principal defaults on its original obligation." The fact that losses resulting from a breach of contract may be catastrophic does not make them any less foreseeable. The majority recognizes that "the parties to a suretyship agreement are on equal footing in terms of bargaining power when they enter into the agreement." Because the loss is foreseeable, the obligee has the opportunity to bargain for provisions protecting against that loss, unlike an insured who is generally required to accept an insurance contract on a "take it or leave it" basis. The inclusion of a bad faith claim in the remedies available against a surety will likely mean that all individuals contracting for a surety bond will be required to pay some additional amount for the tort coverage, whether they want that coverage or not.

The fact that the General Assembly treats sureties similarly to insurers in some contexts should not thereby subject sureties to bad faith liability. * * * These statutes group insurers and sureties together because both enter into contracts to pay a benefit upon a determinable risk contingency, and, hence, both can be similarly regulated. However, it is not the fact that an insurer contracts to pay a benefit upon the occurrence of a particular event that justifies the creation of a tort action for bad faith breach. Rather, in the context of a third-party claim, it is the quasi-fiduciary relationship, and in the context of a first-party claim it is the injured party's vulnerability following an unforeseen calamity and the unequal bargaining power between insurer and insured. Those circumstances are not present in this case.

I view a tort cause of action for bad faith breach of the insurance agreement as a narrow exception to the general rule that breach of contract does not give rise to tort liability. This exception is justified by the special relationship between insurer and insured. Fundamental elements of this relationship are missing from the relationship between surety and obligee. Therefore, I would decline to extend bad faith tort liability to sureties. For this reason, I respectfully dissent.

Chapter 12

LIFE, HEALTH, AND DISABILITY INSURANCE

§ 12.02   LIFE INSURANCE

[G]   Insurance Gothic

Page 832: [Add to § 12.02[G] Note:]

Sometimes, the dark side can be the insurer's side. For example, a famous evidence case that involved a life insurance claim, *Mutual Life Ins. Co. v. Hillmon*, 145 U.S. 285 (1892), featured a battle over the use at trial that could be made of a letter supposedly written by the decedent. The Court resolved the issue by holding that the letter could come in as evidence even though it was hearsay because it reflected the writer's intent to travel to a certain area. Part of the insurer's defense in offering the letter was to suggest that the person insured was not the dead body later found. In effect, the insurer was suggesting that the decedent merely left his wife (the claimant in the case, who eventually prevailed even though the insurer was able to use the letter in question in support of its case) and had not died. Recent scholarship led an evidence professor to conclude that the letter was likely fabricated by the insurer as part of its defense. *See* Marianne Wesson, *The* Hillmon *Case, the MacGuffin, and the Supreme Court*, Litigation, Vol. 32, p. 30 (Fall 2005). The corpse in question in the case (which Mrs. Hillmon contended was her husband and which the insurer contended was another man) has been exhumed from its Kansas grave for DNA testing. As of July 2006, forensic analysis remains ongoing. Stay tuned.

§ 12.04   DISABILITY INSURANCE

[A]   The Meaning of Disability and the Scope of Disability Insurance

Page 864: [Add to § 12.04[A] on page 864 after Phillipe v. Commercial Insurance:]

DOWDLE v. NATIONAL LIFE INSURANCE COMPANY

407 F.3d 967 (8th Cir. 2005)

RILEY, Circuit Judge.

John A. Dowdle, Jr., M.D. (Dr. Dowdle), an orthopedic surgeon, brought this diversity action against National Life Insurance Company (National Life), seeking a declaratory judgment determining Dr. Dowdle is entitled to total disability benefits under the terms of his disability policies with National Life. After National Life removed the action to federal court, the parties cross-moved for summary judgment. The district court granted summary judgment to Dr. Dowdle, concluding he is entitled to total disability benefits, because he cannot perform the material and substantial duties of his occupation. National Life appeals, maintaining Dr. Dowdle is not entitled to total disability benefits. Because we agree with the district court's determination that Dr. Dowdle is totally disabled under the policies as interpreted by Minnesota law, we affirm the district court's grant of summary judgment in favor of Dr. Dowdle.

On December 31, 1987, National Life issued a disability income policy (disability policy) to Dr. Dowdle. In the event Dr. Dowdle became totally disabled, the disability policy would provide a maximum monthly benefit of $13,050. The disability policy defines "total disability" as the inability "to perform the material and substantial duties of an occupation." Dr. Dowdle paid an additional premium to obtain an "own occupation rider" to the disability policy, which expands Dr. Dowdle's protection by defining "occupation" as "the occupation of the Insured at the time a disability, as defined in the Total Disability provision of the policy, begins." Dr. Dowdle also purchased a "residual disability income rider," which defines "partial disability" as the inability "1. to perform one or more of the important daily duties of an occupation as defined in this policy; or 2. to engage in an occupation as defined in this policy for as much time as was usual prior to the start of disability."

On June 30, 1988, National Life issued a professional overhead expense disability policy (overhead expense policy) to Dr. Dowdle. This overhead expense policy would reimburse Dr. Dowdle's overhead expenses in the event he became disabled. The overhead expense policy uses the same definition for "total disability" as the disability policy. The overhead expense policy defines "total disability" as the inability "to perform the material and substantial duties of the Insured's occupation." The overhead expense policy defines "occupation" as "the occupation of the Insured at the time such disability begins." The overhead expense policy defines "partial disability" as the inability "1. to perform one or more of the important daily duties of the Insured's occupation as defined in this policy; or 2. to engage in the Insured's occupation as defined in this policy for as much time as was usual prior to the start of disability."

On the applications for both the disability income and the overhead expense policies (collectively, policies), Dowdle identified his occupation as an orthopedic surgeon. The applications also required Dowdle to list his specific duties. Dowdle identified his duties as seeing patients, performing surgery, reading xrays, interpreting data, and promoting referrals. * * * Before becoming disabled, Dr. Dowdle was a shareholder of Summit

Orthopedics. Dr. Dowdle worked 50 to 60 hours per week, plus call duties. In an average week, Dr. Dowdle devoted 5 half-days to surgery and 5 half-days to office consultations, seeing 15 to 20 patients in each half-day session. Dr. Dowdle earned an average of $85,915 per month from Summit Orthopedics. Surgery and surgery-related care comprised 85% of Dr. Dowdle's practice. * * * Outside his orthopedic surgery practice, Dr. Dowdle also performed independent medical evaluations (IMEs) for EvaluMed, Inc., a company Dr. Dowdle co-founded. Dr. Dowdle devoted an average of 1 hours to an IME: hour for discussion and examination, and 1 hour for review of medical records and preparation of the report. Dr. Dowdle often completed IMEs in the evening at his home. Dr. Dowdle performed an average of 7 IMEs per week. Performing IMEs was not part of Dr. Dowdle's normal duties as an orthopedic surgeon.

On September 9, 2000, Dr. Dowdle suffered injuries, including a closed head injury and a right calcaneal (heel bone) fracture, when the private aircraft he was piloting crashed shortly after takeoff. As a result of Dr. Dowdle's injuries, he is unable to stand at an operating table for an extended period of time. Consequently, he can no longer perform orthopedic surgery. * * * On November 16, 2000, Dr. Dowdle filed a claim with National Life for total disability benefits. National Life started paying Dr. Dowdle $28,050 per month, the maximum total disability benefits.

On February 7, 2001, Dr. Dowdle resumed performing office visits. Initially, Dr. Dowdle worked 1 half-day per week. He now works 6 half-days per week at Summit Orthopedics, seeing 15 to 20 patients during each half-day session. Since Dr. Dowdle resumed working after the accident, Summit Orthopedics considers Dr. Dowdle an independent contractor and pays Dr. Dowdle based upon a percentage of fees he generates. Dr. Dowdle earns an average of about $11,700 per month from Summit Orthopedics. * * * Dr. Dowdle describes his post-accident duties as follows:

> It's taking care of patients who have spinal injury and illnesses and doing the office portion of it and handling them and directing their care. And when they get to a place, if they need surgery, I hand it off to two of my partners who do the surgical treatment. Otherwise I manage their medicines. I manage their work injury and rehab and injections and all the rest, the same thing as I've done previously.

Dr. Dowdle also resumed performing IMEs for EvaluMed.

In light of his ability to resume office consultations, National Life determined that, as of February 7, 2001, Dr. Dowdle was residually disabled rather than totally disabled. National Life reasoned that, because Dr. Dowdle resumed his office practice and performed IMEs, duties he performed before his disability, Dr. Dowdle is only partially disabled. National Life continues to provide monthly residual disability benefits under the policies. * * * National Life argues Dr. Dowdle is not totally disabled under the terms of the policies, because Dr. Dowdle is able to conduct office consultations and other nonsurgical tasks. Conversely, Dr. Dowdle argues that, under Minnesota law, he is entitled to total disability benefits, even though he can perform some non-surgical duties.

Agreeing with Dr. Dowdle, the district court concluded, "since Dr. Dowdle is unable to perform any orthopedic surgery, he is unable to perform the substantial and material parts of his occupation in the customary and usual manner and with substantial continuity. Accordingly, Dr. Dowdle is entitled to 'total disability' benefits" under both policies. National Life appeals, arguing the district court erred in: (1) construing the policies in favor of Dr. Dowdle; and (2) concluding Dr. Dowdle is totally disabled, because he still is able to conduct an office practice and perform IMEs.

As an initial matter, we note the procedural posture of this appeal is different from the cases cited by the parties. In each of these cases, the appellate court reviewed a verdict to determine if the facts supported a finding of total disability. In the instant case, National Life appeals from an order granting summary judgment. We find it appropriate to decide this case on summary judgment, because the parties do not dispute the facts, the parties agree the issues are purely legal, and neither party desires to take this case to trial. * * * We review de novo the district court's grant of summary judgment, viewing the record in the light most favorable to the nonmoving party. Summary judgment is proper if the evidence shows there are no genuine issues of material fact and the moving party is entitled to judgment as a matter of law. We review de novo a district court's interpretation of a contractual provision in an insurance policy as a question of law. We apply Minnesota law in this diversity action.

* * *

National Life argues the district court erroneously construed the policies in favor of Dr. Dowdle, because the district court failed to make a threshold finding that the policy provisions at issue are ambiguous. * * * Under Minnesota law, if the "insurance policy language is clear and unambiguous, the language used must be given its usual and accepted meaning." However, if the "policy language is ambiguous, it must be interpreted in favor of coverage."

The parties agree orthopedic surgery was a material and substantial duty of Dr. Dowdle's occupation. However, the parties dispute whether Dr. Dowdle is totally disabled, because he still can conduct an office practice and perform IMEs. National Life contends the policies require that Dr. Dowdle be unable to perform "all" of the material and substantial duties of his occupation in order to qualify as totally disabled. Conversely, Dr. Dowdle contends the district court correctly held "total disability" means the inability to perform "the most important part" of his occupation.

Our review of the disputed policy language leads us to conclude ambiguity exists. The policies' definitions of "total disability" are susceptible to differing interpretations, because the policies do not speak in terms of "any," "all," "some," or "the most important part" of Dr. Dowdle's duties. Because the policies' definitions of "total disability" are susceptible to multiple interpretations, we conclude the district court properly construed the policies in favor of Dr. Dowdle.

In interpreting total disability policies with similar language, courts have taken one of two approaches. National Life urges us to apply the line of cases in which courts have interpreted similar language in total disability policies to mean an insured must be unable to perform "all" of his material and substantial duties to be considered totally disabled. These courts have held an insured's ability to perform just one material and substantial duty precludes a determination of total disability.

The other approach, adopted by the Minnesota Supreme Court Weum v. Mutual Benefit Health & Accident Ass'n, 54 N.W.2d 20, 31-2 (Minn. 1952), assesses a total disability if the insured's inability to perform certain duties precludes continuation in his or her regular occupation. In Weum, the insured, an obstetrician and gynecologist, sustained an injury which impaired his ability to deliver babies. For some time, the insurance company paid total disability benefits. When the insurance company ceased making total disability benefit payments, Dr. Weum sued. Id. Dr. Weum claimed he was totally disabled because, after his accident, he was unable to perform the work required of an obstetrician.

The policy at issue in Weum provided for total disability "if such injuries . . . *shall wholly and continuously disable the Insured*." The Weum court upheld an instruction to the jury that Dr. Weum should be considered "wholly and continuously disabled" if he was "unable to perform the substantial and material acts necessary to the successful prosecution of his occupation or employment in the customary and usual way." The court also upheld the jury verdict finding Dr. Weum totally disabled, even though he resumed an office practice. The court noted Dr. Weum "was so physically handicapped as a result of his injury that he would have been unable to perform the most important part of his specialty." The Weum court specifically rejected the argument that the fact an insured earns a substantial post-accident income bars a finding of total disability.

In the years since its 1952 decision in Weum, the Minnesota Supreme Court consistently has held, when applying an occupational disability clause like the provision present in the instant case, a determination of total disability does not require "a state of absolute helplessness or inability to perform any task relating to one's employment." Under Minnesota law, an insured may be entitled to total disability benefits, regardless of the number of important duties an insured still can perform in isolation. Under the Minnesota law set forth in Weum and its progeny, the district court correctly concluded Dr. Dowdle is totally disabled. At the time he incurred his disability, Dr. Dowdle was engaged predominantly in the occupation of an orthopedic surgeon. The parties agree Dr. Dowdle's IME practice was separate and distinct from his surgery practice. Therefore, the fact that Dr. Dowdle performed IMEs both before and after the accident has no bearing on whether Dr. Dowdle can perform the "material and substantial duties" of being an orthopedic surgeon. National Life concedes Dr. Dowdle can no longer perform orthopedic surgery, which is clearly the most important substantial and material duty of Dr. Dowdle's occupation as an orthopedic surgeon. Because Dr. Dowdle's disability prevents him from performing the most important part of his occupation, he is entitled to total disability benefits under Minnesota law. We affirm the judgment of the district court.

[C] Disability Insurance and Illusory Coverage

Page 865: [Add at the end of § 12.04[C]:]

(5) One of the authors (Stempel) finds the outcome in *Dowdle v. National Life* both correctly decided and personally pleasing. Dr. Dowdle performed successful knee reconstruction on Stempel more than 30 years ago at the University of Minnesota Hospital when Dowdle was still a resident physician (Stempel was a toddler at the time). As the case illustrates, Dowdle subsequently more than recouped his medical school tuition. Although no one will ever confuse Stempel with Hines Ward, Dowdle's work on the knee has held up pretty well, suggesting that Dowdle was a surgeon who did high quality work that justified a seven-figure income (assuming anyone is worth seven figures a year) as well as the disability insurance benefits sought.

(6) The *Dowdle v. National Life* case also illustrates that for many workers, their vocational talents and opportunites for compensation may vary considerably according to various aspects of their jobs. For example, Dowdle as a surgeon may have had few peers in his community but there may be many more doctors who are comparably skilled at office consultation (this as well as the economics of modern medicine probably helps explain the dramatic difference in his compensation after he could no longer do surgery). As doctors often put it, you either "have good hands or you don't" just as many basketball players can set screens but relatively few can consistently knock down three point shots under pressure. Similarly, a lawyer may have exceptional talents in court but be only a good to average brief writer. After a serious injury (e.g., lost voice, facial disfigurement, chronic fatigue syndrome), the lawyer may no longer be able to try cases, but can still research and write. However, unless this attorney is also a masterful writer or legal theorist, the lawyer's value to the firm and clients may be dramatically lowered even though the lawyer is still "working" after the injury. For that reason, *Dowdle v. National Life* represents a correct approach to construction of "high-end" disability policies that define disability with reference to the policyholder's particular skills at the time the policy is placed rather than by mere ability to be gainfully employed in the field. Of particular importance, of course, is whether the policy is a high-end policy that pays when the policyholder cannot return to specific employment as opposed to a "Brand X" policy that pays only if the policyholder is completely unable to work.

Chapter 13

AUTOMOBILE INSURANCE

§ 13.04   RECURRING ISSUES IN AUTOMOBILE COVERAGE

[A]   Who is an "Insured"?

Page 870: [Add to § 13.04[A] after the second full paragraph:]

See also Cole v. State Farm Ins. Co., 128 P.3d 171 (Alaska 2006) (former wife living with ex-husband after reconciliation is not "spouse" under husband's auto insurance policy).

[C]   Loss "Arising Out of Ownership, Maintenance, or Use" of a Vehicle

Page 892: [Add to § 13.04[C], Note (3):]

State Farm Mut. Auto Ins. Co. v. DeHaan, 2006 Md. LEXIS 341 (Md. June 5, 2006) (injury to policyholder when shot by intruder stealing care not injury arising from "use" of motor vehicle; instrumentality of injury was handgun and not automobile used in normal or intended manner); *Peagler v. USAA Ins. Co.*, 386 S.C. 153, 628 S.E.2d 475 (S.C. 2006) (no auto insurance coverage where wife killed while putting on seatbelt by discharge of firearm being removed from pickup truck cab by husband; insufficient causal connection between truck and accidental shooting); *Lawrence v. State Farm Fire & Cas. Co.*, 133 P.3d 976 (Wyo. 2006) (a relatively easy case in which the court enforces the automobile exclusion in a homeowner's policy regarding a third party claim of negligence in giving "gas money" to unlicensed teenage driver for road trip to Billings resulting in accident causing passenger's death; knowingly funding an unlicensed, underage driver's use of car may have been grossly negligent but the tragic death nonetheless arose out of use of an automobile, which is excluded from general liability coverage under both homeowner and business policies); *Estate of Nord v. Motorists Mut. Ins. Co.*, 105 Ohio St. 3d 366, 826 N.E.2d 826 (Ohio 2005) (injury incurred when paramedic dropped syringe did not arise out of use of ambulance as a vehicle) (but has the Court ever tried to use a syringe at 70 m.p.h.? Curiously, the *Nord* opinion does not describe the incident in any detail; the reader is not even told if the ambulance was in motion at the time); *Foremost Ins. Co. v. Levesque*, 868 A.2d 244 (Me. 2005) (automobile loading exclusion does not defeat coverage under homeowners policy where injury took place in home during delivery of washing machine that had come by truck; injury sufficiently land-based and separated from vehicle use to be outside scope of auto coverage); *Texas Farm Bureau Mut. Ins. Co. v. Sturrock*, 146 S.W.2d 123 (Tex. 2004) (injury to foot that became entangled with truck door while exiting vehicle is covered under auto policies personal injury protection benefits).

While *Lawrence* may be an easy case, what would the Florida Supreme Court that decided *Blish* think of the *DeHaan* and *Peagler* analyses and results? If nothing else, case reports continue to teem with "use or maintenance of an automobile" cases? Why is that? Are courts too zealous in guarding the boundary between auto incidents efforts to obtain auto insurance for non-auto losses? Or are courts too callous toward claimants who may have not other form of compensation? Extensive life insurance and disability insurance is a middle class or upper middle class type of asset—and many injured persons are lower on the economic rung and lack such coverage.

§ 13.05   UNINSURED AND UNDERINSURED MOTORIST COVERAGE

[B]   Nature of Underinsured Motorist Coverage

Page 903: [Add to § 13.05[B] prior to the Notes and Questions:]

UM and UIM disputes continue to provide a steady stream of cases, many of them state specific. Regarding UM coverage, *see, e.g., Gabriel v. Premier Ins. Co. of Mass.*, 445 Mass. 1026, 840 N.E.2d 548 (Mass. 2006) (hit-and-run driver is uninsured, entitling victim to UM benefits under his own auto policy); *Geico Gen. Ins. Co. v. Northwestern Pacific Indem. Co.*, 115 P.3d 856 (Okla. 2005) (UM coverage primary to any available excess liability policies); *Farmers Ins. Co. v. Southwestern Bell Tel. Co.*, 113 P.3d 258 (Kan. 2005) (self-insurer not required by state insurance law to provide UM/UIM benefits to occupants of its motor vehicles). Regarding UIM coverage, *see, e.g., Welin v. American Family Mut. Ins. Co.*, 2006 Wisc. LEXIS 374 (Wis. June 30, 2006) (state statute requires payment of additional UIM benefits to injured policyholder notwithstanding policy language); *Cole v. State Farm Ins. Co.*, 128 P.3d 171 (Alaska 2006) (UIM benefits that would be available to "spouse" not available where victim and claimant merely lived together even though they had once been married); *Eaquinta v. Allstate Ins. Co.*, 125 P.3d 901 (Utah 2005) (UIM benefits not available to motorist for death of adult child that was not part of claimant's household); *Mecca v. Farmers Ins. Exch.*, 329 Mont. 73, 122 P.3d 1190 (Mont. 2005) (availability of UIM coverage turns on policy covering vehicle involved in injury rather than policy covering vehicle's driver); *Gillen v. State Farm Mut. Auto. Ins. Co.*, 215 Ill.2d 381, 830 N.E.2d 575 (Ill. 2005) (payments by employer to victim did not entitle auto insurer to offset UIM benefits by those received by victim pursuant to workers' compensation); *Hartford Casualty Ins. Co.*

v. Farrish-Leduc, 275 Conn. 748, 882 A.2d 44 (Conn. 2005) (UIM carrier may reduce limits payable by amount victim driver received in legal malpractice against arising out of treatment related to auto accident; malpractice action against law firm that missed statute of limitations for commencing what would have been a meritorious tort claim against tortfeasor with adequate insurance); *Continental Ins. Co. v. Murphy*, 96 P.3d 747 (Nev. 2004) (policy exclusion barring UIM coverage if policyholder not occupying own auto set aside on statutory grounds so that policy provides state minimum of required coverage limits).

§ 13.07 THE MEASURE OF RECOVERY FOR DAMAGE TO AN AUTOMOBILE

Page 926: [Add to § 13.07 at the end of the Notes and Questions:]

(5) In the continuing battle over diminished valued coverage, insurers appear to have the momentum. *See, e.g., Allgood v. Meridian Security Ins. Co.*, 836 N.E.2d 243 (Ind. 2005) (standard auto policy does not obligate insurer to pay for diminished valued of car after repairs); *Culhane v. Western National Mut. Ins. Co.*, 704 N.W.2d 287 (S.D. 2005) (no coverage for diminished value unless policyholder can demonstrate that car cannot be repaired to its former physical, mechanical, and operating condition). *Culhane* went so far as to describe rejection of diminished value coverage as not only the majority view but an "almost unanimous" view. That's probably a little overboard, at least historically (*See Stempel on Insurance Contracts* § 22.12) but close to correct regarding modern caselaw.

(6) More important, the argument for diminished value coverage is just not particularly persuasive in that it tends to convert insurance for physical damage into insurance for economic injury that normally is not covered under standard property policies. Stempel feels more strongly about this than Swisher and readers should know that Stempel has been a retained expert for a large insurer in one of these cases. To test the logic of diminished value for auto damage, try a thought experiment substituting home damage. For example, if a family is slaughtered by a serial killer (assume a messy serial killer as in all the *Halloween* and *Texas Chain Saw* movies), there will be the physical damage to the property, which can be cleaned up by ServiceMaster or similar vendors. The home will then be "good as new" but will likely have a diminished market value because of its spooky and tragic past, which not even the best realtor will be able to suppress. The Amityville Horror is logically worth less than the same house down the block unless you really find a niche buyer. Unless Quentin Tarantino is looking to relocate to the neighborhood, the house is probably worth less. But should physical injury insurance compensate the policyholder for this type of loss? Most courts have answered "no" regarding auto insurance.

We could use the same macabre "situs of atrocity" hypothetical for cars and presumably have the same result. The car might be worth less because it was the scene of a crime but if the repairs are adequate, there is no remaining physical damage to the car. The tricky part may be the determination of the quality of repairs. Laypersons may have difficulty knowing when the vendor selected by an auto insurer has truly repaired a damaged vehicle to the extent it is good as new. Anecdotally, drivers who have been in accidents have long complained that even after repair the vehicle "just doesn't drive right like it used to." They may be right and this may well be because their insurers cut corners on repairs. There may even be a small subset of cases where the even with thorough repair, the car seems to perform as if still at least slightly damaged. Most of you have probably seen the Carfax commercials suggesting that buyers want to avoid vehicles that have been previously damaged; the implicit message is that even if repaired these cars are bad news. But notwithstanding popular perception, it appears that repair can restore automobiles to their former condition if the repairs are adequate in scope and done correctly. Where the insurer does this, it should not be obligated to also compensate the policyholder due to a market-based discount imposed on auto resales simply because the car was once in an accident.

(7) There may also be disputes as to the type and quality of repairs and parts used in fixing an automobile after a collision. For a time, it looked like plaintiffs might score a big victory against the nation's largest insurer by challenging the insurer's practice of paying for repair of damaged policyholder vehicles with parts made by manufacturers other than the original automaker. The insurer asserted that the parts were of equal or at least comparable quality and that their use was efficient and justified. A class of nearly five million policyholders certified by the state trial court contended that this violated their policies and amounted for fraud and misrepresentation. A jury awarded more than $1 billion in damages. However, the class certification was subsequently reversed. *See, e.g., Avery v. State Farm Mut. Auto. Ins. Co.,* 216 Ill.2d 100, 835 N.E.2d 801 (Ill. 2005). *See also* Arthur D. Postal, *Did State Farm 'Buy' Auto Policy Parts Ruling? Plaintiffs say campaign contributions influenced deciding vote in Illinois court,* Nat'l Underwriter (Prop. & Cas. ed.), Jan. 16, 2005 (plaintiffs allege that Illinois Justice Lloyd Karmeir received $350,000 from State Farm, its lawyers, and supporters and more than $1 million in additional campaign aid from insurer groups, calling his impartiality into reasonable question; plaintiffs seek certiorari on this ground). Certiorari was denied by the U.S. Supreme Court. *See* 126 S. Ct. 1470 (2006).

(8) The *Avery* trial court decision was rendered in Williams County, Illinois, which has been included in the American Tort Reform Association's list of "judicial hellholes," jurisdictions seen by ATRA (a pro-business group) as excessively pro plaintiff due to an alleged combination of powerful trial lawyers, compliant judges (in need of campaign contributions from powerful trial lawyers) and jurors interested in wealth redistribution. To some extent, both the *Avery* plaintiffs and State Farm (or its supporters like ATRA) seem to be accusing the other side of trying to buy judicial influence.

Like the inspector speaking with Rick's Cafe American proprietor Humphrey Bogart in *Casablanca*, we are "shocked, shocked" (which means we are really not shocked) to read such allegations. In our view, both sides have something to talk about. Certain forums are more favorable to plaintiffs or defendants, which undercuts the American aspiration of fair trials and justice obtained from neutral courts and juries. (There are some pro-defendant judicial hellholes, but they have been less well identified and publicized then their pro-plaintiff counterparts.)

(9) Should state governments and federal courts not take this problem more seriously? How? By seeking less ideological, more competent judges and fairer cross-sectional representation in juries? By appointing judges rather than having judges run for office like legislators? By outlawing campaign contributions (assuming this would survive First Amendment challenge)? Or would this create different, arguably greater problems because of establishment control of judicial selection and reduced public input? But how much does the average member of the voting public know about judicial candidates? How much do you know about your local judicial candidates? Can you figure out where we stand on the matter?

Chapter 14

"BAD FAITH" LITIGATION AND CLAIMS ADMINISTRATION

§ 14.01 THE CONCEPT OF GOOD FAITH AND BAD FAITH—IN GENERAL

Page 936: [Add at the conclusion of § 14.01:]

New York precedent suggests that "gross disregard" of the policyholder's interests or a "reckless failure to place on equal footing the interest of its insured with its own interests" (at least for liability insurers considering a settlement offer) is sufficient to constitute bad faith by the insurer. *See Greenhouse v. Allstate Ins. Co.*, 446 F.3d 356, 362 (2d Cir. 2006) (applying New York law) (collecting cases); *Pavia v. State Farm Mut. Auto Ins. Co.*, 82 N.Y.2d 445, 453, 626 N.E.2d 24, 605 N.Y.S.2d 208 (1993). Although unreasonable insurer behavior is often enough to demonstrate bad faith, many states require both the absence of a reasonable basis for the insurer's conduct or claim denial and that the insurer know it had no reasonable basis or acted with "reckless disregard" of the policyholder's interests. *See, e.g., Cathcart v. State Farm Mut. Auto Ins. Co.*, 123 P.3d 579 (Wyo. 2005).

Although simple negligence in claims-handling or coverage evaluation is not sufficient to constitute bad faith, the duty of good faith requires that insurer respond reasonably to a reasonable claim or requests by the policyholder or third parties. The insurer must act as though it were responsible for the entire claim. *See Badillo v. Mid Century Ins. Co.*, 121 P.3d 1080 (Okla. 2005) (but requiring greater showing of insurer misconduct for punitive damages such as reckless disregard of policyholder interests from which malice may be inferred; divided court finds sufficient unreasonable behavior in failing to take apt steps to protect policyholder from plaintiff's verdict in excess of $10,000 policy limits). However, this standard does not mean that an insurer may not take reasonable steps in aid of investigating a matter and determining coverage. *See, e.g., Mutual of Enumclaw Ins. Co. v. Dan Paulson Const., Inc.*, 134 P.3d 240 (Wash. Ct. App. 2006) (not bad faith for insurer to issue subpoena to arbitrator in effort to apportion arbitration award into covered and uncovered claims).

Statutes may by their textual terms or the statutory design also act to preclude certain actions against insurers or insurance entities. *See, e.g., Maes v. Audubon Indem. Ins. Group, 127 P.3d 1126 (N.M. Ct. App. 2005) (auto insurers providing coverage pursuant to state FAIR plan immune from bad faith tort liability). See also Machan v. Unum Life Ins. Co., 116 P.3d 342 (Utah 2005) (state statute requiring timely payment of claims does not create private right of action for policyholders).*

193

To perhaps state the obvious, a policyholder must actually suffer some injury from an insurer's bad faith conduct in order to recover damages. Some courts address the matter by stating that harm is an essential element of a bad faith claim. *See Werlinger v. Clarendon Nat'l Ins. Co.*, 120 P.3d 593 (Wash. Ct. App. 2005). In our view, it is more accurate to say that a policyholder may prove bad faith without showing injury but can recover no compensation absent a showing of harm.

Individuals working as adjusters for insurers (either as employees or independent contractors generally cannot be sued for bad faith in that they are agents of a disclosed principal (the insurer). *See, e.g., Sherner v. National Loss Control Services Corp.*, 329 Mont. 247, 124 P.3d 150 (Mont. 2005) (independent contractor adjuster and its employee); *Hamill v. Pawtucket Mut. Ins. Co.*, 2005 Vt. LEXIS 316 (Vt. Dec. 30, 2005) (independent contractor adjuster). If the individual has affirmatively committed a tort in connection with the claim (e.g., the assault and battery of shoving the claimant during an argument), the individual may become a defendant, but not an insurance bad faith defendant.

In addition to bad faith exposure, insurers may become defendants for other alleged breaches of tort or contract duty. *See, e.g., Pehle v. Farm Bureau Life Ins. Co.*, 397 F.3d 897 (10th Cir. 2005) (insurance applicants stated cognizable claim against life insurer that denied applications but failed to reveal to them that blood tests obtained by insurer showed applicants to be HIV-positive; insurer has duty to make sufficient disclosure of adverse health information in screening tests so that reasonable applicant may inquire further).

Regarding litigation and proof of bad faith, states vary as to whether expert testimony is required to prove up a bad faith claim, with the majority of states rejecting any such requirement. *See, e.g., American Family Mut. Ins. Co. v. Allen*, 102 P.3d 333 (Colo. 2004) (expert testimony not required; affirming bad faith judgment for policyholder).

§ 14.04   DIFFERENCES AMONG THE STATES REGARDING INSURANCE BAD FAITH

Page 948: [Add at the conclusion of § 14.04:]

A recent study suggests that states permitting bad-faith claims in first party insurance matters generally have higher claims settlement offers to policyholders. *See* Mark J. Browne, Ellen S. Pryor & Bob Puelz, *The Effect of Bad-Faith Laws on First-Party Insurance Claims Decisions*, 33 J. Leg. Stud. 355 (2004). The question remains, of course, whether these higher offers reflect the possibility of a bad faith claim prompting fairer treatment by the insurer or instead reflect the insurer offering more due to the mere fear that a groundless bad faith claim is always a possibility if the policyholder is unsatisfied and refuses to accept the insurer's offer.

§ 14.06 INSURANCE BAD FAITH LITIGATION IN OPERATION

[B] The Contract Law Approach to Bad Faith

Page 978: [Add at the end of § 14.06[B]:]

(4) *See also Machan v. Unum Life Ins. Co.*, 116 P.3d 342 (Utah 2005) (applying *Beck* analysis and permitting consequential damages for breach of policy but denying private right of action under state claims statute).

[D] Punitive Damages

Page 1013: [Add to § 14.06[D] prior to the Notes and Questions:]

CAMPBELL v. STATE FARM MUTUAL AUTOMOBILE INSURANCE COMPANY

98 P.3d 409 (Utah 2004), *cert. denied*, 543 U.S. 874 (2004)

NEHRING, Justice:

We take up this case after remand from the United States Supreme Court, which held that the imposition of a $145 million punitive damages award against State Farm Mutual Automobile Insurance Company in favor of State Farm's insured, Curtis B. Campbell, and his wife, Inez Preece Campbell, was excessive and violated the due process clause of the Fourteenth Amendment to the Constitution of the United States. The Supreme Court directed us to recalculate the punitive damages award under principles articulated in its decision. We have performed this task and reduced the jury's award to $9,018,780.75 in punitive damages, a figure nine times the amount of compensatory and special damages awarded to the Campbells.

* * *

II. DUTY ON REMAND

State Farm suggests that our duty in the face of a remand order demands unwavering fidelity to the letter and spirit of the mandate. We agree. State Farm further argues that the letter and spirit of the mandate erect an impenetrable ceiling on the punitive damages award of $1,002,086.75, based on a 1-to-1 ratio of punitive damages to compensatory damages. State Farm makes two arguments in aid of this contention. First, it invokes what it characterizes as the "mandate rule" which, it claims, elevates all of the statements in the Supreme Court's opinion to the status of a holding, thereby binding us to what would otherwise be properly deemed dicta. Second, having identified and broadly defined a "mandate rule," State Farm then turns to the text of Campbell II which states that "an application of the [relevant] guideposts to the facts of this case . . . likely would justify a punitive damages award at or near the amount of compensatory damages." State Farm claims that, when given the dignity required by the mandate rule, this language limits our punitive damages award to the amount of compensatory damages.

We are both sensitive to our responsibility as an inferior court to honor the Supreme Court's remand order with utmost fidelity and skeptical of claims that our duties can be reduced to an enumerated task list imposed by a "mandate rule." We do not, therefore, interpret the Supreme Court's mandate to be as restrictive as State Farm claims. Had the letter of the Supreme Court's mandate included an express punitive damages award, our responsibilities would be easily discharged. The Supreme Court declined, however, to fix a substitute award, choosing instead to entrust to our judgment the calculation of a punitive award which both achieves the legitimate objectives of punitive damages and meets the demands of due process. We take seriously the Supreme Court's direction that "the proper calculation of punitive damages under the principles we have discussed should be resolved, in the first instance, by the Utah courts."

By assigning to us the duty to resolve the issue of punitive damages by fixing an award, the Supreme Court signaled its intention to vest in us some discretion to exercise our independent judgment to reach a reasonable and proportionate award. To faithfully exercise our discretion, we must properly identify and apply the Supreme Court's principles announced in Campbell II. These principles restated and refined the analytical tools first announced in *BMW of North America, Inc. v. Gore.*

* * *

The Supreme Court has also consistently recognized punitive damages as a means to "further a State's legitimate interests in punishing unlawful conduct and deterring its repetition." Taken together, these themes create a logical underpinning to an interpretation of the Supreme Court's remand order which sanctions and expects us to exercise a considerable measure of independent judgment in fixing the punitive damages award.

Even the Supreme Court's observation that this case "likely would justify a punitive damages award at or near the amount of compensatory damages" does not cause us to retreat from our view that we have been granted discretion to determine the amount of punitive damages. Contrary to State Farm's assertions, this language cannot reasonably be interpreted as a conclusive determination that the magnitude of State Farm's blameworthiness merits a punitive damages award no greater than the compensatory award. These are words of prediction, not direction, and are wholly compatible with a remand order which both instructs us to apply the Supreme Court's standards with fidelity and recognizes that Utah courts are best able to address our state's legitimate interests. Consistent with that view, the Supreme Court has clearly communicated its intention to cede to us the responsibility to assess the reprehensibility of State Farm's conduct, to identify Utah's legitimate interests, and to exercise reasoned judgment in fixing punitive damages.

While authorizing us to determine the amount of the punitive damages award, the Supreme Court leashed us more tightly to the established analytical guideposts of Gore in two ways: by narrowing the scope of relevant evidence which we may consider in evaluating the reprehensibility of State Farm's conduct, and by providing more detailed guidance for determining the relationship between compensatory and punitive damages.

The Supreme Court chided us for basing our reinstatement of the jury's $145 million punitive damages award on State Farm's "nationwide policies rather than for the conduct direct [sic] toward the Campbells." The Supreme Court found impermissible our reliance on State Farm's conduct outside Utah in measuring the reprehensibility of the company's conduct. Drawing on views expressed in Gore, the Supreme Court limited evidence that can properly be weighed in the reprehensibility scale to behavior which took place within our borders and was directed at the Campbells. We are mindful that it was our consideration of irrelevant extra-territorial evidence concerning reprehensibility which attracted most of the Supreme Court's criticism in Campbell II. We therefore reevaluate State Farm's conduct based solely on its behavior that affected the Campbells and took place within Utah.

The Supreme Court stopped well short, however, of punctuating its disagreement with the evidence we considered in our analysis by pinning State Farm's behavior to a particular location along the reprehensibility continuum. It instead simply issued the mandate that "a more modest punishment for this reprehensible conduct could have satisfied the State's legitimate objectives, and the Utah courts should have gone no further."

Had the Supreme Court injected into Campbell II its own conclusive findings concerning the degree of State Farm's blameworthiness, it would have announced a federal standard measuring reprehensibility. By creating such a national reprehensibility standard, however, the Supreme Court would have collided with its own rationale for limiting the scope of relevant reprehensibility evidence to intra-state conduct. The Supreme Court's rejection of our consideration of State Farm's conduct in other states was grounded in the recognition that much of the out-of-state conduct was lawful where it occurred. The Supreme Court respected states' autonomy to make policy choices about the lawfulness of human and corporate behavior within their own borders, and used that deference to justify disallowing out-of-state conduct as an indicator of reprehensibility.

Just as behavior may be unlawful or tortious in one state and not in another, the degree of blameworthiness assigned to conduct may also differ among the states. As long as the Supreme Court stands by its view that punitive damages serve a legitimate means to satisfy a state's objectives to punish and deter behavior which it deems unlawful or tortious based on its own values and traditions, it would seemingly be bound to avoid creating and imposing on the states a nationwide code of personal and corporate behavior. * * * In this instance, we find the blameworthiness of State Farm's behavior toward the Campbells to be several degrees more offensive than the Supreme Court's less than condemnatory view that State Farm's behavior "merits no praise." * * * We reach this conclusion after applying the relevant reprehensibility standards to the facts approved for consideration of State Farm's reprehensibility in Campbell II, and in light of Utah's values and traditions. We now turn to explaining how we exercised the discretion granted us by the Supreme Court to award the Campbells $9,018,780.75 in punitive damages.

* * *

Because any determination of reprehensibility inevitably implicates moral judgments and is therefore susceptible to an arbitrary, inexplicable, and disproportionate outcome, the Supreme Court has fashioned certain measuring tools. These include consideration of whether the harm caused was physical as opposed to economic; the tortious conduct evinced an indifference to or a reckless disregard of the health or safety of others; the target of the conduct had financial vulnerability; the conduct involved repeated actions or was an isolated incident; and the harm was the result of intentional malice, trickery, or deceit, or mere accident.

First, we consider whether the harm was economic or physical. We are mindful of the Supreme Court's observation that "the harm [in this case] arose from a transaction in the economic realm, not from some physical assault or trauma." We do not, however, read this comment to foreclose our value-based assessment of the type of injuries which may flow from the abuse of transactions in the economic realm, nor to bar us from judging the reprehensibility of such abusive conduct. The Supreme Court's observation is carefully phrased. It does not classify the injury inflicted on the Campbells by State Farm as "economic." Rather, it notes that the transaction which gave rise to the injury was in the "economic realm."

If we were to hold the view that insurance has no purpose beyond providing economic compensation for loss, there would be little reason to dwell on this first reprehensibility factor. So interpreted, not only would the harm caused by State Farm be purely economic in nature, but the economic harm sustained by the Campbells would be minimal. State Farm ultimately paid the entire judgment which was awarded against the Campbells, including amounts in excess of the policy limits. However, we do not believe that the Campbells' injuries were limited to their economic loss.

Instead, we recognize that the gravity of harm which an insurer may potentially inflict on an insured is unique to the nature of the product and service that insurance provides. Life is fraught with uncertainty and risk. In Utah alone, our citizens pay nearly $1 billion annually in automobile insurance premiums in an effort to ameliorate the anxiety caused by uncertainty and risk.

We have shaped our law relating to first party insurance contracts to recognize the practical reality "that insurance frequently is purchased not only to provide funds in case of loss, but to provide peace of mind for the insured or his beneficiaries." Peace of mind clearly plays a central role in accounting for the appeal of liability insurance. * * * In insurance each party must take a risk. But it is inaccurate to assert that if the insured event does not occur then the insured receives nothing in return for the premium payment made. Each insured receives at the time of contract formation present assurance of compensation if the loss occurs which is a valuable peace-of-mind protection.

An allegation that one's negligent conduct has caused the injury or death of another inevitably triggers fear and apprehension that insurance succors. * * * Insureds buy financial protection and peace of mind against fortuitous losses. They pay the requisite premiums and put their faith and trust in their insurers to pay policy benefits promptly and fairly when the insured event occurs. Good faith and fair dealing is their expectation. It is the very essence of the insurer-insured relationship. In some instances, however, insurance companies refuse to pay the promised benefits when the under-written harm occurs. When an insurer decides to delay or to deny paying benefits, the policyholder can suffer injury not only to his economic well-being but to his emotional and physical health as well. Moreover, the holder of a policy with low monetary limits may see his whole claim virtually wiped out by expenses if the insurance company compels him to resort to court action.

As the facts of this case make clear, misconduct which occurs in the insurance sector of the economic realm is likely to cause injury more closely akin to physical assault or trauma than to mere economic loss. When an insurer callously betrays the insured's expectation of peace of mind, as State Farm did to the Campbells, its conduct is substantially more reprehensible than, for example, the undisclosed repainting of an automobile which spawned the punitive damages award in Gore. * * * State Farm expressly assured the Campbells that their assets would not be placed at risk by the negligence and wrongful death lawsuit brought against them. The company then unnecessarily subjected the Campbells to the risks and rigors of a trial. State Farm disregarded facts from which it should have concluded that the Campbells faced a near-certain probability of having a judgment entered against them in excess of policy limits. When this probability came to pass, State Farm withdrew its expressions of assurance and told the Campbells to place a "for sale" sign on their house. These acts, all of which the Supreme Court conceded that State Farm had committed, and for which State Farm has not voiced so much as a whisper of apology or remorse, caused the Campbells profound noneconomic injury.

It simply will not do to classify this injury as solely "economic" for the purposes of evaluating it under the first prong of the Gore reprehensibility test, and we decline to do so. We turn now to the remaining Gore indicia for evaluating reprehensibility. The second factor in assessing reprehensi-bility is whether State Farm showed indifference or reckless disregard for the health and safety of the Campbells. There is little doubt that State Farm could reasonably have known that its conduct would cause stress and trauma to a policyholder. State Farm was clearly indifferent to this result, evincing a reckless disregard for the Campbells' peace of mind. The third factor is whether the victims were financially vulnerable. It remains obvious to us that not only were the Campbells financially vulnerable, but their vulnerability enabled, if not motivated, State Farm's conduct. We need stray no further into the record than to the post-judgment advice given to the Campbells by State Farm's adjuster that they put a "for sale" sign on their house to make this point. It is difficult to imagine State Farm making this statement to a sophisticated insured whom State Farm believed to have the wherewithal to protect himself from its predations.

Fourth, we consider whether the reprehensible conduct was repeated or merely an isolated incident. We take up this measure of reprehensibility with considerable caution because, although Gore instructs us to consider whether "the conduct involved repeated actions or was an isolated incident," the Supreme Court expressly found that we erred in determining that State Farm was a recidivist. Repeated misconduct justifies a more severe sanction both because it minimizes the likelihood that the conduct was a unique aberration and because it justifies the imposition of punitive damages as a deterrent. Although we are bound by the Supreme Court's finding that State Farm was not a recidivist, absence of prior bad acts does not mean that State Farm has forsworn the conduct that caused the Campbells' injury, and that the citizens of Utah therefore have no reason to deter State Farm's future conduct. State Farm's obdurate insistence that its treatment of the Campbells was proper clearly calls out for vigorous deterrence.

In Campbell I, we voiced our incredulity over State Farm's protestations of blamelessness. We noted:

State Farm refuses in its brief on appeal to concede any error or impropriety in the handling of the Campbell case. Rather, testimony at trial indicated that State Farm was "proud" of the way it treated the Campbells. Further, State Farm asserts that it is in fact a "victim" in this case because it is the target of the secret "conspiracy" perpetrated by the Campbells, Ospital, Slusher, and their attorneys to bring this bad faith lawsuit and to share any recovery received.

The Supreme Court did not take issue with this observation. Since Campbell I, State Farm has directed us to no evidence suggesting that it has gained insight into the wrongfulness of its behavior or has reconsidered its feelings of pride and victimization.

We will not and, consistent with our duty on remand, cannot invoke deterrence as a justification for punitive damages based on conduct dissimilar to that which State Farm inflicted on the Campbells. We can, however, find ample grounds to defend an award of punitive damages in the upper range permitted by due process based on our concern that State Farm's defiance strongly suggests that it will not hesitate to treat its Utah insureds with the callousness that marked its treatment of the Campbells. *See*

Diversified Holdings, L.C. v. Turner, (Utah 2002) (stating that the chief aggravating factor was "a lack of remorse increasing the likelihood of recidivism").

Lastly, we consider whether the substantial emotional damages sustained by the Campbells were the result of State Farm's intentional malice, trickery, and deceit. We conclude that the damages sustained by the Campbells were no mere accident. At trial, Ray Summers, the adjuster who handled the Campbell case, testified that State Farm resorted to various tactics to create prejudice in the event the case ever went before a jury. For example, State Farm manager Bob Noxon instructed Summers to manufacture the false story that Todd Ospital, who was killed in the automobile accident for which Mr. Campbell was found to be at fault, was speeding because he was on his way to see a pregnant girlfriend. In truth, there was no pregnant girlfriend, nor was Mr. Ospital even speeding; this story was invented only to cause prejudice in the record. This deceitful conduct can only be explained as part of a scheme to reduce State Farm's economic exposure. The possibility that its dissembling would expose the Campbells to an excess judgment must have been apparent to State Farm. To react as it did when the excess judgment became a reality only confirms the toxicity of State Farm's behavior.

We turn now to the second Gore guidepost: the ratio between actual and punitive damages awarded. State Farm focuses its attention on the Supreme Court's statement that "when compensatory damages are substantial, then a lesser ratio [of compensatory to punitive damages], perhaps only equal to compensatory damages, can reach the outermost limit of the due process guarantee." The compensatory damages award to the Campbells was substantial and, in the Supreme Court's view, provided them "complete compensation." This is due at least in part to the possibility, recognized by the Supreme Court, that the compensatory damages award for emotional distress incorporated within it a punitive component.

Such a conclusion, though plausible as an abstract proposition, does not account for the circumstances of the compensatory damages award in this case. The jury awarded the Campbells $2.6 million in compensatory damages. The trial court granted State Farm's motion for remittitur and reduced the award to $1 million: $600,000 for Mr. Campbell and $400,000 for Mrs. Campbell. The trial court's ruling was supported by extensive and detailed findings explaining the basis for the reduced compensatory damages award. Based on this thorough record, we conclude that the trial court's compensatory damages award was purged of elements which may have been more properly placed in the category of punitive damages. We are convinced that the combined efforts of the jury and the trial judge ensured that the compensatory damages award was what it purported to be: compensation based on considered evaluation of the degree of emotional harm inflicted on the Campbells by State Farm. Because it is exclusively for actual harm sustained by the Campbells, the compensatory damages award supports a punitive damages award exceeding $1 million.

In its discussion of the relationship between compensatory and punitive damages, the Supreme Court reaffirmed that ratios exceeding single-digits, which it strongly implied mark the outer limits of due process, may be appropriate only where " 'a particularly egregious act has resulted in only a small amount of economic damages,' " or where " 'the monetary value of noneconomic harm may have been difficult to determine.' " These circumstances are not present here. But, neither is this a proper case to limit a punitive damages award to the amount of compensatory damages. The 1-to-1 ratio between compensatory and punitive damages is most applicable where a sizeable compensatory damages award for economic injury is coupled with conduct of unremarkable reprehensibility. This scenario, likewise, does not describe this case.

Here, the Campbells were awarded substantial noneconomic damages for emotional distress. As the Supreme Court noted, "Much of the distress was caused by the outrage and humiliation the Campbells suffered at the actions of their insurer; and it is a major rule of punitive damages to condemn such conduct." The trial court valued the extent of the Campbells' injury at $1 million. We have no difficulty concluding that conduct which causes $1 million of emotional distress and humiliation is markedly more egregious than conduct which results in $1 million of economic harm. Furthermore, such conduct is a candidate for the imposition of punitive damages in excess of a 1-to-1 ratio to compensatory damages. Simply put, the trial court's determination that State Farm caused the Campbells $1 million of emotional distress warrants condemnation in the upper single-digit ratio range rather than the 1-to-1 ratio urged by State Farm. * * * When considered in light of all of the Gore reprehensibility factors, we conclude that a 9-to-1 ratio between compensatory and punitive damages, yielding a $9,018,780.75 punitive damages award, serves Utah's legitimate goals of deterrence and retribution within the limits of due process.

The application of Gore's final guidepost, the difference between the punitive damages awarded by the jury and the civil penalties authorized or imposed in comparable cases, to State Farm's conduct does not cause us to retreat from our determination that a punitive damages award nine times greater than the compensatory damages is called for here. * * * the Supreme Court pointed to a potential $10,000 fine for fraud as "the most relevant civil sanction" to which State Farm was exposed for its conduct toward the Campbells. According to the Supreme Court, this fine was "dwarfed" by the $145 million punitive damages jury award. It is unclear, however, what amount of punitive damages would be supported by a $10,000 fine. The Supreme Court endorsed a punitive damages award of $1 million, which is one hundred times greater than the $10,000 fine. Presumably, then, this 100-to-1 ratio does not offend due process. Thus, somewhere between $1 million and $145 million, the difference between the $10,000 civil penalty and the punitive damages award becomes so great that the latter "dwarfs" the former. State Farm claims in its brief that the Supreme Court impliedly found that the civil penalty would be dwarfed by a $17 million punitive damages award. Whether or not this is true, we hold fast to our conviction that a punitive damages award of $9,018,780.75 is in line with the third Gore guidepost.

The nature of a civil or criminal penalty provides some useful guidance to courts when fixing punitive damages because it reflects "legislative judgments concerning appropriate sanctions for the conduct at issue." However, the quest to reliably position any misconduct within the ranks of criminal or civil wrongdoing based on penalties affixed by a legislature can be quixotic. For example, while a $10,000 fine for fraud may appear modest in relationship to a multi-million dollar punitive damages award, it is identical to the maximum fine which may be imposed on a person in Utah for the commission of a first degree felony, the classification assigned our most serious crimes. * * * The Campbells invite us to conduct anew an analysis of the potential penalties to which State Farm may be exposed, based on the narrowed range of conduct deemed relevant by the Supreme Court. While we agree that the Supreme Court opened the door to such a reassessment, we believe that it is unnecessary in light of our conclusion that $9,018,780.75 is amply supported by the $10,000 civil penalty.

In sum, the Supreme Court affirmed the authority of a state to "make its own reasoned judgment about what conduct is permitted or proscribed within its borders." It follows, therefore, that each state retains the right and the responsibility to draw on its own values and traditions when assessing the reprehensibility of tortious conduct for the purpose of reviewing the propriety of a punitive damages award, so long as that review conforms to the Gore guidelines and the demands of due process. To the extent that our conclusions about what size punitive damages award best serves the legitimate interests of Utah exceeds an award suggested by the Supreme Court, we are exercising what we interpret to be a clear grant of discretion to do so. We have carefully considered the scope of the Supreme Court's mandate and have endeavored scrupulously to confine ourselves to it.

Finally, we turn to the Campbells' claim that costs and attorney fees incurred in this action, as well as the excess portion of the verdict not covered by insurance, should be included as part of the denominator in calculating a ratio between compensatory and punitive damages. We disagree.

We believe that fairly read, the Supreme Court's opinion forecloses consideration of a compensatory damages number other than the $1,000,000 awarded by the jury. The Supreme Court's analysis of the reasonableness and proportionality of the punitive damages award was grounded in its conviction "that there is a presumption against an award that has a 145-to-1 ratio." While that analysis may not have been different had the denominator been $1,939,518.10 (the amount of the compensatory damages, special damages, excess verdict, and attorney fees combined), and the ratio thereby reduced to 75-to-1, the considerable attention given by the Supreme Court to the issue of compensatory damages and the methodology for arriving at a constitutionally permissible ratio of compensatory to punitive damages convinces us that we would not be at liberty to consider a substitute denominator. We do, however, include the award of special damages as part of our punitive damages award as both parties agree it is part of the overall damages assessment.

To consider attorney fees and expenses in awarding punitive damages also invites unnecessary conceptual and practical complications to an already complex enterprise. In almost every case, including this one, the attorney fees and expense damage component would require its own independent reprehensibility assessment using the Gore standards. The manner in which a defendant conducts litigation bears a rational relationship to the conduct giving rise to the claim for punitive damages and would inevitably lead to an unseemly and time-consuming appendage to the trial.

The incorporation of attorney fees and expenses into the compensatory damages award would substantially alter the manner in which trials are conducted in this state. Under our general practice, the issues of whether attorney fees are available to a party and the reasonableness of the requested fees are reserved for determination by the judge after the conclusion of the trial or other proceedings. We have little doubt that the interests of justice would be subverted by sidetracking the focus of a trial away from the central claims of the parties and onto issues relating to attorney fees and expenses.

In conclusion, we hold that State Farm's behavior toward the Campbells was so egregious as to warrant a punitive damages award of $9,018,780.75, an amount nine times greater than the amount of compensatory and special damages.

Page 1014: [Add at the end of § 14.06[D]:]

(8) *See also Goddard v. Farmers Ins. Co.*, 120 P.3d 1260 (Or. App. 2005) (striking down $20 million punitive damages award as unconstitutionally excessive in relation to net compensatory award of approximately a quarter million dollars due to bad faith regarding insurer's failure to settle serious auto accident claim within policy limits; court orders punitive damages reduced to 3:1 ratio in relation to compensatory damages). In addition, *Goddard*, 120 P.3d at 1283, reviews other Oregon cases dramatically reducing punitive damages awards that exceed the presumptive 9:1 ratio of *Campbell v. State Farm*. See also Martin H. Redish & Andrew L. Mathews, *Why Punitive Damages are Unconstitutional*, 53 EMORY L.J. 1 (2004); Amy Kolz, *Go Figure*, LITIGATION (2005) (discussing Harvard Law Professor W. Kip Viscusi's view that punitive damages are too high and Cornell Law Professor Theodore Eisenberg's view that punitive damages are not excessive).

§ 14.07   ADDITIONAL ISSUES REGARDING THE DUTY TO DEFEND CLAIMS AND SUITS

Page 1019: [Add at the end of § 14.07:]

California has reiterated its view that upon a proper reservation of rights, a liability insurer may defend a case and then seek reimbursement from the policyholder regarding legal expenditures made for claims that are not potentially covered under the policy but are part of a complaint that includes at least one covered claim that triggers the policy's duty to defend. *See Scottsdale Ins. Co. v. MV Transp.*, 115 P.3d 460, 471 (Cal. 2005), 31 Cal. Rptr. 3d 147 (Cal. 2005) ("[W]e conclude that an insurer under a standard CGL policy, having properly reserved its rights, may advance sums to defend its insured against a third party lawsuit, and may thereafter recoup such costs from the insured if it is determined, as a matter of law, that no duty to defend ever arose because the third party suit never suggested the possibility of a covered claim.")

In addition, Montana has backed recoupment while Texas appears to favor recoupment but may be reconsidering the matter as well. *See Travelers Casualty & Surety Co. v. Ribi Immunochem Research*, 108 P.3d 469, 480 (Mont. 2005) ("We likewise conclude the District Court properly determined that Travelers may recoup its defense costs expended on Ribi's behalf for those claims outside the CGL policy's pollution exclusion provision. Travelers timely and explicitly reserved its right to recoup defense costs when it notified Ribi of the reservation prior to the payment of the defense costs in [various] letters. Travelers expressly reserved its right to recoup defense costs if a court determined that it had no duty to provide such costs. Travelers also provided specific and adequate notice of the possibility of reimbursement. Ribi implicitly accepted Traveler's defense under a reservation of rights when it posed no objections. Under these circumstances, the District Court appropriately concluded that Travelers may recoup its defense costs."); *Excess Underwriters at Lloyd's, London v. Frank's Casing Crew & Rental Tools, Inc.*, 2005 Tex. LEXIS 418 (Texas Supreme Court, May 27, 2005), *rehearing granted, 2006 Tex LEXIS 1 (Tex. Jan. 6, 2006). However, one large state has come out squarely against Buss and the recoupment of counsel fees.*

GENERAL AGENTS INSURANCE COMPANY OF AMERICA, INC. v. MIDWEST SPORTING GOODS COMPANY

215 Ill. 2d 146, 828 N.E.2d 1092, 293 Ill. Dec. 594 (Ill. 2005)

JUSTICE THOMAS delivered the opinion of the court.

At issue in this case is whether, following a declaration that an insurer has no duty to defend its insured, the insurer is entitled to reimbursement of the amounts paid for the defense of its insured in the underlying lawsuit. The circuit and appellate courts held that the insurer was entitled to reimbursement. For the following reasons, we reverse the judgments of the circuit and appellate courts.

The City of Chicago and Cook County sued Midwest Sporting Goods Company (Midwest) and other defendants for creating a public nuisance by selling guns to inappropriate purchasers. Midwest tendered defense of the suit to General Agents Insurance Company of America (hereinafter Gainsco), its liability carrier. Gainsco denied coverage. The City of Chicago and Cook County then filed their first amended complaint against Midwest and other defendants. Midwest again tendered defense of the suit to Gainsco. On July 23, 1999, Gainsco responded to Midwest's independent counsel as follows:

> We wish to acknowledge and confirm our receipt and review of the First Amended Complaint that you forwarded to our office on behalf of your client and our Insured, Midwest Sporting Goods, Inc. by letter dated April 28, 1999. This letter will supplement Gainsco's letter of December 3, 1998 denying coverage with respect to the plaintiff's original complaint in this matter. We have had an opportunity to review the allegations of the First Amended Complaint, as well as the policy documentation, and without waiving the Company's rights or defenses under the Policy, would like to call the following points to your attention.
>
> * * * [The letter then quotes certain policy language.]
>
> The policy only applies to damages because of property damage or bodily injury caused by an occurrence. The First Amended Complaint does not seek damages because of property damages or bodily injury. As such, the claim is not covered under the Policy.
>
> The First Amended Complaint alleges that the Insured is liable to the plaintiffs for various acts of intentional and/or willful conduct. As a consequence, and based upon the above-noted policy provisions, the claim may not be covered under the Policy.
>
> Additionally, to the extent that the claim involves periods of time that fall outside of the periods of time to which the coverage afforded by the Company covers, the claim is not covered by the Policy.
>
> Please note that to the extent that the claim seeks injunctive relief, the claim is not a claim for damages and, thus, is not afforded coverage under the Policy. Further, to the extent that the claim is for punitive or exemplary damages, the claim is not afforded coverage under the Policy.
>
> Subject to the foregoing, and without waiving any of its rights and defenses, *including the right to recoup any defense costs paid in the event that it is determined that the Company does not owe the Insured a defense in this matter*, the Company agrees to provide the Insured a defense in the captioned suit. In light of the competing interests between the Company and the Insured in respect of the coverage for this matter, the Company agrees to the Insured's

selection and use of your firm as its counsel in this matter. However, the Company notes its right to associate with the Insured and its counsel in the defense of the underlying litigation.

* * *

Please note that any acts taken by or on behalf of the Company are taken under and pursuant to a full reservation of its rights and defenses under the Policy. Likewise, we will understand that any acts taken by or on behalf of the Insured are taken pursuant to a reservation of rights as well." (Emphasis added.)

Based upon the record in this case, it does not appear that Midwest ever responded to Gainsco's reservation of rights letter. Midwest thereafter accepted Gainsco's payment of defense costs.

On October 28, 1999, Gainsco filed a declaratory judgment action seeking, *inter alia*, a declaration that it did not owe Midwest a defense in the underlying litigation. The declaratory judgment action also asserted a claim for recovery of all defense costs paid to Midwest's independent counsel on behalf of Midwest in the underlying litigation. On June 5, 2000, Gainsco filed its first amended complaint for declaratory judgment. Midwest responded with an answer and counterclaim.

Gainsco then filed a motion for summary judgment in its declaratory judgment action, and Midwest filed a cross-motion for summary judgment. [The trial court held] that Gainsco had no duty to defend Midwest in the underlying litigation. * * * [T]he trial court noted that the issue before it was whether the plaintiffs in the underlying complaint were seeking damages in the nature of economic loss or bodily injury. The trial court held that based upon case law, the damages sought by the plaintiffs in the underlying case amounted only to economic loss, and therefore held that Gainsco was entitled to summary judgment on its declaratory judgment action.

Gainsco then filed a motion for entry of judgment for recovery of defense costs, seeking to recover the defense costs that it had paid to Midwest's independent counsel for Midwest's defense of the underlying litigation. The motion for defense costs included the affidavit of Rita Beck, a senior claims examiner for Gainsco, stating that Gainsco had paid $40,517.34 for the defense of Midwest in the underlying litigation. The trial court stayed consideration of Gainsco's motion for defense costs pending Midwest's appeal of the trial court's finding that Gainsco was not obligated to defend Midwest. * * * On appeal, the appellate court affirmed the trial court's judgment, holding that Gainsco had no duty to defend or indemnify Midwest against the underlying claim. * * * [T]he trial court [subsequently] held that Gainsco had reserved its right to recoup its costs for defending Midwest and therefore granted Gainsco's motion. The trial court ordered Midwest to pay Gainsco $40,517.34. * * * The appellate court, with one justice dissenting, again affirmed the trial court's judgment. On appeal,

Midwest argued that Gainsco had paid the defense costs pursuant to the insurance contract, which made no provision for the recovery sought by Gainsco. In addition, because the relationship between the parties was governed by contract, Gainsco could not recover defense costs under a theory of unjust enrichment. * * * The appellate court rejected Midwest's argument, stating that Midwest misconstrued the payments made by Gainsco.

The appellate court characterized the parties' actions in this case * * * as an "accommodation pending litigation to determine whether Gainsco owed Midwest the cost of defending the lawsuit the City of Chicago brought against Midwest." * * * The appellate court then noted that courts in other jurisdictions had reached a similar result. For example, the court in *Buss v. Superior Court* (Cal. 1997), ordered an insured to reimburse its insurer for defense costs paid on claims that were not within the coverage of the insured's policy. In addition, [the trial court cited other cases consistent with *Buss*] * * * The appellate court rejected Midwest's argument that the court should not adopt the reasoning of *Buss* [and similar cases] because those decisions give an insurance company too much leverage. The appellate court stated that if Midwest had refused to accept the funds under Gainsco's conditions, Midwest could have forced Gainsco to either defend without a right of reimbursement or deny a defense and risk losing its policy defense if it was found in breach of the insurance contract. Finally, the appellate court reiterated that the payments made by Gainsco were not made pursuant to Midwest's insurance policy, but rather were an "accommodation pending litigation to determine whether Gainsco owed Midwest, under the insurance contract, a defense." * * * The dissenting justice disagreed that Illinois law supported the majority's decision. The dissenting justice stated that an insurer's duty to defend its insured arises from and is limited by the express undertaking to defend as stated in the contract of insurance. Here, there was no language in the policy providing for reimbursement of costs.

Midwest argues that Gainsco failed to establish any legal basis that would entitle it to an award of reimbursement of defense costs. Midwest notes that the insurance policy between Midwest and Gainsco contains no provisions allowing Gainsco to recover defense costs. Further, because there was an express written insurance contract between the parties, Gainsco cannot claim that it is entitled to recover defense costs under a theory of unjust enrichment. In addition, Gainsco's reservation of rights letter could only reserve the rights contained within the insurance policy and could not create new rights. In any event, the language in the reservation of rights letter clearly establishes that Gainsco paid the defense costs pursuant to the insurance policy.

Gainsco responds that each of the preceding arguments must fail because there is no contract governing the parties' relationship. Gainsco argues that its duty to defend extended only to claims for damages that were payable or potentially covered under a Gainsco policy. Here, as the circuit and appellate courts found, the Gainsco policies did not apply to the underlying litigation. In addition, Gainsco notes that numerous decisions, including *Buss*, * * * support the trial court's decision.

An insurer's duty to defend its insured is much broader than its duty to indemnify its insured. An insurer may not justifiably refuse to defend an action against its insured unless it is clear from the face of the underlying complaint that the allegations set forth in that complaint fail to state facts that bring the case within or potentially within the insured's policy coverage. A court must compare the allegations in the underlying complaint to the policy language in order to determine whether the insurer's duty to defend has arisen. If the underlying complaint alleges facts within or potentially within policy coverage, an insurer is obligated to defend its insured even if the allegations are groundless, false or fraudulent. The allegations in the underlying complaint must be liberally construed in favor of the insured. In addition, if several theories of recovery are alleged in the underlying complaint against the insured, the insurer's duty to defend arises even if only one of several theories is within the potential coverage of the policy. When the underlying complaint against the insured alleged facts within or potentially within the scope of policy coverage, the insurer taking the position that the complaint is not covered by its policy must defend the suit under a reservation of rights or seek a declaratory judgment that there is no coverage.

In the instant case, as noted, Gainsco chose both to defend under a reservation of rights and to seek a declaratory judgment that there was no coverage. Gainsco's reservation of rights letter provided that it reserved the right to recoup any defense costs paid in the event it was determined that Gainsco did not owe Midwest a defense. The gravamen of Midwest's argument on appeal is that Gainsco could not reserve the right to recoup defense costs because the insurance contract between the parties does not contain a provision allowing Gainsco the right to recoup defense costs. In turn, the gravamen of Gainsco's response is that there is no contract governing the relationship between the parties because both the circuit and appellate courts have held that the policies issued by Gainsco to Midwest did not apply to the underlying litigation. Accordingly, Gainsco maintains that it had no duty to defend Midwest and thus is entitled to recoup the amounts paid for Midwest's defense.

In support of its argument, Gainsco points to decisions from other jurisdictions where courts have held that an insurer may recover its defense costs if it specifically reserves the right to recoup those costs in the event it is determined that the insurer does not owe the insured a defense. Gainsco notes that *Grinnell Mutual Reinsurance Co. v. Shierk* (S.D. Ill. 1998), the only decision interpreting Illinois law on this issue, is indistinguishable from this case and directly supports the circuit court's decision to grant Gainsco's motion for recovery of defense costs. In *Grinnell*, the insured, Shierk, was sued by his wife for negligence in connection with an incident where he discharged a gun in her direction, causing a bullet to strike her in the face. Shierk tendered defense of the lawsuit to Grinnell Mutual Reinsurance Company (Grinnell), claiming coverage pursuant to his homeowner's insurance policy. Grinnell agreed to defend Shierk, but expressly reserved the right to later deny coverage and reserved the right to seek reimbursement from Shierk in the event a declaratory judgment action found that Grinnell had no duty to defend. The district court later determined that Grinnell had no duty to defend.

The district court then considered whether Grinnell was entitled to reimbursement of funds that it had already expended in defending Shierk. The district court noted that there was no Illinois case law addressing the issue, but that such relief was found to be available in other jurisdictions. The district court predicted that this court would order reimbursement of defense costs, observing that Grinnell specifically reserved the right to seek reimbursement and that Shierk, fully aware of Grinnell's reservation of its right to reimbursement, accepted the benefit of Grinnell's defense.

Gainsco notes that the district court in *Grinnell* also relied on a decision from the Supreme Court of California. In *Buss v. Superior Court*, the court also addressed whether an insurer could recover reimbursement of defense costs from its insured. The underlying action in that case asserted 27 causes of action, of which only one claim potentially fell within policy coverage. The insurer accepted defense of the underlying action, but reserved all of its rights, including the right to deny that any cause of action was actually covered and the right to be reimbursed for defense costs in the event it was later determined that there was no coverage.

In addressing the issue, the court first noted that in a "mixed" action, involving claims that are at least potentially covered and claims that are not, an insurer nonetheless has a duty to defend the claim in its entirety. The court then stated that with regard to "mixed" claims, an insurer may not seek reimbursement for claims that are at least potentially covered, but may seek reimbursement for defense costs as to the claims that are not even potentially covered. The court explained that with regard to defense costs for claims that are potentially covered, the insured had paid premiums and the insurer had bargained to bear those costs, so that there was no right of reimbursement implied in the policy or implied in law. The court noted exceptions would exist if the policy itself provided for reimbursement or if there was a separate contract supported by separate consideration. However, with regard to claims that are not even potentially covered, the insured had not paid premiums to the insurer and the insurer did not bargain to bear those costs. Consequently, the court reasoned that the insurer has a right to reimbursement implied in law as quasi-contractual. Under the law of restitution, the insured has been "enriched" through the insurer's bearing of unbargained-for defense costs, an enrichment that must be deemed unjust.

Finally, Gainsco notes that other jurisdictions also have found that an insurer may recover defense costs from its insured where the insurer agrees to provide the insured a defense pursuant to an express reservation of rights, including the right to recoup defense costs, the insured accepts the defense, and a court subsequently finds that the insurer did not owe the insured a defense. See *United National Insurance Co. v. SST Fitness Corp.* (6th Cir. 2002) (insurer was entitled to reimbursement of defense costs where the insurer reserved the right to recover defense costs and the insured accepted payment of defense costs); *Resure, Inc. v. Chemical Distributors, Inc.* (M.D. La. 1996) (insurer was entitled to reimbursement for all costs of defense where it timely and specifically reserved the right to seek reimbursement and insured did not object to the reservation); *Knapp v. Commonwealth Land Title Insurance Co.*, (D. Minn. 1996) (where insurer reserved its right to seek reimbursement of attorney's fees and costs, insured's silence in response to the reservation of rights letter and subsequent acceptance of defense constituted an implied agreement to the reservation of rights); *North Atlantic Casualty & Surety Insurance Co. v. William D.* (N.D. Cal. 1990) (where insurer sent letter to the insured reserving the right to reimbursement, and the insured accepted payment of defense fees without comment, insurer was entitled to reimbursement from insured); *Hecla Mining Co. v. New Hampshire Insurance Co.*, (Colo. 1991) (court states that proper course for insurer that believes it owes no duty to defend "is to provide a defense to the insured under a reservation of its rights to seek reimbursement should the facts at trial prove that the incident resulting in liability was not covered by the policy"); *Colony Insurance Co. v. G&E Tires & Service, Inc.* (Fla. App. 2000) (insurer was entitled to reimbursement of defense costs where it timely and expressly reserved the right to seek reimbursement, and the insured accepted the offer of a defense with a reservation of rights).

In general then, the decisions finding that an insurer is entitled to reimbursement of defense costs are based upon a finding that there was a contract implied in fact or law, or a finding that the insured was unjustly enriched when its insurer paid defense costs for claims that were not covered by the insured's policy. Although such reasoning was not the basis for the appellate court's decision in this case, Gainsco notes that this court may affirm the appellate court on any basis, and urges this court to adopt the reasoning of the courts in the preceding cases.

Gainsco is correct that it would be entitled to reimbursement of the defense costs paid in the underlying action if this court adopted the analysis set forth in the preceding cases. Gainsco timely and expressly reserved its right to reimbursement of defense costs, Midwest accepted payment of those defense costs without objection, and a declaratory judgment action determined that Gainsco did not owe Midwest a defense in the underlying lawsuit. Our research reveals, however, that other jurisdictions, albeit a minority, have refused to allow an insurer to receive reimbursement of its defense costs even though the underlying claim was not covered by the insurance policy and the insurer had specifically reserved its right to reimbursement.

Upon review, we find the analysis of those decisions refusing to allow reimbursement to be more persuasive and more on point with Illinois case law than the cases cited by Gainsco. For example, in *Shoshone First Bank v. Pacific Employers Insurance Co.*, (Wy. 2000), the court declined to allocate costs between covered and uncovered claims, holding that "unless an agreement to the contrary is found in the policy, the insurer is liable for all the costs of defending the action." The court rejected the insurer's claim that it had the right to allocate defense costs for uncovered claims because its reservation of rights letter had specifically reserved the right to allocate the fees, expenses and indemnity payments when the case was resolved. The court stated:

> "The insurer is not permitted to unilaterally modify and change policy coverage. We agree with the Supreme Court of Hawaii that a reservation of rights letter 'does not relieve the insurer of the costs incurred in defending its insured where the insurer was obligated, in the first instance, to provide such a defense.' *First Insurance Co. of Hawaii, Inc. v. State, by Minami* (Haw. 1983). [The insurer] could have included allocation language in the Policy, but it failed to do so. We look only to the four corners of the policy to determine coverage, and where the policy is unambiguous, extrinsic evidence is not considered. [Citation.] The Policy issued to Shoshone by [the insurer] states a duty to defend, and allocation is not mentioned. In light of the failure of the policy language to provide for allocation, we will not permit the contract to be amended or altered by a reservation of rights letter."

Accord *Texas Ass'n of Counties Government Risk Management Pool v. Matagorda County*, (Tex. 2000) (absent provision providing for reimbursement of settlement funds, unilateral reservation of rights letter could not create rights not contained within the insurance policy).

The court in *Shoshone First Bank* then cited an unpublished decision from the United States District Court for the District of Wyoming that clearly articulated the problem with allowing an insurer to reserve the right to seek reimbursement of defense costs. That court stated that:

> "15. A reservation of rights letter does not create a contract allowing an insurer to recoup defense costs from its insureds.
>
> 16. The question as to whether there is a duty to defend an insured is a difficult one, but because that is the business of an insurance carrier, it is the insurance carrier's duty to make that decision. If an insurance carrier believes that no coverage exists, then it should deny its insured a defense at the beginning instead of defending and later attempting to recoup from its insured the costs of defending the underlying action. Where the insurance carrier is uncertain over insurance coverage for the underlying claim, the proper course is for the insurance carrier to tender a defense and seek a declaratory judgment as to coverage under the policy. However, to allow the insurer to force the insured into choosing between seeking a defense under the policy, and run the

potential risk of having to pay for this defense if it is subsequently determined that no duty to defend existed, or giving up all meritorious claims that a duty to defend exists, places the insured in the position of making a Hobson's choice. Furthermore, endorsing such conduct is tantamount to allowing the insurer to extract a unilateral amendment to the insurance contract. If this became common practice, the insurance industry might extract coercive arrangements from their insureds, destroying the concept of liability and litigation insurance.

Order on Plaintiff's Motion for Summary Judgment, *America States Ins. Co. v. Ridco, Inc. Riddles Jewelry, Inc. And Ken B. Berger* (D. Wyo. 1999)."

We agree with the analysis of the court in *Shoshone First Bank*, as well as the United States District Court for the District of Wyoming in *America States Insurance Co.* As a matter of public policy, we cannot condone an arrangement where an insurer can unilaterally modify its contract, through a reservation of rights, to allow for reimbursement of defense costs in the event a court later finds that the insurer owes no duty to defend. We recognize that courts have found an implied agreement where the insured accepts the insurer's payment of defense costs despite the insurer's reservation of a right to reimbursement of defense costs. However, as stated by the court in *America States Insurance Co.*, cited by the *Shoshone First Bank* court, recognizing such an implied agreement effectively places the insured in the position of making a Hobson's choice between accepting the insurer's additional conditions on its defense or losing its right to a defense from the insurer.

The United States Court of Appeals for the Third Circuit, applying Pennsylvania law, also has ruled that an insurer cannot recover defense costs even when it defends under a reservation of rights to recover defense costs if it is later determined there is no coverage. *Terra Nova Insurance Co. v. 900 Bar, Inc.* (3d Cir. 1989). The court reasoned that:

"A rule permitting such recovery would be inconsistent with the legal principles that induce an insurer's offer to defend under reservation of rights. Faced with uncertainty as to its duty to indemnify, an insurer offers a defense under reservation of rights to avoid the risks that an inept or lackadaisical defense of the underlying action may expose it to if it turns out there is a duty to indemnify. [footnote omitted]. At the same time, the insurer wishes to preserve its right to contest the duty to indemnify if the defense is unsuccessful. Thus, such an offer is made at least as much for the insurer's own benefit as for the insured's. If the insurer could recover defense costs, the insured would be required to pay for the insurer's action in protecting itself against the estoppel to deny coverage that would be implied if it undertook the defense without reservation."

Again, we find the reasoning of the *Terra Nova* court to be more persuasive than the authorities cited by Gainsco. We agree that when an insurer tenders a defense or pays defense costs pursuant to a reservation of rights, the insurer is protecting itself at least as much as it is protecting its insured. Thus, we cannot say that an insured is unjustly enriched when its insurer tenders a defense in order to protect its own interests, even if it is later determined that the insurer did not owe a defense. Certainly, if an insurer wishes to retain its right to seek reimbursement of defense costs in the event it later is determined that the underlying claim is not covered by the policy, the insurer is free to include such a term in its insurance contract. Absent such a provision in the policy, however, an insurer cannot later attempt to amend the policy by including the right to reimbursement in its reservation of rights letter.

Moreover, as the Supreme Court of Hawaii recognized, "affording an insured a defense under a reservation of rights agreement merely retains any defenses the insurer has under its policy; it does not relieve the insurer of the costs incurred in defending its insured where the insurer was obligated, in the first instance, to provide such a defense." *First Insurance Co. of Hawaii, Inc. v. State of Hawaii* (Haw. 1983). Gainsco's reservation of rights letter could retain only those defenses that Gainsco had under its policy. Gainsco concedes that the insurance policies at issue did not provide for reimbursement of defense costs. Consequently, Gainsco's attempt to expand its reservation of rights to include the right to reimbursement must fail.

As previously noted, Gainsco argues that we need not look to the insurance contract between the parties to determine whether Gainsco had a right to reimbursement because the circuit and appellate courts have already determined that Gainsco owed no duty to defend. Gainsco maintains that because it had no duty to defend, it follows that there is no contract governing the relationship between the parties. The problem with this argument is that Gainsco is attempting to define its duty to defend based upon the outcome of the declaratory judgment action. Although an insurer's duty to indemnify arises only after damages are fixed, the duty to defend arises as soon as damages are sought. As explained by the Court of Appeals for the Eighth Circuit:

"Liberty remained obligated to defend [its insured] so long as there remained any question as to whether the underlying claims were covered by the policies. Upon determination that *** the claims against [the insured] were therefore excluded from coverage, the district court properly concluded that Liberty's duty to defend [its insured] in this action expired. Because we conclude that Liberty had a duty to defend [its insured] until such determination was made, we reject Liberty's argument that it is entitled to reimbursement of defense costs." *Liberty Mutual Insurance Co. v. FAG Bearings Corp.* (8th Cir. 1998).

We find the analysis of the court in *Liberty Mutual* to be well taken. Although Gainsco implies that it has always maintained that it did not owe Midwest a defense in the underlying matter, we note that Gainsco's reservation of rights letter reveals some uncertainty concerning coverage. With regard to allegations in the underlying claim that Midwest was liable to the plaintiffs for various acts of intentional and/or willful conduct, Gainsco's reservation of rights letter stated that "the claim *may not be covered* under the Policy." (Emphasis added.) Given this uncertainty, Gainsco correctly agreed to pay Midwest's defense costs in the underlying action and sought a declaratory judgment that it did not owe Midwest a defense. Gainsco thus remained obligated to defend Midwest as long as any questions remained concerning whether the underlying claims were covered by the policies. Because Gainsco's obligation to defend continued until the trial court found that Gainsco did not owe Midwest a defense, Gainsco is not entitled to reimbursement of defense costs paid pending the trial court's order in the declaratory judgment action. The fact that the trial court ultimately found that the underlying claims against Midwest were not covered by the Gainsco policies does not entitle Gainsco to reimbursement of its defense costs.

In sum, we acknowledge that a majority of jurisdictions have held that an insurer is entitled to reimbursement of defense costs when (1) the insurer did not have a duty to defend, (2) the insurer timely and expressly reserved its right to recoup defense costs, and (3) the insured either remains silent in the face of the reservation of rights or accepts the insurer's payment of defense costs. We choose, however, to follow the minority rule and refuse to permit an insurer to recover defense costs pursuant to a reservation of rights absent an express provision to that effect in the insurance contract between the parties.

For the foregoing reasons, then, we reverse the decisions of the circuit and appellate courts awarding Gainsco reimbursement of defense costs, in the amount of $40,517.34, expended for the defense of Midwest in the underlying litigation.

NOTES AND QUESTIONS

(1) In spite of *Midwest Sporting Goods*, the scorecard of cases decided is split by insurer rights to recoupment of defense costs (i.e., the *Buss* position) appears to be on the ascendancy. But is it a good idea? In *Frank's Casing*, the Texas Supreme Court was influenced by the writings of Dean Robert Jerry, author of a well-respected insurance law textbook for students (*Understanding Insurance Law* (3d ed. 2002) and a popular law school casebook (which competes with this casebook and thus meets the Voldemort "it shall not be named" standard, even if it is a LexisNexis publication). *See* Robert H. Jerry, II, *The Insurer's Right to Reimbursement of Defense Costs*, 42 Ariz. L. Rev. 13 (2000). Although Dean Jerry's analysis on any insurance topic is always worthy of consideration, many other law professors (us included) are not nearly as enthusiastic about insurer recoupment

actions. Particularly troubling is that the standard liability insurance policy promises to defend "suits" against the policyholder and does not contain specific language.

(2) Where recoupment has been permitted, this has been either on equitable grounds or because the insurer expressed a reserved right to recoupment when it agreed to defend the claim. This is a bit like a surgeon bargaining with a patient that is already anesthetized and on the operating table. After a policy is sold, premiums collected, and a claim arises, the policyholder as a practical matter needs a defense. The policyholder should not be expected to refuse a defense in which the insurer is adding a recoupment reservation that was not expressly in the policy. Arugably, this is changing the rules in the middle of the game. Dean Jerry and others disagree on this point and by now (more than six years after Jerry wrote on the topic) can also argue that sophisticated policyholders purchasing liability insurance now have constructive notice that their liability carriers may seek recoupment of defense expenditures that can be isolated to claims in a suit that are clearly beyond the scope of policy coverage. It's not a bad argument in 2006, even if it was not a good argument in 1997 when *Buss v. Superior Court*, the leading modern pro-recoupment precedent, was decided. But recoupment does give insurers leverage over policyholders by judicial activism and concepts of equity rather than by express terms of a contract agreement. Ordinarily, insurers are seen as the litigants arguing for strict enforcement of contract terms and dismissing appeals to equity (often made by policyholders) as improper.

§ 14.10 POLICYHOLDER PREROGATIVES REGARDING SETTLEMENT

Page 1027: [Add at the end of § 14.10:]

(4) *See also Century Indem. Co. v. Aero-Motive Co.*, 336 F. Supp. 2d 739 (W.D.Mich. 2004) (finding $5 million settlement and consent judgment unreasonable where it was twice the amount of plaintiff's highest prior demand and several times counsel's valuation; concluding that settlement resulted from bad faith conduct by policyholder; *Miller-Shugart* treatment also unavailable because insurer was in fact defending claim when improper settlement made); *Safeway Ins. Co. v. Guerrero*, 106 P.3d 1020 (Ariz. 2005) (rejecting insurer's claim of intentional interference with contractual relations against claimant's attorney negotiating a settlement and assignment of policy rights with policyholder-defendant).

(5) Arizona has perhaps an even more well-developed *Miller-Shugart* jurisprudence than Minnesota, with such agreements known as "*Morris, Damron, or Morris-Damron*" settlements in Arizona. *See Guerrero*, 106 P.3d at 1022; *United Servs. Auto. Ass'n v. Morris*, 154 Ariz. 113, 741 P.2d 246 (1987); *Damron v. Sledge*, 105 Ariz., 151, 460 P.2d 997 (1969). The distinction is that a *Morris* settlement occurs even where the insurer is defending the claim but where the policyholder can credibly assert an anticipatory

breach of the insurer's duty to indemnify. A *Damron* agreement results in situations where the insurer fails to defend at all, making it closer to *Miller-Shugart* and similar case lines in other states.

Chapter 15

REINSURANCE, EXCESS INSURANCE AND SELF-INSURANCE

§ 15.01 REINSURANCE

[A] Introduction

Page 1029: [Add the following at the end of § 15.01[A]:]

"Traditional" reinsurance has existed in some form since at least 1370. *See* Adam B. Leichtling & Laura M. Paredes, *Fundamental Concepts in Reinsurance in Latin American Countries*, 37 INTER-AMERICAN L. REV. 1 (2005) (noting documented existence of maritime insurer's purchase of reinsurance against loss paid in connection with insurance of voyage). By traditional, we mean reinsurance in which the reinsurer takes on a true underwriting risk—the chance that the reinsurer could unexpectedly be called upon to pay fortuitous losses as well as the chance that the reinsurer could make more from ceding insurer's premium payments than the reinsurer paid in connection with losses. When we spoke of risk transfer in Chapter One, we were referring to underwriting risk.

However, in addition to underwriting risk, there is also investment risk and timing risk. Investment risk is the risk that an insurer's investment portfolio might underperform expectations. Timing risk is the risk that an insurance company might pay out for losses more quickly than was anticipated, which of course reduces the amount of investment income earned by the reinsurer and is thus a cousin to investment risk. Because insurers and reinsurers make much of their money because of the "float" or lag time between receipt of premiums and payment of claims, both insurers and reinsurers tend to want longer lag time. That way, insurers and reinsurers can make money even if their underwriters have "guessed wrong" about the number and severity of claims under their policies.

To take a simple example: If a policyholder has two significant bodily injury claims during the policy year rather than the one predicted by the actuaries, the insurer may be in trouble because it assessed premiums based on the prediction of a single claim. However, if the claims are not paid until after several years of litigation, an insurer with a good investment portfolio may nonetheless make money on the account, although this is a little far-fetched in connection with a single policyholder and policy. Even the most efficient defense of a claim will cost significant sums that will probably outpace investment return on a single policy's premium. But where risks are pooled, the years of interest or other investment wealth created while a pool of claims is adjusted or litigated can be particularly significant. As a result, insurers have a strong incentive to delay paying claims as long as possible so long as this does not create bad faith exposure (see **Chapter 14**).

To take a larger, more complex example: even though asbestos liability claims have been the largest "mass tort" in history, they are estimated to be only a 3-5 percent drag on liability insurer earnings. Why? Because liability insurers have in most cases not been required to pay these claims until years or even decades after the injuries took place. Furthermore, when it has come time to pay the piper, insurers pay with dollars that are worth less because of intervening inflation. Consequently, although long-tale claims bother insurers because of their potential to trigger more than one liability policy, the long-tale claims also enable insurers to have a greater float, larger investment returns, and to pay in inflation-diminished dollars.

Reinsurers face the same situation and hence have an interest in paying claims later rather than earlier. Consequently, reinsurers are happy to have insurers take their time in paying claims and seeking payment from the reinsurers. Because reinsurers are ordinarily held not to have a contractual relation with the underlying policyholder, the reinsurer often has little or no bad faith exposure unless the reinsurer has been involved in claims processing or is acting in concert with an insurer committing bad faith (more on this later in the Chapter). A prudent reinsurer may even enjoy having the ceding insurer delay claims payments for years as this normally gives the reinsurer economic advantage while the risk of a bad faith punitive damages award is shouldered by the ceding insurer.

However, even with the advantages of the time value of money, insurers face investment and timing risk. For example, in one case involving bankruptcy of asbestos defendant policyholders, a federal appeals court ruled that confirmation of the bankruptcy debtor's Chapter 11 Plan triggered the debtor's liability policies and required the insurers to immediately pay policy proceeds into the trust fund established to pay the policyholder-debtor's asbestos claims liability even though many of those claims would not actually be processed until years in the future. See *UNR Indus., Inc. v. Continental Cas. Co.*, 942 F.2d 1101 (7th Cir. 1991) (applying Illinois law law). As you might imagine, insurers were not too happy about that result. But, perhaps viewing the case as an apparition, the insurance industry made relatively little protest. But when a Los Angeles trial court followed the *UNR* approach, insurers vigorously objected in the trade press and legal periodicals and successfully challenged the result on appeal, obtaining a ruling that implementation of a bankruptcy reorganization did not operate to trigger or accelerate insurer payment obligations for asbestos claims. See *Fuller-Austin Insulation Co. v. Highlands Ins. Co.*, 135 Cal. App. 4th 958, 38 Cal. Rptr. 2d 716 (Cal. Ct. 2006). Similar coverage battles remain active so it is too early to say which side will prevail. See generally *Stempel on Insurance Contracts* § 12.09[E] (3d ed. 2006 & Supp. 2007).

Our point is simply that the investment and timing risk are significant. Even in relatively simple situations, timing and investment risk can matter. For example, Acme Insurance may provide fire coverage on the home of Anthony Aardvark. Even if Anthony is well-known for smoking in bed (and has had three prior house fires because of it) and was charged a high premium, timing risk can matter. For example, if Anthony nods off while smoking on Day 2 of the policy period, this is much worse for the insurer than if he makes it to Day 364, lengthening the time before which the insurer will be called upon to pay the claim. The insurer's substantive investment decisions are also important. If the insurer invested substantially in Enron stock, it will have substantially less investment income than anticipated, no matter when misfortune strikes the Aardvark home.

All this becomes important for reinsurance purposes because insurers would prefer to smooth out the rough ups and downs of their risks, not only underwriting risks but investment and timing risks as well. "Financial" or "Finite" reinsurance can assist in this regarding the latter two risks even when there is no shift of underwriting risk. By purchasing finite reinsurance, the ceding insurer gains a commitment for future payments at specified times, effectively transferring investment risk and timing risk to the reinsurer. Without more, however, some timing risk remains with the ceding insurer in that the insurer may be called upon to pay claims sooner than it receives its scheduled payments from the reinsurer. There is also at least some investment risk in that the insurer may have been able to earn more with the premium money than it received in return from the reinsurer. However, as discussed above, some finite reinsurance contracts provide limitations on timing risk, retroactively increase premiums, or return excess premium payments. Provisions of this type may effectively strip away even timing and investment risk transfer from the resulting "reinsurance" products. When this happens, the resulting transaction looks very much like a favorable loan (or a CEO's compensation package approved by a board of directors violating its fiduciary duty to shareholders): there is little or no risk transfer and the contract is simply a financing vehicle.

So what, you say? If that's your reaction, do not apply for a job with New York Attorney General Elliot Spitzer (who will probably be Governor by the time this Supplement is in print). Spitzer's famous investigations of AIG and other insurers centered in part around finite reinsurance. Most offending to Spitzer and other regulators was finite insurance that did not transfer underwriting risk. Although there is nothing illegal about entering a contract that addresses investment and timing risk alone or that is simply a loan, there is a problem if one treats such a contract as insurance with underwriting risk for tax purposes. This is because American tax law permits an insurer to deduct premium payments. When an insurer purchases traditional reinsurance, the amount of reinsurance is treated as a reserve and results in a considerable tax savings for the insurer in return for the insurer's payment of premium to the reinsurer. But if there has been no transfer of underwriting risk because over time premiums equal reinsurance policy or treaty benefits, the insurer has improperly taken a tax deduction simply for lending money to itself through a third party. This is not all that different from the things that Enron did that earned criminal convictions for Andrew Fastow, Jeffrey Skilling and the late Kenneth Lay. The transaction creates the impression of income, profit, or balance sheet that does not exist. Of course, loans or financial reinsurance programs that transfer only investment and timing risk are not the equivalent of Enron's phony profits from special purpose entities. But when insurers or reinsurers treat pure financial reinsurance as if it were risk-shifting traditional reinsurance, this can be tax fraud as well as fraud upon the investment community. Now you know why Spitzer and other regulators get upset if finite reinsurance is improperly treated as traditional reinsurance.

The Spitzer perspective was expressed by the Financial Accounting Standard Board (FASB) long before Spitzer became a household word. In FASB Statement No. 113 (1992), the Board stated that a reinsurance contract can be considered an insurance contract rather than an investment contract based upon (1) the amount of underwriting risk to which the reinsurer is exposed and (2) the timing of the reinsurer's reimbursement claims.

> For short-duration reinsurance contracts to be considered [true] insurance contracts [for tax purposes], the reinsurer must assume significant insurance [i.e., underwriting] risk, and it must be "reasonably possible that the reinsurer may realize a significant loss from the transaction." For long-duration reinsurance contracts to be considered insurance contracts, they must satisfy the same criteria as for short-duration contracts, and in addition, the insurer must be subject to mortality or morbidity risks.

> If a reinsurance contract fails to meet the conditions stated above, then it is considered to be an investment contract. In accounting for an investment contract, the primary insurer would report the premium paid, less the premium retained by the reinsurer, as a deposit.

See Heather M. Hulburt, *Financial Reinsurance and the AIG/General Re Scandal*, CPCU EJOURNAL, Nov. 2005 at p. 1 (endnotes omitted). Because financial/finite reinsurance "seldom involves the transfer of underwriting risk," these reinsurance transactions generally should not have the same tax benefits accorded to traditional reinsurance. What got AIG, General Re, other insurers and certain individuals in trouble with Spitzer and other regulators was not the use of financial reinsurance but treating it like traditional reinsurance. *See* Hulbert; supra, at 1, 5-6, Diana Reitz, *Why Do Finite-Risk Deals Raise Eyebrows?*, NATIONAL UNDERWRITER (Prop. & Cas. ed.), April 18, 2005 at p. 58; Ianthe Jeanne Dugan & Theo Francis, *How a Hot Insurance Product Burned AIG*, WALL ST. J., March 15, 2005 at C1, col. 1.

The *Wall Street Journal* article cited above also contains a short history of the development of the financial/finite insurance product in Bermuda during the 1980s. Beginning in the 1980s, reinsurers began to offer so-called "financial" or "finite" reinsurance, products that almost always carried at least some investment risk and timing risk but where the reinsurer might bear no underwriting risk. Some finite reinsurance contracts are sufficiently modified so that even investment or timing risk was not particularly significant. In such cases, the finite "reinsurance" functions more like a straight-out loan in which a ceding insurer pays "premiums" to a reinsurer and is relatively certainly assured of being repaid over time irrespective of the loss experience of the underlying policyholders. Finite reinsurance became a popular means for insurers to spread the investment and timing risks of their business even if the reinsurance "policies" functioned more like loans. But like any innovative product, financial/finite reinsurance can be abused, as the events of 2005 reflect.

On a technical level, there are "five distinct types of financial reinsurance contracts": (1) time and distance contracts; (2) loss portfolio transfers; (3) retrospective aggregate contracts; (4) prospective aggregate contracts; and (5) financial quota share treaties. *See* Hulburt, *supra*, at 2. Professor Hulburt explains them succinctly and well.

In the **time and distance** contract, the primary [ceding] insurer pays an agreed-upon premium to the reinsurer at the inception of the contract. In return, the reinsurer promises to make one or more payments to the primary insurer in the future. The timing and amount of these future cash flows are determined upfront, and are based on the investment income that the reinsurer expects to earn on the premium it receives from the primary insurer. The premium paid by the primary insurer, then, is equal to the present value of all of these future cash flows, plus a loading for the reinsurer's expense and profit. * * * The risk transferred in the time and distance contract is reinvestment rate risk.

In the **loss portfolio transfer**, the primary insurer transfers its liability for a block of reported underwritten losses to the reinsurer. The premium paid by the primary insurer to the reinsurer is based on the present value of the (expected) future loss payments, plus a loading for expenses and profits. ["loading" is the "overhead or administrative expenses of an insurer that is included in the cost of a policy." *See* JAMES S. TRIESCHMANN, ROBERT E. HOYT & DAVID W. SOMMER, RISK MANAGEMENT AND INSURANCE G-11 (12th ed. 2005)] * * * Note that the loss portfolio transfer can be structured so as to also transfer underwriting risk [if the] reinsurer accepted liability for paying out on both expected **and** unexpected future claims. If a true underwriting risk transfer exists, then the primary insurer can deduct the premium paid to the reinsurer for tax purposes.

The **retrospective aggregate** contract works much like the loss portfolio transfer, except that it covers primary insurer reserves for both (1) reported losses (as in the loss portfolio transfer); and (2) incurred-but-not-reported (IBNR) losses.

In the **prospective aggregate** contract, the reinsurer agrees to make specified payments in the future to assist the primary insurer in paying future losses. Even though the future losses are not known at the time that the contract is drawn up, the contract can still be created to cover investment risk only. This would be accomplished by including aggregate limits, payment schedules, and/or profit-sharing commissions in the contract.

Financial quota share treaties are similar to traditional quota share treaties, in that the primary insurer transfers a fixed, predetermined percentage of every risk covered in the treaty. What makes the financial quota share treaty different from the traditional quota share treaty is that the treaty is structured in such a way as to protect the reinsurer from any underwriting risk. This is accomplished by setting the reinsurer's aggregate liability equal to the reinsurance premium plus the reinsurer's anticipated investment income.

[F]inancial reinsurance contracts can be written on a one-time basis, or they can be written on a recurring basis. If written on a recurring basis, then the primary insurer would make periodic premium payments to the reinsurer, typically on an annual basis, over a three-to-five year period. The reinsurer would deposit the payments into an earmarked account on behalf of the primary insurer (after deducting its loading fee) and would pay interest on the account at a pre-arranged rate of return. As the primary insurer incurred losses over time, the losses would be covered by funds from the earmarked account. If losses in a given year were greater than the balance in the account, then the reinsurer would cover the excess, but would get reimbursed by future premium payments made into the account by the primary insurer. If losses were less than the remaining balance in the account at the end of the contract period, then the surplus would be returned to the primary insurer. Thus, in the longer-term financial reinsurance contracts, the primary insurer is still covering its own losses, but is able to effectively smooth the payments on these losses (and, hence, on earning) over time.

See Hulburt, *supra*, at 2-4 (endnotes omitted; boldface in original).

[B] Contractual Relationship Between the Insured and the Reinsurer

Page 1034: [Add at the end of § 15.01[B]:]

Additional Potential Reinsurer Liability to Policyholders

Although reinsurers may not be in strict contractual privity to policyholders, they may face bad faith liability where they step into the shoes of an insurer and act in bad faith or where they work in concert with an insurer in a manner that exhibits bad faith toward the policyholder. Similarly, a reinsurer may be liable in damages to policyholders if the reinsurer tortiously interferes with the insurer-policyholder relationship or induces bad faith by the insurer where the reinsurer unreasonably attempts to convince an insurer to refuse coverage, undervalue a claim, attempt to intimidate a policyholder into a low settlement, or other misconduct.

Many reinsurers would perhaps dispute this analysis, arguing that under the traditional rules of privity of contract they are beyond the reach of the policyholder. Some reinsurers may even expect consultation by insurers and expect to have a voice regarding claims. However frequent reinsurer participation in claims decisions may be, it remains inconsistent with the basic premises of the insurer-policyholder relationship and the insurer-reinsurer relationship. Although it is correct that there is no contractual relationship between reinsurer and policyholder, the need for a reinsurer to stay outside the circle of policyholder and insurer follows as a natural corollary of the nature of reinsurance in relation to insurance. Consequently, reinsurers that "meddle" in an insurer's coverage and claims decisions may be liable to the extent the insurer is or would be liable to the policyholder for bad faith conduct.

Recall a key operating premise of reinsurance, as essentially "codified" through the follow-the-fortunes doctrine and express follow-the-fortunes language in reinsurance treaties and contracts. The assumption is that the insurer will make reasonable determinations regarding coverage and claims handling, including settlement of claims and litigation. After the insurer has settled, the matter of coverage liability is essentially over. According to longstanding custom and practice (often reflected in express contract language) the reinsurer is bound by the insurer's decisions, so long as those decisions are made in good faith. If an insurer pays a suspicious claim, the reinsurer cannot second-guess the insurer. Conversely, if the insurer spurns an early settlement offer but the plaintiff then recovers a large verdict, the reinsurer is also bound by the decisions of the insurer and their consequences. If a reinsurer thinks an insurer makes poor claims or coverage decisions, the reinsurer's remedy is not to contest those decisions in subsequent litigation but to cease doing business with insurers in which the reinsurer lacks confidence.

These are well-established norms of reinsurance. Only if the insurer's payment is palpably unreasonable, in bad faith or is for a loss clearly outside the scope of the policy can the reinsurer avoid the force of the follow-the-fortunes principle (see § **15.01[D]**, *supra*). The rationale of the doctrine is to prevent a second round of coverage litigation between insurer and reinsurer and to prevent either reinsurer or insurer from raising issues in their intramural dispute that may adversely affect underlying tort or coverage litigation. An additional value of the doctrine is that it discourages reinsurers from medling in the insurer-policyholder relationship. The expectation is that insurer and policyholder will work together in connection with claims and that after the matter is finalized, the reinsurer will follow the insurer's fortunes.

If a reinsurer interjects itself into the insurer-policyholder relationship, the reinsurer has not only undermined the basic premises of reinsurance and the follow-the-fortunes doctrine but has also interfered with the fiduciary-like relationship between insurer and policyholder. Consider this scenario: a policyholder's home or business burns down. The insurer concludes that the fire was intentionally set and must determine whether it was the work of local juvenile delinquents or policyholder arson. Normally, the insurer alone must decide what it believes was the cause of the loss and pay or deny the claim accordingly.

Consider what happens if the reinsurer inserts itself into the claims decision. The reinsurer may view the evidence as tilting toward the arson explanation rather than the vandalism explanation and correspondingly urge the insurer to deny the claim. If the arson evidence is so weak as to make denial unreasonable, the insurer has committed bad faith toward the policyholder. Logically, the reinsurer has also committed bad faith because it has been part of this unreasonable coverage denial.

Alternatively, the reinsurer may not be completely immersed in the sifting of evidence as to the cause of the loss but may intercede and strongly criticize the underwriting decisions of the insurer, perhaps suggesting that the policy should never have been issued. The reinsurer may even express concern about continuing to work with an insurer that it regards as a poor underwriter. The effect of such conduct by the reinsurer will not be lost on even the dullest insurer. The insurer will likely take the hint and attempt to display its resistance to claims disliked by the reinsurer and deny coverage or seek to pay as little as possible regardless of the strength of the claim.

To the extent anything like this hypothetical scenario takes place, the reinsurer has acted improperly by interfering in the insurer-policyholder relationship. Where the reinsurer's meddling induces the insurer to act in bad faith, the reinsurer is logically responsible as well. At a minimum, the insurer has acted in bad faith simply by willingly permitting a third party to intrude into its near-fiduciary relationship with the policyholder. Whether one views this as sounding more in tortuous interference with the insurer-policyholder contract or as bad faith because the reinsurer has elected to act as an insurer in connection with the claim, the effect is the same. To the extent the policyholder is treated in bad faith (through unreasonable decisions or unreasonable claims conduct), the reinsurer is at least partially at fault.

Although insurers of course prefer to have good relations with reinsurers, the insurer cannot validly permit its claims or coverage decisions to be determined by the reinsurer. The policyholder is the one to whom an insurer owes a duty of good faith. The insurer must make coverage decisions with an eye toward the policyholder's interests and fair treatment of the policyholder. Within that framework of giving at least equal consideration to the interests of the policyholder, the insurer must "call it as it see it" (not as its reinsurers see it) regarding claims. An insurer violates its duties to the policyholder if it gives reinsurers power over the policyholder's claim. The insurer is required to make a good faith decision on each claim, giving equal consideration to the interests of the policyholder. Even the mere solicitation of the reinsurer's opinion on a claim is inconsistent with the insurer's duty to the policyholder.

In addition, a court may find the reinsurer and the insurer to be in a "joint venture" regarding a claim or their operations and thereby consider the reinsurer and the insurer essentially one entity regarding operations, including any bad faith treatment of policyholders. In *Albert H. Wohlers & Co. v. Bartgis*, 114 Nev. 1249, 969 P.2d 949 (Nev. 1998), one court held that an insurance intermediary (a general agent in the case but its rationale would apply to other types of agents, brokers, and reinsurers as well) can be liable on a bad faith claim or other insurer responsibility to the same extent as would the insurer if the intermediary and the insurer are in a "joint venture." In determining whether a joint venture exists, the court considered whether the intermediary (1) developed promotional material for the insurer; (2) issued policies; (3) billed premiums; (4) collected premiums, (5) adjusted claims; (6) paid claims, (7) assisted the insurer with development of the policy or insurance product line, (8) shared in the profits of the insurer; or (9) otherwise had a pecuniary interest in keeping claim costs down. *See* 114 Nev. 1249, 969 P.2d 949, 959 (Nev. 1998).

Unfortunately, the *Wohlers v. Bartgis* Court did not comment explicitly on the relative strength of these factors or whether a specific number of factors must be shown to establish a joint venture. The logical reading of the opinion suggests that there is no rigid formula but that the existence of a critical mass of these factors establishes a joint venture. It also appears that profit-sharing or an economic incentive to suppress claim costs is the most important factor in determining whether an intermediary acts in a joint venture with an insurer. *See also Farr v. Transamerica Occidental Life Ins. Co.*, 145 Ariz. 1, 699 P.2d 376 (Ariz. Ct. App. 1984). Applied to reinsurers, this list of factors strongly suggests that insurers and reinsurers are always engaged in a joint venture and become more closely linked if the reinsurer is involved in an insurer's claims decisions. Consequently, reinsurers subject to *Wohlers* or similar precedent undoubtedly face bad faith exposure when they become part of the claims adjustment process or have a joint economic self-interest in suppressing claim costs and that a reinsurer may face bad faith exposure when it aids and abets bad faith conduct by a primary insurer.

Unfortunately, some reinsurers and insurers appear to have forgotten the basic groundrules of the follow-the-fortunes doctrine and insurer duties to the policyholder. Some reinsurance contracts contain "control clauses . . . . intended to give more power and involvement to the reinsurer" regarding claims, "traditionally an area left exclusively to the ceding insurer." *See* Adam B. Leichtling & Lara M. Paredes, *Fundamental Concepts in Reinsurance in Latin American Countries*, 37 INTER-AMERICAN L. REV. 1, 24 (2005). Control clauses may: (1) "[r]equire the ceding insurer to inform the reinsurer of modifications to the underlying insurance contract and materialization of the risk;" (2) "[r]equire the ceding insurer to consult with or give the reinsurer final decisions regarding the adjustment of catastrophes and losses and selection of the adjuster or attorney;" or (3) "[g]ive the reinsurer the final decision on acceptance or rejection of a claim or the amount of covered loss." *See* Leichtling & Paredes, *supra*, at 24-25. Where a reinsurance policy or treaty contains this type of "control" language, the reinsurer is obviously in a joint venture with the insurer under the *Wohlers v. Bartgis* analysis and has in essence codified a regime of bad faith toward the policyholder.

§ 15.02   EXCESS INSURANCE: DUTIES OF THE PRIMARY INSURER AND THE EXCESS INSURER

Page 1074: [Add at the end of § 15.02:]

NOTES AND QUESTIONS

(1) Which is more persuasive: the *Megonnell* majority opinion or the dissent? Why? Does the answer become more apparent when one knows more about insurance theory, history, custom and practice?

(2) Can you have a valid umbrella policy with holes? Can you have a skinny excess policy with coverage narrower than the underlying policy? At the risk of answering our own question, we think the answers are (a) "No" and (b) "Not unless there is an express and clear understanding to this effect by the parties."

(a) The very notion and nomenclature of an "umbrella" policies implies that it provides coverage beyond the contours of the underlying insurance. Perhaps that's too timid a statement. Calling a policy an "umbrella" policy in effect promises that its scope of coverage will exceed that of the underlying insurance. *See* EMMETT J. VAUGHAN & THERESE VAUGHAN, FUNDAMENTALS OF RISK AND INSURANCE 532-33 (8th ed. 1999). There may also be combination or hybrid excess umbrella policies. *Id.* at 631-32. This is the general view of insurance authorities and establishes an industry-wide understanding of what it means to provide (umbrella" coverage. *See, e.g.*, JAMES S. TRIESCHMANN & SANDRA G. GUSTAVSON, RISK MANAGEMENT & INSURANCE 286-87 (9th ed. 1995) (excess umbrella policy usually follows form or (provides coverage on conditions identical to those of the underlying lawyers of coverage.() (Umbrella liability insurance, designed for business use, is first excess insurance over the insured's more conventional liability insurance of various sorts, such as general liability insurances . . . . Second, umbrella insurance coverage hazards not covered under other liability insurance . . . .). *Accord*, ALBERT H. MOWBRAY, RALPH H. BLANCHARD & C. ARTHUR WILLIAMS, JR., INSURANCE: ITS THEORY AND PRACTICE IN THE UNITED STATES 244 (6th ed. 1969); *See* JAMES L. ATHEARN, S. TRAVIS PRITCHETT & JOAN T. SCHMIT, RISK AND INSURANCE 514 (6th

ed. 1989); *See* JAMES S. TRIESCHMANN, ROBERT E. HOYT & DAVID
W. SOMMER, RISK MANAGEMENT AND INSURANCE 306 (12th ed.
2005); *See* GRIFFIN COMMUNICATIONS, INC., THE UMBRELLA BOOK
12 (2002). *See also id.* at 12 (noting that standard CGL form underlying typical umbrella policy excludes coverage for claims of property damage to policyholder's own work but that ([t]he exclusion
does not apply if the damaged work or the work out of which the
damage arises was performed by a subcontractor on the insured's
behalf.(). *Accord*, SCOTT E. HARRINGTON AND GREGORY R. NIEHAUS,
RISK MANAGEMENT AND INSURANCE 285 (2d ed. 2004) (If losses
exceed primary policy limits, (then the umbrella policy will pay
losses up to its limit. Most umbrella policies also provide some
coverage for liability exposures not covered under the insured's primary policies (e.g., libel or slander) subject to a self-insured retention that operates like a deductible.() and 510 ((Umbrella liability
coverage is similar to excess coverage in that the policy provides
excess coverage over other policies or self-insured retentions.();
GEORGE E. REJDA, PRINCIPLES OF RISK MANAGEMENT AND INSUR-
ANCE 321-22 (9th ed. 2004) (ISO umbrella form tracks ISO CGL
form regarding available general liability coverage); JAMES S.
TREISCHMANN, ROBERT E. HOYT & DAVID W. SOMMER, RISK MANAGE-
MENT AND INSURANCE 304-307 (12th ed. 2005); MARK S. DORFMAN,
INTRODUCTION TO RISK MANAGEMENT AND INSURANCE 374 (8th ed.
2004) (umbrella policy defined as having coverage at least as broad
as underlying insurance) and 484 (glossary defines umbrella liability policy as (covering losses in excess of the limits provided by
underlying liability insurance().

(b) Just as "umbrella" insurance suggests broader coverage, the
term "excess" suggests that an excess policy provides more of the
coverage contained in the underlying policy. Consequently, unless
there is a specific agreement to the contrary, an excess policy should
be congruent in scope to the underlying policy. In a particularly
"hard" market where obtaining coverage is difficult, a policyholder
may need to accept restrictions on normal, "follow-form" excess
coverage as to some risks. In a very hard market, insurers may only
be willing to right lower levels of coverage for some risks perceived
as particularly difficult. This is not to say that all follow-form excess
policies are carbon copies of the underlying insurance (although
many excess policies consist only of a Declarations Sheet). An excess
insurer writes coverage on its own form rather than simply signing
on to the underlying form. However, the excess policy should not
deviate in material respects from the followed form absent an
express agreement to that effect. Frequently, an excess policy may
have some insurer-specific language regarding the mechanics of
notice, proof of loss, or other ministerial aspects of a claim. Rarely
will an excess policy be substantively narrower in scope than the
underlying policy.

(c) Because the terms "excess" and "umbrella" have such well-established meanings, the sentiments expressed above are the conventional wisdom (and we mean it in a good sense without the potentially negative implications attached to the term by the economist John Kenneth Galbraith or sociologist Robert Merton, who saw conventional wisdom as received orthodoxy that was often inaccurate) of the insurance world. Where there is deviation from this norm, it should not be the result of mere different in the text of the excess or umbrella insurance policy. As stated in Chapter Two, the policy is only a memorialization of the insurance contract; it is not the contract itself. The contract is the agreement of the parties. Where the parties agreed to a normal and rational insurance program, this means excess insurance co-extensive with underlying insurance and umbrella insurance that is somewhat broader than the underlying insurance. This intent of the parties and this general understanding of policyholders, brokers, and insurers, cannot be altered by an excess insurer simply providing a policy form weeks or months later with language at variance from the underlying or followed policy. At best, this is a nullity. At worst, it may indicate fraud and deceit by an excess or umbrella insurer.

(d) This is not to say that some policies titled "excess" or "umbrella" policies are not intentionally narrower than the underlying coverage. But when this takes place and is enforceable, it is because the scope of coverage reflected in the contract documents accurately captures the agreement of the parties, agreement that should be express and clear. However, even if there is an agreement to have a "skinny" excess policy or an "umbrella with holes," labeling these policies "excess" or "umbrella" is misleading. To properly reflect an understanding of this sort, the policies should be labeled "limited excess" or "restricted excess policies." As discussed previously, these sorts of policies are normally found only in a hard market. Where a market is even moderately soft, rational policyholders and brokers will insist upon excess or umbrella coverage at least as extensive as underlying coverage and will be able to obtain it at acceptable prices.

PREMCOR USA, INC., v. AMERICAN HOME ASSURANCE CO.

400 F.3d 523 (7th Cir. 2005)

MANION, *Circuit Judge.* Premcor USA, Inc., and The Premcor Refining Group, Inc. (together, "Premcor") sued American Home Assurance Company ("AHA") for coverage of litigation defense costs under an "umbrella" insurance policy (the "AHA policy"). Premcor argued that the AHA policy required AHA to pay more than two million dollars in costs that Premcor incurred while defending itself in an Illinois state court case. Premcor also argues that AHA had a duty to indemnify it for any liability incurred. The parties filed cross-motions for summary judgment. The district court granted judgment in favor of AHA. Premcor appeals.

In 1995, two Premcor employees were fatally injured while working at a Premcor facility in Blue Island, Illinois. Subsequently, their estates initiated negligence actions in Illinois state court to recover damages under the Illinois Wrongful Death and Survival Act. The state trial court granted summary judgment to Premcor in January 2004, but the case presently continues on appeal. To date, Premcor has spent over two million dollars defending this action. * * * At the time of the accident, Premcor was covered by several insurance policies. The initial layer of insurance was composed primarily of a two million dollar commercial general liability policy (the "Reliance policy") from Reliance National Indemnity Company ("Reliance"). In addition, Premcor had several other insurance policies covering discrete areas such as employers' liability and automobiles. Premcor also contracted with AHA for an umbrella insurance policy that would provide ten million dollars in excess coverage. An umbrella policy is a type of policy that acts both as an excess insurance policy and, in certain circumstances, as a primary insurance policy. Regarding the latter aspect, an umbrella policy provides coverage for those incidents left uncovered by other insurance policies, filling gaps in underlying insurance.

When the accident occurred, Premcor filed a claim with Reliance. The Reliance policy contained a "duty to defend" provision, which provided that Reliance would pay defense costs for any actions covered by the Reliance policy. Reliance, however, subsequently became insolvent, which left Premcor itself to pay the defense costs in the Illinois state court action. After Reliance became insolvent, Premcor filed a declaratory judgment action against AHA in the Northern District of Illinois, arguing that, under the AHA policy, AHA had to "drop down" and pay all defense costs above the amount Premcor received from Reliance, which because of the insolvency was zero.

As this case turns on the precise coverage of the AHA policy, we examine the applicable provisions in some detail. The AHA policy begins with a broad description of its coverage: "to pay on behalf of [Premcor] that portion of the ultimate net loss in excess of the retained limit as hereinafter defined . . . ." Several provisions of the AHA policy add specific contours to this general description. The Declarations page sets forth the Limit of Liability of the AHA policy. This Limit of Liability states that AHA will provide ten million dollars in coverage for any loss in excess of either:

　　(1) the amount recoverable under the underlying insurance as set out in the attached Schedule A

　　or

　　(2) $25,000 US ultimate net loss in respect of each occurrence not covered by underlying insurance.

A second provision in AHA's policy further explains AHA's obligation to provide coverage. Specifically, the AHA policy's "retained limit" clause states:

A. [AHA] shall be liable only for that portion of the ultimate net loss excess of [Premcor's] retained limited defined as either:

1. the total of the applicable limits of the underlying policies listed in the Schedule of Underlying Insurance hereof, and the applicable limits of any other underlying insurance providing coverage to [Premcor]; or

2. the amount stated in Item 3(A-2) of the Declarations as the result of any one occurrence not covered by such underlying policies or insurance; and then up to an amount not exceeding the amount as stated in Item 3(A) of the Declarations as the result of any one occurrence.

The AHA policy defines "ultimate" net loss as:

the total sum which [Premcor], or any company as its insurer, or both become obligated to pay be [sic] reason of personal injury, property damage, . . . and shall also include . . . expenses for doctors, nurses, and investigators and other persons, and for settlement, adjustment, investigation and defense of claims. . . . [AHA] shall not be liable for expenses as aforesaid when such are covered by underlying policies of insurance whether collectible or not.

In short, by defining ultimate net loss, the AHA policy restricts its coverage to situations where either damages or costs exceed the total of the applicable limits of the underlying policies.

Another relevant portion of the AHA policy addresses AHA's liability in instances of insolvency by any underlying insurers. Endorsement 10 provides:

The liability of [AHA] shall not be increased by the refusal or inability of [Premcor] to pay its Self-Insured Retention (or retained limit) or by the refusal or inability of any underlying insurer to pay, whether by Reasons of Insolvency, Bankruptcy, or otherwise.

This endorsement indicates that insolvency by an underlying insurance provider has no effect on the amount of AHA's liability.

In addition to these provisions regarding excess insurance, the AHA policy, as an umbrella insurance policy, also supplies primary coverage in some circumstances. Under a section designated "Defense, Settlement, Supplementary Payments," the AHA policy provides primary coverage "to occurrences covered under this policy but not covered by any underlying policies. . . ." The primary coverage aspect of the AHA policy therefore only exists where there is a hole in the coverage of the underlying insurance.

Notwithstanding the policy language that seems to address insolvency of underlying insurers, Premcor argued in its declaratory judgment action that AHA was required to pay all defense costs because Reliance was insolvent. Premcor maintained that the amount recoverable language in the AHA policy meant that AHA was responsible for all amounts above that which was actually recovered from the underlying insurance. As the underlying insurance paid nothing in this case, Premcor argued that AHA should be responsible for the entire two million dollars.

The parties filed cross-motions for summary judgment and the district court decided in favor of AHA. The district court found that the amount recoverable language in the AHA policy was ambiguous as a matter of Illinois law, but that Endorsement 10 expressly forbade increased liability because of the insolvency of underlying insurance. This appeal followed.

* * *

The law of Illinois applies to the interpretation of these contracts. The construction of the provisions of an insurance policy is a question of law, subject to *de novo* review. "In order to ascertain the meaning of the policy's language and the parties' intent, the court must construe the policy as a whole and take into account the type of insurance purchased, the nature of the risks involved, and the overall purpose of the contract." If the language of the policy is susceptible to more than one meaning, it is considered ambiguous and will be construed strictly against the insurer who drafted the policy and in favor of the insured. However, [a] court 'will not strain to find ambiguity in an insurance policy where none exists.' "* * *

The parties' dispute over the scope of coverage of the AHA policy focuses on the interpretation of the "amount recoverable" language. This language is critical to determine when AHA's obligation to provide excess coverage begins. In the past, Illinois courts have interpreted such amount recoverable language, considered alone, to be ambiguous. *See Donald B. MacNeal, Inc. v. Interstate Fire & Cas. Co.* (Ill. App. Ct. 1985). In the *MacNeal* case, the Illinois appellate court indicated "that language might possibly be interpreted either to expose [the excess insurer] only for amounts over the dollar limits of the underlying insurance or to expose [the excess insurer] for amounts which the insured is not able to actually recover from the underlying insurer because of its insolvency." (quoting *Reserve Ins. Co. v. Pisciotta* (Cal. 1982). Faced with two plausible interpretations of this language, and with no other terms in the policy shedding light on which was proper, the Illinois court found an ambiguity and strictly construed the amount recoverable language against the insurer.

Premcor argues *MacNeal* controls and that this court must interpret the "amount recoverable" language to provide coverage. However, the AHA policy is distinguishable from the policy in *MacNeal*. Here, the AHA policy contains several provisions informing the meaning of the "amount recoverable" language, offering the guidance that was lacking in *MacNeal*. A cardinal rule of contract interpretation is that a document "should be read to give effect to all its provisions and to render them consistent with each other." In this case, the relevant [*528] provisions show that the AHA policy only covered costs in excess of the limits of the underlying policy, and the amount recoverable language must be interpreted consistently.

Like the district court, we consider Endorsement 10 to be significant. It states that AHA's liability should not be in-creased "by the refusal or inability of any underlying insurer to pay, whether by Reasons of Insolvency, Bankruptcy, or otherwise . . . ." Any interpretation of the AHA policy that would lead to an increase in liability because of the insolvency of one of the underlying insurers would not be valid, as it would contradict the express terms of this endorsement. Yet such an increase is what Premcor's interpretation of "amount recoverable" would require. In its brief Premcor acknowledges that if AHA is called upon to pay defense costs "previously owed by the insolvent primary insurer" (Reliance), "this theoretically could increase the excess carrier's total monetary obligation." The language of Endorsement 10, however, prohibits such a result.

A second clause in the AHA policy confirms that AHA's responsibilities are not changed by insolvency. The definition of ultimate net loss in the AHA policy states that "[AHA] shall not be liable for expenses as aforesaid when such are covered by underlying policies of insurance whether collectible or not." The insolvency of Reliance does not require AHA to drop down and pay all defense costs. Rather, the AHA policy specifically provides that AHA will not be liable for defense costs in the case of insolvency, even if Premcor cannot recover from the underlying policy.

The retained limit language is a final provision that demonstrates that the AHA policy does not cover costs in the event of an insolvency of an underlying insurer. "[AHA] shall be liable only for that portion of the ultimate net loss excess of the Insured's retained limit," which in this case is defined as "the total of the applicable limits of the underlying policies listed in the Schedule of Underlying Insurance hereof." In *MacNeal*, that court commented on cases in which the insolvency of the primary insurer did not require the excess insurer to assume the primary's obligation. The *MacNeal* court distinguished its case from these cases based on policy language nearly identical to the AHA policy retained limit provision.

* * *

Premcor attempts to minimize the effect of the retained limit language by referring to a case from the Fifth Circuit involving an insurance policy with both amount recoverable and retained limit/ultimate net loss provisions. See *Sifers v. Gen. Marine Catering Co.* (5th Cir. 1990). In *Sifers*, the Fifth Circuit concluded that the amount recoverable language was not ambiguous, but in fact required the excess insurer to cover any amounts above what the underlying insurance actually paid. The Fifth Circuit then decided that this language controlled over the retained limit language that the policy also contained. * * * This is obviously not our case. In *Sifers*, the Fifth Circuit attempted to reconcile seemingly conflicting provisions that each had a clear meaning under Louisiana law. Under Illinois law, that is not our task because Illinois law has found the amount recoverable language to be ambiguous in isolation. Our task is to determine whether this provision remains ambiguous when viewed in the context of the entire AHA policy. It does not.

Interpreting the amount recoverable language in light of the contract as a whole removes the apparent ambiguity when the amount recoverable language is viewed out of context. Unlike *MacNeal*, this case features several contractual provisions that illuminate the true meaning of this phrase. Endorsement 10, the definition of ultimate net loss, and the retained limit language show that the AHA policy would not assume additional responsibilities to cover defense costs in the event of the insolvency of an underlying insurer. The proper interpretation of the amount recoverable language, which is most consistent with these provisions of the AHA policy, is that AHA only covers costs in excess of the limits of the underlying policy. Therefore, AHA is not required to pay the defense costs that Premcor incurred in the underlying litigation. * * *

Premcor asserts that, at a minimum, the AHA policy covers the cost of defense to the extent it exceeds the two million dollar limit of the underlying Reliance policy. However, the Reliance policy provides unlimited defense costs—it does not limit its coverage to the first two million dollars. And the AHA policy provides, "The Company [AHA] shall not be liable for expenses as aforesaid when such are covered by underlying policies of insurance whether collectible or not." Thus, under the policies, Premcor is not entitled to recover the cost of defense in excess of two million dollars because Reliance's policy covered such costs. This interpretation accords with common sense as well. If Premcor's argument is correct, there would be duplicate coverage by AHA and Reliance for all cases exceeding two million dollars in defense costs, since the Reliance policy provides for the payment of unlimited costs and AHA's obligation, according to Premcor, begins once the costs reach the two million dollar level. * * *

Premcor offers another argument on this appeal—that the AHA policy provides primary insurance in cases where underlying insurance does not. Premcor contends that this gap-filling provision should apply here, alleging the Reliance policy could be read to exclude work-related injuries. Premcor, however, fails to provide any information about other underlying insurance policies and whether they could cover this situation. No matter. We need not tarry over this argument; it was not presented to the district court and was, therefore, waived. * * *

Finally, Premcor argues that the district court should not have granted summary judgment on the issue of AHA's duty to indemnify. As the underlying state action remains pending on appeal in the Illinois courts, Premcor is correct—the district court acted precipitously. Therefore, we reverse the distrct court's judgment on this point and remand for either dismissal without prejudice of this issue or a stay of the proceedings relating to this issue until the underlying action in the Illinois state court has become final (and any liability is determined). * * *

Interpreted as a whole, the AHA policy contains no ambiguity. Instead, it provides for excess coverage only after the underlying insurance has been paid to the policy limits. AHA is not required to pay the two million dollars in defense costs, which would have been the obligation of Reliance in the absence of the insolvency. Summary judgment for AHA on the duty to defend issues was correct. Summary judgment on the duty to indemnify issue was premature, and we remand that issue to the district court for proceedings consistent with this opinion.

NOTES AND QUESTIONS

(1) As the *Premcor* opinion reflects, the text of an excess or umbrella policy is important to determining the question of whether the policy "drops down" to fill a lower layer of coverage when an underlying insurer becomes insolvent. But apart from the particular text of a specific policy form, which approach (drop-down or no drop-down) as a matter of insurance theory and principles? Think about the logic of insurance pricing when formulating your answer.

(2) Where a guaranty fund covers the insolvency of liability insurers, this usually means that the policyholder remains liable to the third party claimant for any amounts above the guaranty fund maximum up to the amount of the claimant's judgment or settlement. *See, e.g., Goodyear Tire & Rubber Co. v. Dynamic Air, Inc.,* 702 N.W.2d 237 (Minn. 2005) (answering certified question submitted by federal district court) (defendant policy-holder of insolvent insurer must fill gap between $300,000 guaranty fund maximum and $2 million sought by claimant).

§ 15.03   SELF-INSURANCE AND RISK RETENTION GROUPS

[A]   Introduction

Page 1080: [Add at the end of § 15.03 on page 1080:]

The popularity of risk retention groups tends to ebb and flow according to whether the market for conventional insurance is "soft" (where insurance is easy to obtain at relatively low rates) or "hard" (where insurance is difficult to obtain or available only at high rates or with more exclusions or sub-limitations than usual). One illustration from 2004 is the formation of the Henry Hudson LTC Risk Retention Group, which was formed to address the insurance needs of long-term care facilities in New York in response to "tough conditions . . . with fewer commercial insurers offering coverage and rases escalating" according to a representative of Uni-Ter, the consultant group that will administer the new RRG and obtain reinsurance for the group. See Jerry Geisel, N.Y. *LTC facilities to get new RRG,* BUSINESS INSURANCE, April 26, 2004 at 4. The new RRG planned to charge members $375 per bed in annual premiums for New York City and Long Island facilities and $175 per bed for facilities located elsewhere in New York.

Illustrative of the more free-flowing, "write-your-own" atmosphere attending risk retention groups, the "Henry Hudson" RRG formed by New

York-based businesses that specialize in care of the elderly is domiciled in Nevada, which was chosens "because of the quality and interest of the state's insurance department", which the RRG found to be "more friendly and responsive than other states" although the RRG could have been located in New York pursuant to that states" captive insurer statute. Critics of the status quo have suggested that businesses forming risk retention groups or captive insurers may be "forum shopping" too much and too easily in order to find states with less regulatory supervision.

For the moment, however, the political climate and insurance regulatory opinion appears to favor RRGs and captives as a means of providing greater risk management flexibility to businesses. Although 2004 Democratic presidential candidate John Kerry lambasted one-time rival Howard Dean for "turning Vermont into a snowy Bermuda," a reference to Vermont's status as the chief U.S. domicile of captive insurance companies, this charge was not one that resonated. Governor Dean may have had electoral problems, but his support for captives appeared not to be one of them.

But just what is the distinction between a captive and a risk retention group? The two are so close, both in concept and in technicality that observers tend to use the terms interchangeably. The distinction is that a true captive tends to operate as a separate insurance company while an RRG is more responsive to member wishes and direction (subject to the applicable bounds of regulation). Whatever the precise definitional nomenclature, there is no doubt that captives are big business, and not only in Bermuda and Vermont. A.M. Best has estimated that perhaps half of all U.S. risk transfers are held by captives, and captives appear to be catching on in areas outside their traditional base of the Carribean, North America, and Europe.